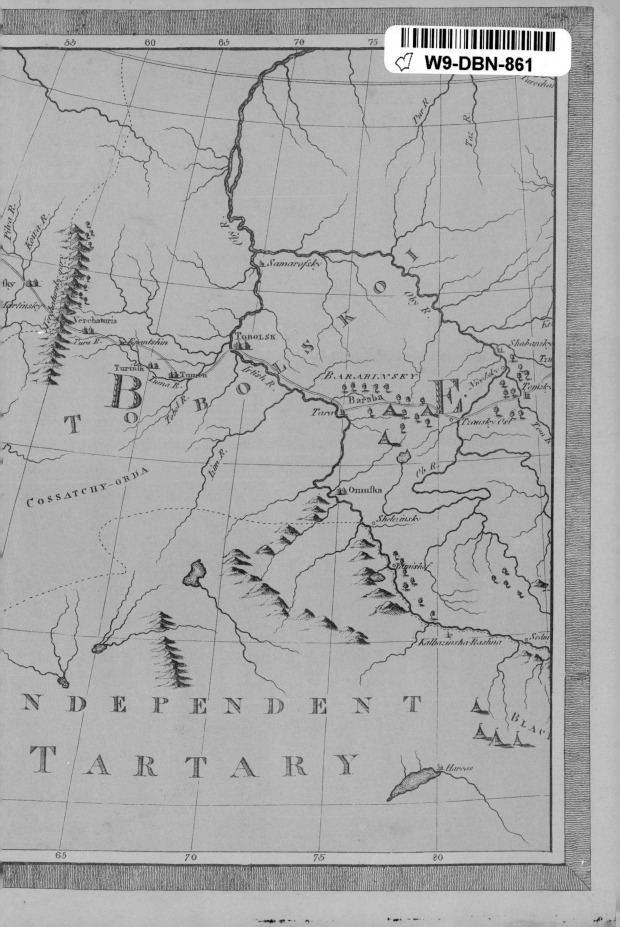

A JOURNEY FROM ST PETERSBURG TO PEKIN

A JOURNEY

From

ST PETERSBURG

To

PEKIN

◯

1719-22

by

JOHN BELL

of Antermony

*Edited with
an introduction by*
J. L. STEVENSON

BARNES & NOBLE, INC.
New York

Printed in Great Britain
by T. & A. Constable Limited
Printers to the University of Edinburgh

FOREWORD

JOHN BELL, a Scottish doctor, travelled overland from St Petersburg through Siberia and Mongolia to Peking and back again in the years 1719-1722 in the suite of a Russian Embassy from Peter the Great to the Chinese Emperor K'ang Hsi. Over forty years later, in 1763, Bell published an account of this long journey and his stay in Peking as a self-contained section of his *Travels from St Petersburg in Russia to Diverse Parts of Asia*, two handsome volumes which had a considerable success in the later eighteenth and earlier nineteenth centuries, and which have long enjoyed a deserved reputation for the accuracy with which Bell reported what he saw. 'The veracity of Mr Bell's narrative', wrote Sir George Staunton in 1821, 'may perhaps be considered to be too well established to need at present any further confirmation'. The *Quarterly Review* in 1817 described Bell's book as 'the best model perhaps for travel-writing in the English language'.

John Bell's *Travels* have since fallen into a wholly unmerited obscurity with the general reading public, although, of course, they have never been forgotten by the scholars, in several fields, to whom they offer a great deal of invaluable first-hand evidence. His *Journey to Pekin* is now reprinted first and foremost because it is an eminently readable book in itself. It was a fascinating journey, along the overland caravan route between Russia and China, through regions which few of his countrymen have traversed and none has so well described. It took place, moreover, at one of the turning-points of history, when Peter the Great's restless energy was successfully reshaping Russia's destiny, when the heartlands of Asia still sheltered nations, more or less independent, which might even then have been welded together into a formidable new Mongolian Empire, and when the Chinese Empire under the recently established Manchu Dynasty had risen to one of its great peaks. John Bell's book throws light on all of these themes, and particularly on Sino-Russian relations – as interesting a study in the eighteenth century as they are today. But his *Journey to Pekin* is not just for the historical specialist. He wrote it for the ordinary intelligent reader of his day, and the spiritual descendants of the subscribers to his volumes in 1763 will find in it what they found then, a good story well told.

THE honour of introducing this edition of one of the Travels of John Bell was entrusted to me by the Edinburgh University Press at the instance of my old teacher, Professor W. L. Renwick. Without his encouragement I would not have attempted it; without his guidance I should have missed much; and without his criticisms I should have been guilty of more errors than may hereafter appear. It is both a duty and a pleasure to record my great debt to him, in this as in a wider context.

In preparing this edition I have incurred many other debts. In particular, I should like to express my gratitude to the Rev. Dr A. A. Morrison of the High Church of Campsie and to other local correspondents, to whom he introduced me, for several helpful communications on John Bell's Scottish background.

I am particularly grateful also to Miss Fu Lo-shu for permission to quote from her translation of the *I Yü Lu*, and for the illustrations reproduced on pp. 130-1 and facing p. 179. For the present-day photographs of Mongolia and the Great Wall I am no less indebted to Sir Fitzroy Maclean and to Mr John Massey-Stewart. It is a pleasure to acknowledge the generosity with which they have put their material at my disposal.

I have made considerable use of the facilities of several Departments of the British Museum; of the School of Oriental and African Studies; of the Bodleian Library; the Edinburgh University Library; and of the National Library of Scotland. On all sides I have met with great courtesy and helpfulness, and if I do not name the individual scholars in these institutions who have dealt so patiently with my enquiries it is only because I would not wish to appear to be sheltering under their great authority. I have been indebted likewise to several Foreign Office colleagues whom, for similar reasons, I also leave anonymous, with the exception of Miss Violet Connolly, whose kindness and helpfulness must not go unrecorded. Special tribute is due also to Miss Blayney and other members of the staff of the Foreign Office Printed Library for the way in which they met my many (and from a professional point of view eccentric) requests for out-of-the-way books. I am most grateful to Mr Ian Scott for drawing the very fine map.

To Winifred, my wife, I owe more than I can publicly acknowledge.

J. L. S., London, *April* 1965

PUBLISHER'S NOTE

THE text reprinted is that of the edition of 1763 (incorporating the original corrigenda, and with a few literal errors corrected). Bell's punctuation and spelling have been retained throughout. The map reproduced on the endpapers is also from the 1763 edition.

CONTENTS

ILLUSTRATIONS

INTRODUCTION

INTRODUCTION

JOHN BELL was born at Antermony, a small estate in the Parish of Campsie, Stirlingshire, in 1691. He was the second son of the Reverend Patrick Bell and Annabella Stirling, daughter of the Laird of Craigbarnet. (It is probably relevant to Bell's future career that his father was deprived of his charge as Minister at Port of Menteith in 1689 for refusing to recognize the accession of Their Majesties William and Mary, and that he evidently stubbornly maintained his Jacobite sympathies thereafter.) His paternal grandfather was Alexander Bell, described in 1657, before he acquired the lands of Antermony, as a 'writer', (that is, solicitor) in Edinburgh. Alexander Bell had married Grizal, herself a Bell by birth, daughter and, with two other sisters, joint heiress of James Bell, Provost of Glasgow.*

The Bells of Antermony were thus a well-found if minor country family, thanks it may be in part to the prudent choice of wives by Patrick and Alexander Bell. When John Bell in due course succeeded Patrick – his elder brother having died in his father's lifetime – he inherited what the local Minister, the Reverend James Lapslie, was later to describe as 'a considerable paternal estate'.

John Bell, of course, and particularly as he was a younger son, had to make his way in the world. He went to Glasgow University at the age of sixteen (he is on record as being a member of the Fourth Class in 1710) and must have completed his degree course in 1711. He then turned to medicine, and is said to have 'passed as a physician' in 1713. It is logical to assume, in the absence of any evidence to the contrary, that he obtained his medical qualifications in Glasgow, but this cannot be positively confirmed as the records of the Faculty of Physicians and Surgeons for the period are lost.

The next phase in John Bell's life is well documented – it is the only phase that is so – from his own writings. He was gripped, like so many Scots before and since, by the desire to see 'foreign parts'. On the motivation of this desire I cannot do better than quote his contemporary M'Ure. 'It is well known', he wrote in 1736, 'that the *Scots* made a greater Figure Abroad than any other Nation in *Europe*. This has been generally ascribed to the Barrenness of the Country, as not being able to maintain its Inhabitants; but this is a vulgar Error; for 'tis entirely owing to the Fineness of their Education. A Gentleman in *Scotland*

---

* On the Bell genealogy, see the article by Joseph Bain in *Scots Lore*, Glasgow (William Hodge) 1895. On Patrick Bell see *Notes and Queries*, 10th Series, iii, 12.

having Four or Five Sons, gives them equal Education, the eldest Son, though often not the finest Gentleman, succeeds to the Estate, and the Rest being bred above Trades, go to seek their Fortune in Foreign Countries, and are thereby lost to their own.'* M'Ure then lists the countries in Europe in which the Scots were prominent, among them Russia. It was indeed to Russia that Bell turned. Why he did so and what prospects he could expect there are discussed later. For the present it is enough to observe that the following nine years in the service of the Russians, if they did not make his fortune, certainly took him to enough foreign parts to have satisfied most appetites.

Bell arrived in Russia in 1714, and in 1715 was appointed physician in a Russian Embassy to Persia. This appointment lasted for three years, and Bell's description of the 'long, tedious and dangerous journey' that it entailed forms the first part of the *Travels* that he was eventually to publish in 1763. Tedious as the journey may have been – and perhaps I should remind the modern reader that Bell uses the word in Dr Johnson's primary definition of 'wearisome by continuance', which was no doubt physically true of the progress of the Embassy, but which cannot be applied to Bell's admirably clear and far from wearisome account of it – Bell's appetite for travel was not sated. When he returned to St Petersburg in 1718 he learned that another, and even more attractive, Embassy, to China, was being planned. He at once set to work to secure a place on it, and was successful, the only difficulty being over the question of salary. For the Persian Embassy he had been paid a salary of 300 roubles. For the Chinese Embassy he was offered a salary of 200 roubles, take it or leave it. He took it.

The Chinese Embassy lasted from 1719 till January 1722, and Bell's account of the journey, now reprinted, is the acknowledged highlight of his *Travels*. On his return from China, Bell went almost immediately on a third mission, this time accompanying Peter the Great on an expedition to Derbent. Bell describes this journey in the third section of his *Travels*. This section is much shorter than the first two, but is of considerable interest in particular for some shrewd observations at first hand on the character and habits of Peter the Great, for whom Bell had a profound admiration.

Bell returned to St Petersburg from Derbent in December 1722, and the first phase of his career, the Russian service, seems to have ended a year or so later. I can find no contemporary authority explaining why he left Russia or describing how he spent the next ten years or so. The

* John M'Ure, *A View of the City of Glasgow*, 1736, p. 345.

Dictionary of National Biography says that he returned to Scotland soon after the mission to Derbent. This seems inherently probable, for Bell's father had died in 1722, and that fact, coming at the end of nine strenuous years in the Russian service, may have determined Bell that it was time he had some home leave. In 1724 a considerable number of curiosities that Bell had picked up in the Far East found their way into Sir Hans Sloane's collection and this gives further support to the probability of Bell's return from Russia at this time. Thus a note,* dated at London, the 6th of August, 1724, records that Bell had presented the following items to Sir Hans Sloane:

1. a large fly
2. a flower certificate
3. a root called pinglang qh the chineses chaw in cold weather to keep them warm
4. a pebble stone, wt a picture supposed to be done with the urine of ye land tortoise
5. a sort of root growing in Siberia in a place called Shamansky porogul (or the magicall water fall) being poudered and given inwardly causes drunkeness

Bell, then, was clearly back in Britain. What is not so clear is what, apart from arousing the interest of the curious, he was doing. It is probable that, his wanderlust cured for the time being, he simply settled down on the paternal estate to live the life of a Scottish country gentleman.†
Whatever he did, one thing is reasonably certain, and that is that there can have been little temptation to return to the Russian service. Peter the Great died in 1725, and the conditions of service of the numerous expatriate experts – which had sometimes, even under that enlightened autocrat, been rather difficult – soon deteriorated. Claudius Rondeau, later to become British Minister Resident at St Petersburg, wrote to

---

* British Museum, Sloane MS 4019, f. 46. This is far from representing the total of Bell's benefactions to Sir Hans Sloane's collections. Apart from the scrolls and the mammoth's tusk referred to on pp. 50 and 205 of the present volume, there are, as the Keeper of the Department of Oriental Antiquities has pointed out to me, several references in the original Sloane register of 'Miscellanies' which show Bell as the source of other small items in the collection. Unfortunately none of these can be definitely identified in the collection as it now exists.

† This presumption is strengthened by the reference in M'Ure, *A View of the City of Glasgow*, p. 132, to 'John Bell *now* of Antermainy a Phisician, who was long abroad, and lately come home' (my italics). M'Ure's book was published in 1736, but this passage must have been drafted a few years earlier, since by 1734 Bell was back in Russia.

Lord Townshend from St Petersburg in May 1729 that 'several good foreign officers who are in this service daily ask their discharge to return home, and it is granted them without any difficulty, which shows the politics of this country are strangely changed since the death of the late Czar'.

Bell did, however, go back to Russia eventually, in 1734, but no longer to the Russian service. He became instead Secretary to the Claudius Rondeau just mentioned. This was by the practice of the time a private appointment by Rondeau, and does not mean that Bell was a member of H.M. Diplomatic Service. Rondeau for his part was fortunate in having so well qualified an assistant, and appears, from passing references in his despatches, to have thought highly of Bell. There was the additional advantage that Bell was known to and trusted by the Russians. This trust was important, for it led to Bell's next journey (the fourth and last in his *Travels*). In 1737 Bell was sent to Constantinople, essentially as a courier between Rondeau and Sir Everard Fawkner, British Minister at Constantinople. This mission was a part of the complicated negotiations, to which Britian as a mediating power was a party, to end the war between Russia and Turkey. In so far as the proposals that Bell carried to Constantinople had been worked out with the Russians in St Petersburg, he may be said to have undertaken the journey on their behalf. In any case, no Russians were allowed to enter Turkey. Bell himself was not, however, a negotiating agent either for the Russians or for the British.

Bell returned to St Petersburg from this journey, which was a particularly arduous one, and one which he said he would not advise any man to undertake at such a season and in time of war as he did, in May 1738. He resumed his duties as Secretary to Rondeau until the latter's death in October 1739, when he assumed charge of Rondeau's affairs, writing as follows to Lord Harrington:

> Mr Rondeau died the 5th inst . . . and until such time as it shall please His Majesty to appoint another to succeed him I shall take particular care of his papers and the letters that may come addressed to him from the office or other parts. I shall open and make proper use of them. In this step I have the approval of Count Osterman [the Russian Chancellor].

John Bell thus became in a sense the British representative in Russia, though not of course formally accredited as such in any way, and he later received a payment of £100 from the Treasury for his services in this capacity. His despatches* for the period when he was in charge are, as was proper, limited almost exclusively to administrative matters. Rondeau's successor, Finch, arrived in St Petersburg in April 1740, and Bell then became Finch's Secretary, though not apparently for very long. Perhaps Finch wanted to fill the post with a protégé of his own, or perhaps Bell had tired of the job – or of Finch.

Whatever the reason, Bell now turned to a new career, as a merchant in Constantinople. How he fared there is not known. The Editors of an edition† in 1830 of M'Ure's *A View of the City of Glasgow* say they had seen a volume of Bell's letters in manuscript 'written during his last Residence abroad from 1734 till 1743' which would no doubt go a long way towards clearing up the mystery if it were found. Unfortunately it does not seem to have survived, and no indication of its contents is given. Bell's mercantile career did not last very long. He abandoned it in 1746, at the age of 55, marrying in that year Marie Peters, by all accounts a Russian lady, with whom he returned to Scotland to spend the rest of his long life as a retired country gentleman at his seat of Antermony.

Antermony House no longer exists – its site is now occupied by a market garden – but it must in its day have been a pleasant retreat. It was described thus in an advertisement of 1827:

TO BE LET

THE MANSION HOUSE OF ANTERMONY – The house which stands in a pleasant situation, amid fine old timber, consists of dining room, drawing room, five bedrooms, laundry, kitchen, etc., with good accommodation for servants and suitable offices, and there is a good garden with a fine south exposure.

Antermony is distant from Glasgow ten miles, two miles from the post town of Kirkintilloch, from which there is daily communication to Glasgow by coaches, and the great canal is within the same distance, where passage boats betwixt Edinburgh and Glasgow also pass within a mile of the house.

Due allowance being made for house-agents' hyperbole, it sounds most attractive, and the easy access to Glasgow and to civilisation beyond is

---

* Bell's despatches are printed, in English and Russian, in Vols. 80 and 85 of *Sbornik Imperatorskago Russkago Istoricheskago Obshchestva*. Rondeau's despatches are at Vols. 66, 76 and 80 of the same collection. For details of the manuscript sources in Britain see D. B. Horn's *British Diplomatic Representatives, 1689-1789* and C. H. Firth's pamphlet *Notes on the Diplomatic Relations of England with the North of Europe* (Oxford, Blackwell, 1913).

† MacVean and Wylie, Glasgow, 1830, p. 114, note. (Reproduced also in Gordon's edition of 1872, p. 850.)

B

particularly to be noted. John Bell in his retirement was by no means isolated.

The most important fruit of John Bell's retirement was, of course, the *Travels* which he published in 1763. The background to their publication is discussed later, and it is enough here to observe that one way in which Bell certainly passed his time was, as he says in his Preface, in conversation with his friends. He must have had many an interesting tale to tell that he was far too discreet to put in his book.

Apart from the pleasures of conversation, and, no doubt (though I have found no examples surviving), correspondence, John Bell had other occupations appropriate to his status. In particular he was long remembered for the trees he planted. A very fine avenue of lime trees planted by him stretched along the public road to Antermony Lodge until recent years, when, despite local efforts to preserve them, they were cut down on the grounds that their roots were interfering with road surfacing. A Cedar of Lebanon grown from a seed brought home by him still stands, carefully tended, on the nearby Glorat Estate. And according to the last surviving inhabitant of Antermony House, one of the features of the estate was the trees, sycamore, elm and oak, said to have been grown from seed which John Bell brought home from Siberia.

Other physical memorials of Bell in the parish include a well which he caused to be dug as an act of philanthropy, and which still exists. Less tangible memorials also persisted in the parish for quite some time. Thus J. P. Cameron in *The Parish of Campsie*, published in 1892, records that Bell was remembered as a warm-hearted, benevolent sociable man, and that he was known locally as 'Honest John Bell'. This squares with the Reverend James Lapslie's brief eulogy in the *Old Statistical Account* (1795) where John Bell is described as having been 'remarkable for an amiable simplicity of manners, in private life, and the most sacred regard to truth in all he said and did'. Since Lapslie himself left a reputation behind him as being no respecter of persons, the eulogy may not be overdrawn.

One other tradition recorded by Cameron is that John Bell sometimes rode out dressed in oriental costume. If he did so, it need not be taken necessarily as a sign of eccentricity. Bell noted in his *Journey to Pekin* that Chinese clothes were much more suited to really cold weather than European, and he may simply have dressed accordingly to face the Scottish winters.

His good works and his costume apart, one business deal recorded by Cameron bears witness to Bell's shrewdness. Having no issue, he sold Antermony, subject to his own tenancy for life. Since he lived to the ripe age of 89 the purchaser, who was none too pleased, had a long time to wait before coming into his share of the bargain.

Bell made his will in 1777, at the age of 86. It is a model of simplicity. He left £50 sterling to the poor of the parish, a year's wages to each of his servants, and everything else (unspecified) to his wife. He died in 1780 and his wife in 1802, and both are buried in the parish.

Many of Bell's most valuable effects passed ultimately to the Stirlings of Craigbarnet, his mother's family, by whom, according to Cameron, they were still carefully treasured and highly prized at the end of the nineteenth century. Craigbarnet has now gone in its turn, and with it John Bell's treasures to unknown destinations. Some personal relics remain in the family's possession – Bell's watch, and a large glass vase and two smaller glasses said to have been given to him by Peter the Great. If these seem but small memorials for so long, varied and (one can fairly assume) happy a life, there is, fortunately, his book.

The Russian Service. It is time now to consider why and how the newly-qualified John Bell came to enter the Russian service in 1714. The short answer, though the analogy should not be pressed too far, is that in many respects Russia under Peter the Great was like an underdeveloped country of modern times – urgently in need of the help of foreign experts of many kinds to allow her to realize her own vast potential and enable her to pull herself up to the level of her neighbours. Peter the Great's main pre-occupations lay in the naval and military spheres, and for that reason the soldiers of fortune or mercenaries, the shipbuilders and the engineers are among the most important and best known of his foreign experts. They served him and Russia well, but they and their deeds, apart from an occasional encounter in Bell's pages, lie outside the scope of this book.

Peter's vast if somewhat haphazard ambitions to modernize Russia (it would be going too far to call them development programmes) called for foreign experts of all kinds. We need look no further than Bell's *Travels* – the book as a whole, not just the *Journey to Pekin* – for some individual examples that illustrate the range. Thus Bell notes at Astrakhan a French expert in viticulture; at Klinof a German shepherd complete with German sheep; at Kazan an English tanner to teach the natives how to dress the local hides; also at Kazan an English carpenter (exiled there on suspicion of intending to desert the Russian service); and at Udinsky in Siberia German miners engaged to experiment on the local ores. It reads, *mutatis mutandis*, like a list of Colombo Plan projects today.

Russia, then, was a land of opportunity for the suitably qualified, and if the Russian service had its disadvantages – in particular the difficulty of getting home leave and the fact that the Russians were often bad pay-masters – there were many who accepted the challenge. Prominent among them were the Scots. Peter the Great's General Staff and Admiralty were, it has been said,* almost a Scottish institution. One explanation of this phenomenon, most applicable perhaps to the soldiers of fortune, may lie in the possibility (in some cases the known fact) that they were Jacobites for whom their native land was in any case somewhat uncomfortable. There was, however, more to it than that: the connection already existed in the seventeenth century. Also, Peter the Great seems to have had a genuine personal predilection for the Scots. One reason for this may have been that his mother was brought up by a Scotswoman, a Mary Hamilton, who never lost touch with her native land and no doubt infected her charge with her own feelings towards it. Peter himself, whatever he got from his mother on this score, may have got as much again from General Menesius (a russianization of the Scots patronymic Menzies) in whose charge he was left on his father's death.

However it came about, Peter was to have many good Scots in his service, and to make close friends of some of them. The important contribution which the Scots for their part made to the development of Russia merits further study than it has so far received.† One Scot in particular, however, must detain us at this point, and that is the great Doctor Areskine, personal physician to and confidant of the Czar, the *doyen* of the foreign medical corps in Russia – and the man to whom the young John Bell had a letter of introduction.‡

During the first seventeen years of Peter the Great's reign, no fewer than eleven doctors, eighty-seven surgeons, one eye-doctor and nine apothecaries from foreign countries arrived in Russia. Among them was Robert Areskine (as the family had chosen to spell their name since about 1625: they later reverted to the older form Erskine). He was the

* Crankshaw, *Russia and Britain*.

† See Crankshaw, *op. cit.*; also A. F. Steuart, *Scottish Influences in Russian History*, and James Grant, *The Scottish Soldiers of Fortune*.

‡ The invaluable account of Areskine's career by Robert Paul in the *Miscellany of the Scottish History Society*, II (*1904*), antedates the publication of those Reports of the Historical Manuscripts Commission (*Stuart Papers, II-IV; Polwarth MSS, I*) which provide abundant documentation of Areskine's Jacobite activities. Further contemporary references to Areskine may be found in *Sbornik Imperatorskago Russkago Istoricheskago Obshchestva*. Thus, when Norris was charged with the difficult diplomatic assignment of persuading the Russians to withdraw their troops from Mecklenburg, he wrote to the Earl of Sunderland (*Sbornik*, Vol. 61) that 'it will be best to try for it in a private way, by means of the physician'.

sixth surviving son of Sir Charles Erskine of Alva, Bart., and a relative of the Earl of Mar. He was educated at Edinburgh University and obtained his medical qualifications in Edinburgh (where he served an apprenticeship) and in Paris. In 1704, at the age of 26, he set off for Russia, and first entered the service of Prince Menschikoff, the Czar's favourite. Prince Menschikoff soon parted with him to the Czar, and was later to be called a fool for doing so. Thereafter Areskine's rise was rapid. He became the Czar's personal physician, and was soon deep in his confidence, acquiring public honours and a fair fortune on the way. Outside his purely medical duties, which were extensive enough, he seems also to have been employed by the Czar in a diplomatic capacity. He died in 1718 at the comparatively early age of 41.

A less public aspect of Areskine's life – although it was something of an open secret, and one which called forth an official protest from the British Government – was his deep involvement in Jacobite plotting. In October 1718, when he lay dying, M. Weber, Hanoverian Resident at St Petersburg, wrote to Lord Polwarth: 'His Majesty [the Czar] will lose a skilful physician and our Court a very dangerous enemy.' How dangerous Areskine's Jacobite activities really were, and in particular how far he carried Peter the Great with him, are open questions. An equally open question, though of somewhat lesser importance, is whether Areskine's Jacobite persuasion made him show any special favour to the young Bell, who, whatever his own personal political inclinations may have been, was the son of a non-juror who had suffered for his sympathies. It could have been against this background that Bell secured so attractive a first appointment as the Embassy to Persia.

Before leaving the subject of the Russian service for the Embassy to Peking, I must pause briefly on one other Scottish doctor in the Russian service, if only because it is to him and not to John Bell that falls the honour of being the first Scottish doctor to be sent to Peking by the Russians. This was Thomas Girvan or Garvine, an Ayrshire physician who served as a surgeon at the Hospital at St Petersburg. (His name appears in the standard histories in a strange variety of mutilations – for example 'Harwing' – as a result of transcription from the Russian.) Bell met him during his Persian journey, before he went to China, and gives his name as Girvan. He is also the subject, named as Garvine, of a letter of recommendation to Areskine written by the Earl of Loudon.* Whether or not the Earl of Loudon's recommendation had anything to do with it, Girvan was sent to Peking towards the end of 1715, together with de Lange (of whom we shall hear more), in response to a request

* *Miscellany of the Scottish History Society, II* (1904), p. 403.

from the Chinese Emperor to the Czar to send him a western physician.* The two stayed about a year and a half in Peking, returning to Moscow in June 1718. Girvan left no account of his experiences, however, so that John Bell, if not the first Scotsman in Peking was at least the first Scot to write about it.

The Embassy. It is characteristic of Bell that he does not say very much about the purposes of the Embassy to China in which he took part, and that while his account is an indispensable primary source for the main events of the Embassy he does not try to tell the whole story – and indeed in Peking is careful to disclaim any intention of describing events of which he was not an eye-witness. This does not mean that he did not know what was going on. It is simply that his purpose was to write a travel book, not history or diplomatic memoirs. Bearing in mind his later diplomatic career and the advantages of forty years of hindsight when he came to publish his book, there can be no doubt that he could have said more than he does if he had wanted to do so.

History and diplomatic memoirs have, however, an interest of their own, especially when the subject is of such importance as that of Sino-Russian relations, and I make no apology now for departing for a space from Bell's principles and practice to dwell on the background† to his book. To do so will not harm his text, which stands in its own right as a first-rate story of a fascinating journey.

Throughout the seventeenth century, particularly as the vacuum of Siberia began to fill, China and Russia had become increasingly aware of each other's existence, and with the awareness had come inevitably friction and incidents – due more, it should be noted, to the excesses of frontiersmen than to any desire by either Empire to engage the other. The Treaty of Nerchinsk of 1689 – the first treaty ever concluded by China with a European power – established a fairly satisfactory *modus vivendi* on the political front, and also attempted to regulate the not inconsiderable caravan trade from Russia to China. The political settlement lasted well enough, despite a certain amount of Chinese suspicion

* According to the Rev. Isaac Kimber, *A New History of the Life and Reign of the Czar Peter the Great*, the Chinese asked not only for 'an able physician' but also for 'some medi cines that provoke to venery'.

† The indispensable study of the diplomatic background, to which I am heavily in-debted, is Gaston Cahen's *Histoire des Relations de la Russie avec la Chine sous Pierre le Grand*, Paris, 1912, well documented from the Russian material and with an invaluable bibliography. Baddeley's *Russia, Mongolia, China* is no less indispensable for the wider background—even though it nominally sets its historical limit at the year 1676—and for its exhaustive examination of the geographical links.

of Russian dealings with the Mongolian Kalmuks, who were a real threat to the north-west frontier of China's recently established Manchu dynasty. The arrangements for the caravan trade, though of less national importance, proved to be less mutually satisfactory. On the one hand were the Russian merchants, eager to expand their profitable trade, but not always too scrupulous in their behaviour, and on the other hand was Chinese officialdom, anxious (while not averse to some private gain on the side) to have as little as possible to do with these troublesome adventurers. Thus the caravan trade, though not without advantage to both economies, failed to run smoothly.

Within three years of the Treaty of Nerchinsk one attempt was made by the Russians to put the caravan trade on a better footing. Everard Isbrandt Ides, a German merchant adventurer, was, on his own initiative, invested with the character of 'Envoy' and led a caravan to Peking in 1692 in the dual capacity of merchant and diplomat. The Chinese received him with considerable formal courtesies, including several Imperial audiences, but declined to conduct any diplomatic business with him on the grounds that the Emperor's titles had been written below those of the Czar in his credentials. Ides therefore achieved next to nothing on the diplomatic front, and after his failure the caravans, running every second year to Peking, were left to look after themselves for the next quarter of a century without benefit of official Russian intervention on their behalf.

The next event of diplomatic importance was a Chinese Embassy — the first ever sent by them outside the confines of Asia. This was the Embassy associated with the name of T'u Li-shen, whom we shall meet in Bell's pages. T'u Li-shen was the official historian rather than the leader of this Embassy, which took place in the years 1712-1716. Its main purpose was to negotiate with the Torguts, who were a considerable offshoot of the Kalmuks and at that time were living on the banks of the Volga — and whom it was very much in China's interests to keep from joining their kinsmen among China's enemies on the north-west frontier. T'u Li-shen's journey through Siberia to the banks of the Volga could not, of course, have been undertaken without Russian permission, and in fact the Russians did a good deal to facilitate the progress of the Embassy. It was not, however, thought necessary to invite the Embassy either to Moscow or to St Petersburg to be received by the Czar, though it may be noted that the Embassy was in fact equipped with instructions to meet such an eventuality had it offered itself. As it was, the Chinese were probably quite satisfied with what they achieved of their main purpose, and, no less important, with what they had learned of the Russian dispositions in Siberia in particular and of the relations between Russia and the Torguts and other peoples who formed a buffer between the two Empires.

The time had clearly come for a Russian initiative in this field, and it took the form of the Embassy under Leon Vasilievitch Izmailov in which John Bell took part. Izmailov's mission, unlike that of his predecessor Ides, was to be entirely official, and he was not to engage in any private trade. His instructions were, however, heavily weighted on the commercial side. Those from the College of Foreign Affairs may be summarized* as follows.

So far as ceremonial matters were concerned, his credentials would be written to conform with the Chinese practice, thus avoiding the mistake that had been made with those of Ides. Izmailov was to make every effort to be received according to his rank as he would have been as an Ambassador in any European Court, but he was to submit to Chinese etiquette – the kowtow, etc. – if necessary.

On the military side, Izmailov was to observe (secretly) the country, its resources and its armaments. He was also to assure the Chinese that the new Russian strongholds along the Irtysh were intended merely for defensive purposes against the Kalmuks and the Cossack Horde.

At Peking, Izmailov was to ask for a site for an Orthodox church, to be built at the Czar's expense.

He was to concentrate particularly on commercial matters. First, he was to stay as long as he judged necessary to obtain solid information about the merchandise in which the Russian Treasury was most interested – gold, silver, precious stones – and their rates of exchange. Then he was to enter into direct negotiations with the Emperor's ministers to increase business and to send the caravans yearly instead of every second year. If the Chinese complained of the expense to themselves of catering for the caravans (which they insisted on doing in order to maintain the principle that they were admitted not of right but as Chinese guests) Izmailov was to assure them that thenceforth the caravans would pay their own expenses – though Ambassadors and official envoys (in deference to the same principle) would continue to be quartered at Chinese expense.

So far Izmailov's instructions look reasonable enough, at least as an opening bid after a silence of over a quarter of a century. In more ambitious vein, however, he was also instructed to ask for complete free trade throughout China, on a basis of reciprocity. This instruction was quite unrealistic, as the subsequent history of the China Trade was to

* Following Cahen, *op. cit.*

show. Less ambitious, perhaps, in Russian eyes – though it too struck deep at a Chinese principle – was his final instruction from the College of Foreign Affairs, which was to try to obtain permission to establish a resident Russian agent or consul in Peking, and to leave one of his suite there in that capacity.

In addition to the foregoing instructions from the College of Foreign Affairs, Izmailov also received minutely detailed instructions on commercial matters from the College of Trade. Even more minutely detailed and ambitious instructions were given by the College of Trade to his deputy, de Lange, who, it was hoped, would become the Russian presence in Peking after Izmailov's departure. The instructions to de Lange, while covering much of the same ground as Izmailov's also included, as a Chinese historian has pointed out, an egregious piece of wishful thinking in the instruction that he should propose that the Russian consul should have jurisdiction over all Russian subjects in China – the principle of 'extra-territoriality' finally forced on China in 1844 and bitterly resented always as a national humiliation till its final disappearance during the Second World War.

Izmailov, then, did not lack instructions when he set off for Peking in July 1719, and great care was also taken over the presents for the Emperor and in all the administrative arrangements necessary to ensure the success of the Embassy. He travelled as much as possible, as a glance at the map and Bell's account show, by river – in fact by the well-established caravan route. Of all the accounts of that route, Bell's cannot be bettered, and there is no need here to trace the physical progress of the Embassy. The reader may wish to note, however, that both Ides and T'u Li-shen left accounts* of much of the same route. Neither is as detailed as Bell's, and neither is wholly reliable in itself, but both provide convincing contemporary testimony to the accuracy of Bell's observation and description of many of the points of the journey.

On the 18th of March 1720 (Old Style, as with all Bell's dates) the Embassy reached Irkutsk. There supplementary instructions caught up with Izmailov, on a subject which was to give him a good deal of trouble,

---

* Full bibliographical details in Cahen. The account of Ides was published with admirable illustrations, some of which I have not scrupled to borrow for the present volume. (In so doing, I follow the precedent of the publisher of the *Travels* of Corneille le Brun, into which a version of the narrative of Ides was interpolated.) Adam Brand, Secretary to Ides, also published an account of the Embassy.

T'u Li-shen's account survives in several versions. One was translated into English by Staunton in 1821 under the title *Narrative of the Chinese Embassy to the Khan of the Tourgouth Tartars*, with interesting footnotes comparing T'u Li-shen's text with that of John Bell. A rare Chinese version of T'u Li-shen's account is referred to hereafter.

the solution of which in fact largely obscured the main purposes of the Embassy. A Russian caravan under Istopnikov, which had set out for Peking in 1718 – almost a year before the Embassy – had been held up by the Chinese on the border since July 1719. The reasons for this lay partly in Chinese dissatisfaction with the deteriorating behaviour of the merchants in recent caravans and partly in Chinese suspicions of Russian involvement with the Kalmuks; but whatever the reasons, and whether or not they were justified, the Chinese were going so far as to talk of suspending commercial relations entirely. Izmailov was instructed to join with the Governor of Siberia in trying to persuade the Chinese to let the caravan into China; but if (as was expected) this proved unavailing he was to proceed without it to Peking and try there, in addition to his other instructions, to get permission for it to enter.

Izmailov and the Governor of Siberia duly sent off their joint letter to the Chinese from Irkutsk, and Izmailov then proceeded on his way to the border, hoping perhaps to receive a favourable answer *en route*. What actually happened was that he was met at Selenginsk by T'u Li-shen, who since the successful conclusion of the Embassy to the Torguts had become, and was to remain, one of China's Russian experts.

It was an interesting encounter. Bell describes it very briefly (page 97 of the present volume) and there is a detailed Russian version of it. But T'u Li-shen's account is also worth reading, not only for itself, but as being the only authoritative Chinese account of Izmailov's Embassy.* Here it is, in the form of a despatch from T'u Li-shen to his Emperor:

When Your servant went from Kurun, the residence of the Hutu-khtu, to Selenginsk, he heard that the *Ch'a-han Khan* [the Czar] had despatched an envoy thither. On the twenty-eighth day of the fifth month (July 3, 1720) Your servant arrived at Selenginsk, where people were saying that the Chief of Selenginsk, *Lo-pu-so*, had already been summoned to Tobolsk by the Governor-General, and that in the suite of this Embassy *Lang-k'o* [Lange] who had formerly come to Peking with the Western physician *Ka-er-fei-yin* [Garvine] was serving as an envoy.

* I quote, with permission, the translation of Fu Lo-shu in her unprinted work *A Documentary Chronicle of the Celestial Empire: Sino-Western Relations as Revealed in Chinese Sources, 1644-1820*. (Available in microfilm – British Museum, Dept. of Oriental Printed Books and MSS, Spool 528; Washington, Library of Congress, Microfilm 7771 DS. Reviewed in *T'oung Pao*, LI, No. 2-3). Miss Fu's book contains, among much other valuable material, extracts from a rare Chinese edition of T'u Li-shen's book, the *I Yü Lu*, which I have not myself seen. The references here quoted do not appear in Staunton's version.

Thereupon, the Ambassador sent by the *Ch'a-han Khan*, the chief of the merchants, *Fei-yüeh-to-er* [Feodor (Istopnikov)] and the Acting Chief of Selenginsk, *P'ai-fa-er Ssu-t'ieh-pan* [Stephan] and other officials respectfully asked after the Imperial health of the Great Emperor of the Middle Kingdom. Your servant returned their greetings by asking after the health of the *Ch'a-han Khan*, of his Lady, and of his son, *O-li-k'o-hsieh P'iao-to-er-yü-chih* [Alexis Petrovitch]. Their Ambassador said that the *Ch'a-han Khan* and his Lady were both well, but that the son had died during the past year. Thereupon, Your servant asked about the position of the Ambassador, what his name was, who sent him, where he had come from, how many months he had spent on his journey, and on what errand he had come. According to the Russians this Ambassador is a Captain, a rank somewhat equivalent to the *Tso-ling* of China. His name is briefly spoken as *Wa-shih-li-yü-ch'ih I-ssu-mai-lo-fu* [Vasilievitch Izmailov]. The Vice-Ambassador is *I-fan-I-fan-no-ch'ih Lang-k'o* [Ivan Ivanovitch Lange]. Under them are three officers, one physician,* and over a hundred menservants. They are all specially sent by the *Ch'a-han Khan* to Peking.

The Ambassador Izmailov and others said:

'Last year the *Ch'a-han Khan* of our country said: "The August Emperor of China has reigned for so many years with a sublime virtue and has enjoyed such great happiness and long life that I am somewhat his junior. Since the peace treaty many years ago, our people have received so many favours from His Imperial Majesty that I feel very grateful." Thereupon he specially sent us to respectfully ask after the health of the August Emperor and to present a memorial and native products as tribute. We were sent from *San-pi-ti-li-p'u-er* [St Petersburg] and we have spent eleven months on the journey.

'On the eve of our departure [from St Petersburg] the great Board [i.e. Li-fan Yüan†] of your country had transmitted a communication to our *Ch'a-han Khan* saying that the merchants of our country at Peking had behaved lawlessly. We received the written order of our *Ch'a-han Khan* inquiring: "How can these merchants who go to the Great Empire disobey the law and behave wrongly and unreasonably? Perhaps this was because the commissars and the

---

* Perhaps the only Chinese reference to John Bell.

† This has been translated as 'Office for the Regulation of Barbarians', the nearest equivalent in early Ch'ing administration to a Ministry of Foreign Affairs.

chiefs who have commanded them cannot restrain them. When you arrive at the Middle Kingdom, you should petition the August Emperor that hereafter, if the merchants behave unreasonably, they must be strictly admonished and restrained. You must settle this matter properly before you return home.

"Moreover, in that above-mentioned communication it also says, when our merchants went to China, the August Emperor sent official soldiers to welcome them, and as soon as they arrived at Peking, the people were provided with food and the horses with fodder at government expense. When they returned to our country the August Emperor despatched soldiers to escort them out of the territory. They were not official envoys, but only profit-seeking traders. Why should they enjoy the privileges of official provisions and fodder for their horses? Since the August Emperor has bestowed on them so much favour, how dare they behave so unreasonably and violently? We imagine that after explanation the caravans may be allowed to proceed to China. If you are allowed to bring them into China together, then you should go forth together." '.
I have already reported this situation to the Great Board in a written letter, and I also reported it to the Tushetu Khan over ten days ago. I have in my possession the memorial of the *Ch'a-han Khan*. . . .

T'u Li-shen's account now turns to political and military affairs into which it is unnecessary for present purposes to follow him. The meeting was inconclusive, with evasions on both sides (the Russians refusing to be drawn on the question of their relations with the Kalmuks, and T'u Li-shen being equally non-committal on the question of the caravan). T'u Li-shen departed a few days later. Izmailov finally received on the 9th of August couriers informing him that he, but not the caravan, was admitted to China. So Izmailov at last set off for Peking with his suite – having first, incidentally, borrowed 10,000 roubles from the caravan for expenses in Peking.

John Bell's narrative now takes us to the gates of Peking, but does not mention one episode which could have wrecked the Embassy's prospects at the last moment. This arose on the 7th/10th of November, after the Chinese had handed over to Izmailov four Russian prisoners whom they had taken from the Kalmuks in their recent victory over them. Probably in an excess of zeal the Chinese sought to extract the maximum political advantage from this gesture by trying to induce Izmailov to indicate to a Kalmuk ambassador, whom T'u Li-shen was at that time receiving at Kalgan, that Russia and China were in understanding against the Kalmuks. Izmailov declined, and T'u Li-shen in a rage, real or pretended, threatened to halt the Embassy there and then. Izmailov remained unmoved, and after several unsuccessful attempts at intimidation the Chinese gave way. It was perhaps fortunate from the point of view of saving the Chinese face that at this point Izmailov had fallen ill. This gave the Chinese the opportunity to do more than withdraw gracefully from an awkward position of their own making, and they went accordingly to the other extreme. The Emperor not only sent a doctor to Izmailov – it is perhaps not surprising that John Bell does not mention this – but also sent his own horses to bring Izmailov into Peking, this last being an unprecedented honour.

Thus after all the Embassy finally made an auspicious entry into Peking. It was a magnificent spectacle, as Bell's admirable description shows. Other shrewd eyes besides those of the Chinese were watching also. The Jesuit de Mailla described the scene as follows:

> Le vingt-neuf de novembre, un ambassadeur Russe fit son entrée à Peking avec une suite d'environ cent personnes, vêtues d'habits superbes à l'européenne. Des cavaliers qui l'escortoient l'épée nue à la main offroient un spectacle d'autant plus curieux, qu'il étoit nouveau & extraordinaire à la Chine. . . .*

There is, I think, implied malice here, as Father de Mailla was well aware, from his long residence in Peking, that the Chinese could not but regard drawn swords in Peking as a barbarous breach of etiquette. Bell specifically states that only the officer in charge of the escort was allowed a drawn sword, and even though de Mailla's version is repeated by another Jesuit historian, du Halde, and by Father Ripa, I would prefer to trust Bell on the point.

The Jesuits were an important factor in the Court of the Emperor K'ang Hsi. Indeed Izmailov had been specifically instructed to get them on his side over the question of the ceremonials at his Imperial audience by promising them free passage for their mail through Siberia. How important they were, both as interpreters and as advisers to the Emperor on European affairs emerges clearly enough from references

---

* de Mailla, *Histoire Générale de la Chine*, XI, p. 335. Although de Mailla's book was not published till 1780, he was an eye-witness of the events described, having arrived in Peking in 1702. A very similar account of the Embassy's arrival is in du Halde, *Description de L'Empire de la Chine*, I, p. 549.

throughout Bell's account of the proceedings of the Embassy. Their role is spelled out in even greater detail in Father Ripa's account* of the Embassy's reception, reprinted in the Appendix to the present volume.

John Bell and Father Ripa may be left between them to describe in their equally vivid ways, if from different viewpoints, the events of the Imperial audience which was the first hurdle Izmailov had to cross before he could get down to business. The Chinese insistence on the performance by foreign Ambassadors of the full kowtow ceremony was, as the reader may wish to be reminded, no empty formality, but a positive underlining of the essential doctrine that they were admitted to China not as of right and not as representatives of powers equal to China, but as bearers of tribute to the Middle Kingdom.† (T'u Li-shen, as has been noted, makes Izmailov describe himself as coming to China 'to present a memorial and native products as tribute'.) Unrealistic as the West always found this principle, it was for long the *sine qua non* to the transaction of any business – though it may also be noted that the mere performance of the kowtow was not in itself any guarantee of success in one's mission.

Izmailov at any rate made the best of it, and the real business of the Embassy began. After the first public Audience, Izmailov had no fewer than eleven other audiences with the Emperor during his stay of over three months in Peking, not to speak of separate discussions with Chinese officials. The upshot of all these complicated negotiations was, in Izmailov's view, satisfactory. He obtained permission for the entry of Istopnikov's caravan (in exchange for advising the Governor of Siberia that the Chinese desired the return of seven hundred Mongolians who had fled across the border into Siberia); he obtained permission for de Lange to remain behind after his departure; he was promised a site for a Russian church in Peking; and he was given a hundred seals, each valid for the admission of one Russian caravan to Peking (and without which no Russian caravan could enter). Furthermore, after the disagreeable business of the kowtow had been settled he had throughout been treated with the highest courtesy and respect. The Chinese on their side had exacted no immediate *quid pro quo*. Apart from tidying up the caravan question by the device of the seals referred to above, and the request for the return of the seven hundred Mongolian fugitives, they had stressed

---

* Matteo Ripa, *Storia della Fondazione della Congregazione e del Collegio dei Cinesi etc*, Naples, 1832. The version in the Appendix to the present volume is from the abridged English translation by Fortunato Prandi under the title *Memoirs of Father Ripa*, London, John Murray, 1844.

† On the Ch'ing tributary system see J. K. Fairbank and S. Y. Teng, *Ch'ing Administration: Three Studies* (Harvard University Press, 1960).

throughout the negotiations two questions – Russian relations with the buffer tribes and the Mongolians, and the need for a more precise definition of the frontier. Izmailov was not required to give any specific assurance on either question, but undertook faithfully to represent the Chinese views to the Czar.

On the whole, then, although he had by no means achieved every target in his over-ambitious instructions, Izmailov had reason enough to leave Peking, loaded with presents, a satisfied man.*

De Lange. John Bell rounds off the story of Izmailov's Embassy, which had apparently ended so satisfactorily, by reprinting a version of the journal of de Lange, who, as has been noted, was left behind as the Russian presence in Peking after Izmailov's departure. Not without reluctance I have refrained from following Bell's example, largely because Bell's text of de Lange's journal runs to some hundred and fifty pages in the edition of 1763, and even so is incomplete. Lorenz de Lange was one of the earliest and one of the most interesting of 'Old China Hands', and a study of his complete extant journals would be a most worth-while undertaking.† I confidently recommend them to the attention of anyone who is interested in the day-to-day difficulties of diplomacy in early eighteenth-century Peking.

The trouble was quite simply that although the Emperor personally had given permission for de Lange to remain in Peking the entire Civil Service was up in arms against the fundamental breach of Chinese tradition which his accreditation as a resident diplomatic agent would have implied. In fact the Civil Service's formal position was precariously maintained, since de Lange was never allowed – though he tried hard enough – to present his credentials. The absence of a defined status did not prevent de Lange from trying to do the job for which he had been left in Peking, and he embarked with considerable energy and ability on his consular duties, the most immediate of which was to negotiate the entry of Istopnikov's caravan (in which he was finally successful) and to arrange subsequently for it to trade on a proper basis (in which he was far less successful). This major preoccupation apart, he was also considerably exercised simply in administering his own affairs – repairs to his house, his rations, the behaviour of the guards at his gate, and so on.

---

* As Cahen observes, Izmailov was curiously dilatory in furnishing to his masters a proper account of the achievements of the Embassy, although in August 1725 he was to recall with pride his services and the exceptional advantages he had won, and to complain that he had been insufficiently paid.

† The essential starting-point is again Cahen's bibliography.

The ingenuity, obstinacy and courtesy with which his efforts were thwarted at every turn defy description. De Lange kept his head and – usually – his temper, but in the end he was beaten and sent away from China, after a residence of seventeen months, with nothing achieved except that Istopnikov's caravan had been permitted to trade after a fashion, and with all of Izmailov's apparent other gains eroded in the face of the hostility of the Chinese bureaucratic machine. Sino-Russian political relations, in fact, were in a worse state than before Izmailov had set out.

For de Lange personally it was not all unpleasantness. His personal, as distinct from official, relations with some members of the administration were good, and above all the Emperor showed him some considerable personal marks of favour. I have little doubt that he enjoyed his tour in Peking, frustrating and difficult as it was. Perhaps the last word on it may be left with the mandarin T'u Li-shen, who escorted him out of China, and who on the 16th of October, 1722, submitted the following despatch* from Selenginsk to his Emperor:

Your servant escorted the Vice-Ambassador of Russia, Lange, to Selenginsk. On the day of his return [i.e. to Russia] Lange called at Your servant's residence and kowtowed towards the south-east to return his thanks for the Imperial favour. Then he said to Your servant:

'I am a petty humble man of a remote and backward foreign land. Previously I had accompanied the Western doctor Garvine to Peking, and I received extraordinary honour from the heavenly great August Emperor. Yet again, when our *Ch'a-han Khan* specially sent us to enquire after the health of the Great August Emperor and present our local products, I was loaded with great favours, such as nobody had ever enjoyed here-to-fore. I have lived in Peking for two years, and I have eaten the most delicious food that anyone ever tasted in his life. Moreover I saw many places which few people in the world have seen. The great grace of the great August Emperor is as immense as the sea and the mountains. Food, clothes and various objects His Majesty bestowed on me in such abundance that I cannot enumerate them. Therefore I can find no words to express my thanks. As to the honour which His Majesty conferred on me and the

* From the rare Chinese edition of the *I Yü Lu*, in the translation of Fu Lo-shu, *A Documentary Chronicle*, II, p. 166.

Sundry Anecdotes of Peter the first

written by ~~Lord Hyndford~~

The dates with this attribution impossible. the M.S. was probably written by Patrick Bell, M.D. Anstruther [...] Petersburg

In the year 1714. on my arrival at Crownstadt, the Czar, as he was then called, came on board next morning, Ac=
=companyed only by Doctor Areskine
his chief Phisician & Interpreter on
the occasion, he went directly into the
Cabbin, & asked the Captain many quest=
=ions concerning the Swedish Fleet
he Breakfasted on bread & cheese sailors
fare, & drank a glass of Ale, which he
liked so well that he bespoke all ye Cargo
he examined every thing on board and
about the Riggin & approved much of
the Cabbin being flush with the quarter
Deck, he had been up very early as
he came that morning from Petersburg
in a ten Oar pinnace, and after
Staying

1. The first page of the 1779 manuscript an extract of which is transcribed on page 23. The attribution to Lord Hyndford has been scored out and a further, but still inaccurate, attribution added in pencil (see footnote page 22)

occasions, without prejudice to his Dignity or authority.

To pretend to give the character of Peter the first, is a task too high for me, farther than some few outlines which happened to come under my own observation, without formality or order, as I can recollect them

In his person he was tall & well made, something above six foot high, streight & well turned limbs, a brown complexion with a large hazle eye & agreeable features, strong built & fit for any exercise, or even labour—

In his apparell plain & clean, and the same in his dyet, John Felton a Dane was his master Cook for many years, who dressed his frugal Meals.

Four of Clock in the morning was his hour of getting up, tho' he seldom eat any breakfast & ten at night the hour of going to Bed, and twelve of clock at noon rather before than after, was his dinner time.

It was on a holy-day that I happened to be at Court, the Cloth was laid in the Dining—

2. Two consecutive passages from pages 12 and 13 of the 1779 manuscript including a description of Peter the First (or Great)

kindness which His Majesty bestowed on me, personally they are engraved indelibly on my heart. I shall thank and remember His Majesty all day long, and only pray for long life for the great August Emperor who has given me this great happiness. May His Majesty be strong and healthy for millions and millions of years. I shall sincerely pray to Heaven and the Buddha for His Majesty from morn till night. I, Lange, beg Your Honour to forward the sincere thanks of an ant-like insignificant person to the ears of the Buddha-like great August Emperor.'

T'u Li-shen's despatch was no doubt written on the principle that one should only report what the recipient may be expected to find palatable, and it may be doubted if de Lange, Old China Hand as he was, could have contrived to produce quite such appropriately flowery expressions of gratitude as are here attributed to him. Still, it is a seemly ending to one chapter in Sino-Russian relations. The next chapter, which saw de Lange back in China in the suite of a considerably more successful Ambassador, Sava Vladislavitch (1725-1728), does not here concern us.

The Book. So I leave Sino-Russian relations, recalling that they are, after all, only part of the background to John Bell's travel book. There is another background which needs only the briefest of mentions, so little influence does it have on the book, and that is the vision of 'Cathay', that perfect land ruled by philosophy, which remained a powerful literary convention throughout most of the eighteenth century,* though the convention outlasted the belief that such a place existed. John Bell takes no account whatever of it, carefully setting down only what he saw, and recording, sometimes with qualification, only what he believed to be true of the things he was told, and with no sideways glances at the nonsense – often, it is true, engaging nonsense – that was still in his day being written about China by those who had never been there.

John Bell's account of how he came to write his *Travels* is in his own Preface, here reprinted. It is at first sight curious that he waited so long to publish his book, but there seems to be no good reason to doubt his account. The question inevitably arises, however, whether after so long an interval what he published in 1763 faithfully reflects what he saw some forty years earlier. And the answer to that question hinges on what sort of notes the young Bell took at the time of his travels, and to what extent they were embellished in later years.

* See, for example, Hugh Honour's *Chinoiserie*, London, 1961.

C

There can be little doubt that Bell's original notes, none of which are known to survive, must at the least have taken the form of a careful and detailed travel diary, paying particular attention to such entirely practical points as the distances between the various stages of the journey and the difficulties and problems of the route. No sensible traveller on such a journey would have done less. He had obviously done so on his earlier Persian journey, and such a log of the Chinese journey forms the clear – and unfalsifiable – skeleton of Bell's book.

The flesh on this skeleton – the 'notes and observations' which Bell distinguishes in his Preface – might perhaps be more suspect to those who were ungenerous enough not to be willing to accept John Bell's own word for it, since it is in this aspect that he might, in theory at least, have been tempted to introduce 'improvements' and falsifications of his original material. These are subjective matters in which, in default of hard evidence, the reader must form his own impressions. Bell certainly reworked his original material in preparing it for publication, and he occasionally departs from his own time-scale, as when he interpolates a reference to the date of Izmailov's death. In my view, however, he certainly did not go beyond the limits of decency, and what he printed in 1763 is a substantially faithful reproduction of what he wrote at the time of his journey.

There are indeed occasional errors of fact in Bell's text – not all of which I have thought it necessary to draw to the attention of the reader – which argue for its being a genuine record and not the product of the scholar's lamp and imagination. The most striking example is perhaps his statement that the Great Wall was built 'about six hundred years ago', when two thousand years would have been nearer the mark. This is not the kind of mistake that anyone writing up the passage from literary sources, of which by the 1760's there were enough, would have made.

The most convincing testimony to the honesty and scrupulousness with which John Bell reworked his original material lies in a manuscript in his own handwriting, written at Antermony in 1779 when he was 88 years of age, to which he gave the title *Sundry Anecdotes of Peter the First*.* This manuscript, of forty pages, is, as its title suggests, a somewhat random series of reminiscences of Peter the Great and his times, and it bears every sign of having been written in rather a hurry at two or three sessions. What lends it a particular interest in my present context is

---

* National Library of Scotland, MS 109, ff. 10-29, formerly attributed to one Patrick Bell. Not reprinted in the present volume, since its contents deserve to be more closely studied in relation to Bell's other *Travels*, in particular the *Journey to Derbent*.

that two passages in the manuscript of 1779 use exactly the same material as had appeared in the printed text of the *Travels* of 1763. Two brief extracts will illustrate the point:

Text of 1763 (Vol II, p. 357)
About the middle of October, 1714, I arrived at Cronstadt in an English ship. The Czar, having notice of the ship's arrival, came on board, the next morning, from St Petersburg; being attended only by Dr Areskine, who was his chief physician at that time, and, on that occasion, served him as interpreter. After his Majesty had enquired news about the Swedish fleet, &c. he eat a piece of bread and cheese, and drank a glass of ale, then went on shore to visit the works carrying on at Cronstadt; and returned, the same evening, to St Petersburg, distance about twenty English miles.

Manuscript of 1779
In the year 1714 on my arrival at Crownstadt, the Czar, as he was then called, came on board next morning, accompanied only by Doctor Areskine his chief Phisician and Interpreter on the occasion, he went directly into the Cabbin, & asked the Captain many questions concerning the Swedish Fleet —— he Breakfasted on bread & cheese, sailors fare, & drank a glass of ale, which he like so well that he bespoke all ye Cargo he examined everything on board and about the Riggin & approved much of the Cabbin being flush with the quarter-deck, he had been up very early as he came that morning from Petersburg in a ten Oar pinnace, and after staying about an hour on the Island returned directly in the same pinnace. . . .

It is obvious that the manuscript of 1779, with its additional if minor details, was not copied from the printed text of 1763. If indeed the manuscript were not dated 1779 the natural assumption would be that the printed text had been edited from it. Obviously, in fact, both texts derive from a common original, and that original must have been some considerably detailed notes written very near the time they describe – events, be it noted, of half a century before the appearance even of the printed text.

John Bell, then, from his earliest years, kept detailed notes of his experiences, and for that matter was still drawing on them and reworking them at the end of his long life. The next question, which is raised by an extraordinary story in the *Quarterly Review* of July 1817, is whether anyone else had a hand in the reworking of his notes for the publication of his *Travels*. The *Quarterly*, after describing Bell's *Travels* as 'the best model perhaps for travel-writing in the English language', goes on (expanding some of the detail in Bell's own Preface) to say that for many years after his return he used to amuse his friends with accounts of what he had seen, 'refreshing his recollection from a simple diary of occurrences and observations'. 'The Earl Granville', the *Quarterly* continues, 'then president of the Council, on hearing some of his adventures, prevailed on him to throw his notes together in the form of a narrative, which, when done, pleased him so much that he sent the manuscript to Doctor Robertson, with a particular request that he would revise and put it in a fit state for the press. The literary avocations of the Scottish historian at that time not allowing him to undertake the task, he recommended Mr Barron, a professor in the University of Aberdeen; and on this gentleman consulting Doctor Robertson as to the style and the book of travels which he would recommend him to adopt for his guide, the historian replied "Take Gulliver's Travels for your model and you cannot go wrong".'

So circumstantial a story, with the great authority of the *Quarterly* behind it, cannot perhaps be dismissed out of hand; though I hope I shall not be suspected of undue partiality if I find it hard to accept what is here implied – that the hand of the ghost-writer lies on John Bell's pages. I simply do not believe this. That John Bell unaided could write a good story in a good plain style is in fact demonstrated in the manuscript of 1779 to which I have referred. He had also, it will be recalled, years of diplomatic experience which, if they did not necessarily foster a 'literary' style, certainly gave him plenty of experience of straightforward reporting of events (I wonder how many of Rondeau's admirable despatches he drafted?). The *Quarterly* story, too, appeared more than fifty years after the publication of Bell's *Travels*, and its writer therefore cannot have had any first-hand experience of the circumstances he so plausibly describes.

My guess as to what actually happened is that Bell may well have written to Principal Robertson with a copy of his manuscript, to ask him what he thought of it and for advice on presentation and style – a perfectly sensible way of ensuring that his book, when it appeared, would have the *imprimatur* of learned authority. (Robertson, I observe, later subscribed for a copy: if he had in fact rendered Bell any special services, one might have expected him to get a free copy.) Robertson, in my guess, was too busy to look at it – he must have received plenty of similar approaches – and farmed it out to Professor Barron. Either Barron or Robertson eventually replied to Bell with the perfectly orthodox but really superfluous advice that for a book of travels one could not have a better model than Swift – and Bell then went ahead and prepared his manuscript for printing in his own way. There is no evidence either way, of course, and on such subjective matters the reader must form his own opinion. I will only say that no one would have suspected the hand of a ghost-writer in Bell's *Travels* were it not for the *Quarterly's* story – and that if Professor Barron really did rewrite Bell's manuscript he made a good job of it.

John Bell's book came out in 1763 in two handsome quarto volumes, printed by the distinguished Glasgow printers, Robert and Andrew Foulis, and sold by subscription at one guinea the set. The list of subscribers, reprinted in the present volume, is sufficient indication of the demand for the book. Testimony to its immediate impact, too, lies in the fact that both the *Gentleman's Magazine* and the *Annual Register* for 1763 reprinted long extracts from it — a distinction somewhat akin to serialization in the Sunday papers in more recent times. An Irish (pirate) edition by Robert Bell of Dublin followed in 1764, and in the same year W. Homer of London also reprinted it. There was a French translation, published in Paris in 1766, and in 1776 a Russian translation. In 1788, William Creech of Edinburgh brought out a new edition, commenting as follows in his 'Advertisement':

> The high character which these Travels bear in point of authentic information, and the great variety of curious matter to be found in them, respecting those countries through which the Author travelled, by a route which as yet is very little known, joined to the extreme scarcity of this Book, from the demand for it upon the Continent, were the motives for the publication of this new Edition.

William Creech reprinted it again in 1806, and the complete text was reprinted for the last time in 1811 in Volume VII of J. Pinkerton's *Voyages and Travels*.

Since the early nineteenth century, John Bell's *Travels* have dropped strangely from the consciousness of the general reader, and Bell finds no place in the histories of literature. I am at a loss to account for this, since his book remains, in my opinion, a classic — minor, perhaps, but still a classic — of eighteenth century travel literature in the unflamboyant manner.

It is, perhaps, as much a matter of the personality of John Bell as of anything else, for in a travel book the attitudes of the traveller are more important than the things he writes about. He based himself from the outset on an admirable philosophy of how travel books should be written: 'It is the business of a traveller', he writes, 'to describe places and things without prejudice or partiality; and exhibit them fairly, as they really appear. This principle it shall be my study to keep always in view.' It follows that there is no sensationalism and no purple patches in John Bell's text, and remarkably few judgments either, except for those —and they are not few — which emerge in characteristic asides.

John Bell had a sharp eye, and a mind trained originally in the medical disciplines that have produced so many fine writers of English prose.

He had also an edge to his tongue that will not escape the discerning reader – witness his beautifully restrained description of the shaman's performance at page 79 of the present volume; or his aside, when describing the Buraty (p. 76), 'I should like them much better if they were a little more cleanly'; or how, after describing a hunt he lets fall an indication of his own attitude* to blood sports – 'if killing harmless animals can be called diversion, this may properly be reckoned one of the finest'. Examples could readily be multiplied.

Another characteristic of Bell's approach to his task is the scrupulousness with which he qualifies his remarks on subjects where his knowledge was not first-hand. An example of this characteristic is noted on page 94 hereafter, when Bell's repetition of what must have been a current propaganda line on the importance of the Panchen Lama is, savingly, qualified by being introduced with the words 'I am informed that. . . .' A no less striking illustration of his caution in these respects is to be seen when, after repeating (p. 204) the current old wives' tales of the habits of the mammoth he adds: 'I only mention these things as the reports of a superstitious and ignorant people.' Even the pragmatic T'u Li-shen, in a strikingly similar account of the mammoth (pp. 70-71 of Staunton's edition) reported these tales as fact, without the vital qualification.

To sharpness of eye and an innate caution Bell added an intensely practical interest in the things he saw, which he viewed always from the standpoint of their relevance, real or potential, to the needs and circumstances of his native society. It is in this practical spirit that he looks at rhubarb, tea, porcelain, ginseng and other commodities, like the merchant he was later to become. He would, if I may be forgiven a modern analogy, have made an admirable addition to the Commercial Section of any Embassy today.

But the characteristics which perhaps emerge most clearly of all from Bell's pages are the tolerance and equanimity with which he accepted all that he saw. These qualities were, no doubt, innate in him, but they may well have been fostered and strengthened by his own Scottish background. The Scotland of his day was, after all, as many a traveller in it has made clear, a wild and barbarous enough place in many of its regions. It could well have provided the young Bell, if he knew anything of his native land, with a spectrum of experience of men and manners ranging

---

* Peter the Great also shared this rather untypical attitude. Bell notes in the manuscript of 1779 that 'He had no notion of sport or hunting, tho' the Russian gentlemen are very fond of that diversion, he could employ his leizure hours to better purpose than in pursute of innocent creatures & consequently he kept but few useless hounds & horses'.

from the highly civilized to near savagery. With such a background behind him, he was perhaps better equipped to encounter without bias the hovels and palaces, the princes and peasants, of his various journeys than would have been an observer from the more sheltered and ordered England of his time.

Be that as it may, I have stood long enough in the way of John Bell's text, and it is time that I withdrew to let its undoubted merits speak for themselves in clearer language than I can command. I must, to do justice to his achievement, end with the reminder that the *Journey to Pekin* is only one of his *Travels*. I hope I need offer no apology for leaving the others aside in the present volume to concentrate on the *Journey to Pekin*, which is a proper book in its own right. They too deserve to be read and, if I may say so, reprinted; but the honour of introducing them must fall to some other hand than mine.

NOTE

On the map overleaf, in order to relate to the text,
the place-names given are those used by Bell and not
their modern equivalents. Also, the spelling
of these names is Bell's, although in many cases
this varies from chapter to chapter
and from page to page.

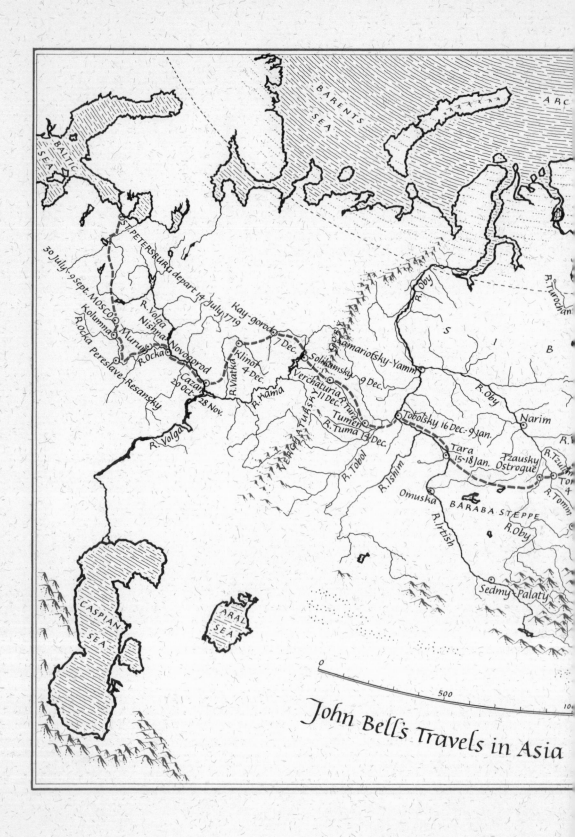

John Bell's Travels in Asia

OCEAN

R. Lena

Ochotsky

SEA OF
OKHOTSK

(EASTERN OCEAN)

Kamtzatsky

Yakutsky

R. Aldan

Podkamena-Tongusta

R. Tongusta

Ostrogue

Krasno-Yarr

Elimsky 9-12 Mar.

R. Elimoa

Vercholensky
Ostrogue

Ballagansky

Irkutsky
18 Mar-15 May

Lake Baikal

Udinsky 26 May

R. Ingoda

Albazin

R. Amoor

R. Amoor

Nertzinsky

R. Argun

Selinginsky
Streaka

29 May-9 Sept.
18 Sept.

Saratzyn 20-22 Sept.

Lake Delay

R. Idyr

R. Selinga

R. Orchon

23 Sept.

R. Tola

SEA OF
JAPAN

MONGOLIA

Khododu

HUNGRY

Oudey

DESERT

1500 Statute Miles

KOREA

Kalgan
5 Nov.

1722

PEKIN
18 Nov. 1720

·IGS·

A
JOURNEY
FROM
St. PETERSBURG
IN
RUSSIA,
TO
PEKIN
IN
CHINA,
WITH
AN EMBASSY
FROM HIS
IMPERIAL MAJESTY,
PETER THE FISRT,
TO
KAMHI
EMPEROR OF CHINA,
IN THE YEAR MDCCXIX.

A facsimile of the title-page to the *Pekin* journey from the 1763 edition
of Bell's *Travels from St Petersburg in Russia to Diverse Parts of Asia.*

NAMES OF THE PRINCIPAL PERSONS WHO COMPOSED
THE TRAIN OF THE AMBASSADOR.

LEOFF VASSILOVICH ISMAYLOFF.

LAURENCE DE LANGE,	Secretary of the Embaffy.
IVAN GLAZUNOFF,	the Ambaffador's Secretary.
KNEAZ ALEXANDER SASECKIN,	
NICOLAUS DE PAULI KRESTITZ,	
LUKIAN NESTEROFF,	Gentlemen of the Em-
ALEXIE DIVOFF,	baffy.
DAVID GRAVE,	
The AUTHOR of this JOURNAL,	
GREGORY,	a Prieft.

Interpreters, clerks, a band of mufic, valets, footmen, &c. in all to the number of about fixty perfons; befides a troop of twenty five dragoons, for our efcort from TOBOLSKY to PEKIN, and back.

A facsimile of the verso of the title-page
to the *Pekin* journey from the 1763 edition.

THE PREFACE

In my youth I had a strong desire of seeing foreign parts; to satisfy which inclination, after having obtained, from some persons of worth, recommendatory letters to Doctor Areskine, chief physician and privy-counsellor to the Czar Peter the First, I embarked at London, in the month of July 1714, on board the *Prosperity* of Ramsgate, Capt. Emerson, for St Petersburg. On my arrival there, I was received by Doctor Areskine in a very friendly manner; to whom I communicated my intentions of seeking an opportunity of visiting some parts of Asia, at least those parts which border on Russia. Such an opportunity soon presented itself, on occasion of an embassy, then preparing, from his Czarish Majesty to the Sophy of Persia.

Artemy Petrovich Valensky, a gentleman of a family of distinction, and a captain of the guards, was appointed ambassador by his Majesty. Upon his nomination, he applied to Doctor Areskine to recommend a person, who had some knowledge in physic and surgery, to go, in his suite, in the embassy. As I had employed some part of my time in those studies, the Doctor recommended me; which he did in so cordial a manner, as produced to me, from the ambassador, many marks of friendship and regard, which subsisted not only during the journey, but also continued, from that time, to the end of his days. The Doctor, at the same time, recommended me to the college of foreign affairs at St Petersburg, by whom I was engaged in the service of Peter the First.

Having acquainted the reader with the manner of my entering on the travels, which are the principal subject of the following sheets, I shall take the liberty to say, that I have, through the whole, given the observations, which then appeared to me worth remarking, without attempting to embellish them, by taking any of the liberties of exaggeration, or invention, frequently imputed to travellers.

I took notes of the subject of the following treatise, by way of diary, from time to time, during the course of my travels; intending nothing further, at that time, than to keep them as helps to my memory, that I might, as occasion offered, communicate, in conversation with my friends, what I had observed worth remarking; and that I might be capable of giving information to others, who might be desirous of it, on their being to make the same journies.

About four years ago, spending some days at the house of a Right Honourable, and most honoured, Friend,* the subject of my travels

* The Earl of Granville.

took up a great part of our conversation; during which, upon his enquiring occasionally, whether I had taken any notes of the places, &c. through which I had passed in my several journies, and, upon my answering in the affirmative, he was pleased to take some pains to engage me to promise that I would collect my notes and observations, and form them into journals, as complete as the time elapsed would admit, and communicate them to the world.

It was not without reluctance that I set about this work; which, had I thought it worth the public's acceptance and perusal, I would have done long ago. Such as it is, I now offer it to them; and flatter myself, (with hopes at least,) that the plainness of style, in which it is wrote, will be of no prejudice to it with candid readers, who may find in it some things new, and of which they would chuse to be informed.

In regard to the translation of Mr de Lange's Journal,* I have given it for two reasons; first, because it continues the negociation begun by Mr de Ismayloff, in the course of which Mr de Lange furnishes the reader with a distinct detail of the manner of transacting affairs with the ministers of state, of their chicaneries, &c. at the court of Pekin. Secondly, because I do not apprehend it hath ever appeared in the English language; at least, I have made what enquiries I could, to find if it had been translated, which have been all fruitless.

As I well knew the worthiness and integrity of Mr de Lange, and am fully persuaded that his Journal was genuine, though perhaps obtained surreptitiously by the editor, I have closed the translation with the end of Mr de Lange's Journal, on his arrival at Selinginsky on the frontiers of Siberia; having omitted an addition to it, made by the editor, of the trade and monies of China; concerning which, the editor, when he enters upon it, acquaints the reader that he had not the means necessary for sufficient information. For the rest, the translation is just, as may be seen by comparing it with the original.

ANTERMONY
October 1st, 1762

JOHN BELL

---

* Not reprinted in the present edition.

CHAPTER I

From ST PETERSBURG *to* TOBOLSKY *the capital of* SIBERIA

When I arrived at St Petersburg from Ispahan, I met with a very sensible mortification, on finding that my very worthy friend, Dr Areskine, was no more; he died about six weeks before my arrival. Not long after which, upon being informed that an embassy was preparing for China, and that his majesty had nominated Leoff Vassilovich Ismayloff, a gentleman of a family very well known and much respected in Russia, and a captain of the guards, for that employment, I became very desirous of making that journey in his train.

Upon my acquainting my very good friend, Artemy Petrovich Valensky, with my desire, he, without loss of time, recommended me to Leoff Vassilovich Ismayloff, the appointed ambassador, in such a manner as produced, on all occasions, marks of friendship and regard for me, as well during the journey, as also after our return, untill he died in 1736.*

The time, between my return from Ispahan and my setting out for Pekin, I spent with much satisfaction with my friends and acquaintance at St Petersburg. Among whom I esteemed as such, not only several worthy persons of my own countrymen, as well in trade as in the service of his majesty; but also not a few of the Russian gentry, to whom I became known on occasion of my journey to Persia, and of whom I found many to be persons of much worth and honour.

At length the presents for the Emperor of China being got ready, as well as the ambassador's dispatches, I set out from St Petersburg the 14th of July, 1719, in company with Messieurs Lange and Grave, attended by a few servants; the first was a native of Sweden, and the other of Courland.† We travelled to the city of Mosco in small parties, the more easily to procure post horses. The weather being very hot obliged us to make short stages, confining us mostly to the mornings and evenings. Having in my Persian journal described what is most remarkable on this road, I have nothing to add to what I have there observed.

Nothing material happened during our journey to Mosco, where

* Izmailov was a professional soldier, born in 1686, who had served in 1710 in a diplomatic mission to Denmark. After the conclusion of his mission to Peking he resumed his military career, rising to the rank of Lieutenant-Colonel before his death in 1738 (not 1736 as stated by Bell).   † Then, two duchies belonging to Poland; later part of Latvia.

we arrived on the 30th of July, and joined the ambassador, who had arrived there two days before, having passed us on the road. We took up our lodgings at the house of Mr Belayof, near the triumphal arch. Here we spent five weeks in preparing barques to go by water to Cazan, and necessaries for so long and unfrequented a road. This interval we passed very agreeably, being invited to all the entertainments the place afforded.

September 9th, having shipped our baggage, and prepared every thing for our departure, we went ourselves on board; and, after firing nine guns, rowed down the river Mosco. There is a shorter way from Mosco to Siberia through Yaroslave; but, as we were incumbered with heavy baggage, consisting chiefly of presents from his majesty to the emperor of China, it was thought best to proceed as far as possible by water.

Accordingly we continued our course down the Mosco river to Kolumna, then into the river Ocka; and passing Pereslave-Resansky, Murum, and other towns of less note, we arrived at Nishna-Novogorod, situated to the right hand, on a high bank of the Ocka, at its confluence with the Volga. Leaving Nishna, we entered the river Volga and proceeded towards Cazan.

After a voyage of six weeks we arrived at Cazan on the 20th of October. We intended to have continued our route farther down the Volga to the river Kama, which falls into the Volga about sixty verst below Cazan, and then up the Kama to Solikamsky; but the advancement of the season, and the frost coming on apace, made us resolve to remain at Cazan till the winter set in; least we should run the hazard of being frozen up near some uninhabited place on the Kama.

In consequence of this resolution the barques were discharged, and we took up our lodgings in the city. Here I found many of my old friends and acquaintance, particularly the Swedish officers; among others, general Hamilton,* general Rosen, and baron Wachmaiter, who still remained prisoners of war, regretting the hard fate of their long captivity. We staid here about five weeks, waiting for the snow falling to smooth the roads, and in the mean time were employed in preparing sledges, and other necessaries for our journey. Having formerly made my remarks on this route, and particularly on Cazan

* A reminder that Scottish soldiers of fortune were engaged on the Swedish side also. Hugo Johan Hamilton, Major-General of the Swedish cavalry, had been taken prisoner at the Dnieper in July 1709. He had fought at Narva, Clissow, Frauenstadt and Poltava. After his release he rose to the rank of Field-Marshal in the Swedish service. He died in 1748.

and its neighbourhood, I shall now pursue our journey towards Siberia.

November 24th, we sent off the heavy baggage: but Monsieur Ismayloff, with a few of the gentlemen, remained some days longer; because it was disagreeable travelling on rough roads with loaded sledges. At last on the 28th, late in the night, the ambassador quitted Cazan, keeping to the north-eastward. There being many villages on the road we changed horses as often as occasion required.

The 29th, we travelled through woods, consisting chiefly of tall oaks, fir, and birch. This part of the country is very fruitful, producing plenty of cattle, corn, and honey. The hives are not made like those in England: the inhabitants take the trunk of a lime-tree, aspin, or any soft wood, of about five or six feet long; having scooped it hollow, they make a large aperture in one side, about a foot in length and four inches broad; they then fix cross rods within the trunk, for the bees to build upon, and, having done this, close up the place carefully with a board, leaving small notches for the bees to go in and out. These hives are planted in proper places, at the side of a wood, and tied to a tree with strong wythes, to prevent their being destroyed by the bears who are great devourers of honey. The wax and honey exported yearly from Cazan make a very considerable article of trade. I have seen above an hundred hives near one village; and was informed, that they have a method of extracting the honey and wax without killing the bees, which would certainly be worth knowing; but I was told it so indistinctly, that I could not understand it, and had no opportunity of seeing it practised.

The villages, through which we passed, were mostly inhabited by the Tzeremish and Tzoowash Tartars, whom I have formerly mentioned. The three following days the roads were rough and narrow, lying through dark woods, interspersed with some villages and corn-fields. We passed the Ick and several smaller rivers, and then the Viatka, a pretty large one, all which discharge themselves into the Kama.

After a tedious journey of six days, we came to a small town called Klinof, or more commonly Viatka, from the river of that name running near it. The situation of this place is very pleasant, having round it corn-fields, and fine pasture, and the rivers in the neighbourhood abounding with great variety of fish.

The country about Klinof is reckoned so proper pasturage for sheep, that his majesty ordered some thousands of German sheep, most esteemed for their wool, to be bought and sent thither, with a view to establish a manufactory at this place for clothing his army. He also caused a German shepherd to be engaged in his service, who is settled here, and enjoys a considerable salary. The flocks are already so numerous, that I am persuaded they will in time answer the end proposed. A thousand other instances might be produced of the unbounded genius of this great and active Prince, who spares no expence, and overlooks nothing that can contribute either to the honour or advantage of his empire. I cannot omit another seemingly inconsiderable article, I mean pump leather: this commodity was formerly brought from England and Holland at no small charge; to save which, his majesty gave orders to engage an English tanner for a certain number of years, whom he sent to Cazan, where the best hides are, to teach the natives the art of dressing them. This scheme has fully answered the end in view, and produced abundance, not only of pump leather, but of every other kind of leather whereof that country hath any need.

There being no verst posts on this, though on most other roads in Russia, I compute the distance between Cazan and Klinof to be about five hundred verst; each verst measures one thousand one hundred and sixty yards and two feet English. Here I met with several Swedish officers, who passed a solitary life in a pleasant and plentiful country. We halted one day to refresh ourselves, and the next, being the 5th of December, we left the baggage to follow leisurely, and set out again toward Solikamsky. On the 7th, we reached Kay-Gorod, a small town. We perceived the cold becoming daily more intense as we proceeded northward along the banks of the Kama.

The 8th, we quitted Kay-Gorod in a vehement cold. Though there was little wind and a thick fog, the frost continued so penetrating that several of our people, who were most exposed, had their fingers and toes frozen. Most of them recovered by the common method of rubbing the numbed parts with snow: but had we not halted from time to time, at villages to let them warm themselves, they must have perished by cold. On the 9th, we arrived at the town of Solikamsky, derived from Sole salt and Kama the river, on the banks of which it is situated. Our arrival was a most agreeable circumstance, as the piercing frost still prevailed.

Solikamsky is a large and populous town, and the capital of a province of that name; which is at present annexed to the government of Siberia. Its situation is very pleasant, upon the eastern bank of the Kama. This river is of great fame in these parts of the world. It rises far to the north, and, in its course, receives the Parma, Pilva, Koyva, and many other rivers, which together form a mighty stream, very

3. MOSCO. 4. CAZAN. 5. KOLUMNA

(From the *Voyages* of Corneille le Brun, Amsterdam, 1718)

6. TOBOLSKY

The Gateway to Siberia (see page 46)

(From Ides, *Three Years' Travels from Moscow overland to China*, London, 1706)

nearly equal to the Volga; into which it discharges itself, about sixty verst below the city of Cazan, and loses its name. Its long course to the south-west is now turned short, by the current of the Volga, and carried toward the south-east. The Kama is well stored with variety of excellent fish. On the banks are fine corn-fields and pasture-grounds; but often interrupted by thick woods, especially to the north. These woods are stocked with different kinds of game, and wild beasts, natural to the climate.

Solikamsky is famous for having many salt-pits in its neighbourhood, the property of my worthy friend Baron Stroganof, by virtue of a grant from his majesty. The Baron has brought these works to such perfection, that he is able to serve all Russia with salt; and could besides furnish a considerable quantity for exportation, were there any demand. The salt is of a brownish colour, and very good of the kind.

The common method of procuring this salt is as follows: They dig pits in the earth till they come to the salt-rock, which seems to ly in these parts at a certain distance from the surface, as coals do in other places of the world. When the pit is finished, it is naturally, and of course, filled with water; which standing for a convenient time, till it is sufficiently impregnated with the salt, is then drawn out with pumps and other engines, and put into large iron caldrons, where it is boiled to a proper consistence; when, the water being evaporated, the salt is left upon the bottom.

I was informed of another curious and extraordinary process, by which they draw salt-water from a fresh-water river, which I cannot omit taking notice of. In the rivers near this place there is a mixture of salt-water arising from the springs, which either have their source in the salt-rocks, or run through them: it is the business of the inhabitants to discover the places where these springs empty themselves into the rivers, which they do by diving, or some other manner; having done this, they make a large frame of strong thick balks or beams joined very close, about fifteen or twenty feet square, and of depth enough to reach the bottom of the river, while part of it remains above the surface; when the ice is very strong they sink this machine into the river, over the place where the salt spring issues, and drive strong piles of wood all around, to hinder its being forced from this position by the current, or by floating ice in the end of winter. During the winter they draw out all the water, mud and sand, contained within the machine, and sink it still deeper until it hath penetrated the bottom of the channel of the river, and prevented all further communication between it and the salt spring: the frame is now filled only with the salt-water,

D

issuing from the spring, from whence it is drawn, and the salt extracted as formerly described.

However tedious and expensive this process may seem, these people perform it with great readiness and ease; and, what is still more extraordinary, without regular instruction in any art subservient to that purpose, but by the mere force of natural genius. The Baron has a great number of hands constantly employed in this service. And the woods for fewel are inexhaustible.

When the salt is made, it is laid up in granaries, till the season of transporting it to Mosco, St Petersburg and other places: the barques, for this purpose, called by the Russians Lodia, are of a construction somewhat uncommon. I have seen some of them longer and broader than any first rate man of war in England, and not one iron-nail in the whole fabrick. All of them are flat-bottomed, having one tall tree for a mast, and a sail of light canvass in proportion. To manage this mighty machine, six or eight hundred men are necessary; the rudder is nearly as long as the barque; and so unwieldy, that sometimes it requires forty or fifty men to steer it. They load these ships very deep, and let them float down the Kama into the Volga; where, if the wind is not favourable, they are obliged to draw them, against the stream, to the place of their destination.

I cannot leave Solikamsky without mentioning the rich iron-mines in the country adjacent, at Katherina-Burg, and other places of that district, which produce iron, equal perhaps in quality to the best in the world. These works have of late been brought to great perfection, by the skill and indefatigable industry of Mr Demidof, a native of Russia, enabled and encouraged to carry them on by a beneficial grant from his majesty; who is always ready to assist and protect those, who, by their ingenuity, form projects to the advantage of his country.

These works, I am informed, are still capable of great improvement. The ore is very good, and rises in many places to the very surface of the earth, and may be dug at a small expence. As for wood to smelt it, no place in the world can have greater advantage. Besides, all the machines may be driven by water; and there is an easy communication by the rivers, to St Petersburg for exportation, and to many other parts of Russia, for inland consumption.

In these mines are often found magnets of various sizes. I have seen some of them very large, and of high virtue.

There are several other iron-works in Russia; for instance, at Tula, Olonitz, and other places; but the metal is of an inferior quality to that of Siberia. Besides these of iron, there are also rich mines of excellent copper at this place, which, being lately discovered, are capable of great improvement. The copper-ore also rises to the very surface.

In the neighbourhood of Solikamsky is found the fossil called asbestos; of which is made a kind of cloth like linen, that may be put into the fire and taken out again unconsumed. This cloth was known among the ancients, and used by them on several occasions. At present, it goes by the name of the incombustible linen.

The asbestos, like many both curious and useful discoveries, was found out by mere accident in these parts. I shall briefly relate in what manner: A certain huntsman being about to load his fowling-piece, and wanting wadding, observed a great stone in the woods, which seemed to have some flakes upon it like loose threeds; he soon found that by rubbing it turned into a soft downy substance fit for his use: he therefore filled his pocket with it; but having fired his piece, was surprised to see that the gun-powder had no effect upon the wadding: this raised his curiosity so far, that he kindled a fire on purpose, into which he put the asbestos; but still took it out intire, and of the same use as formerly: this experiment so frightened the poor sportsman, that he imagined the devil had taken possession of the fossil. On returning home, he narrated what had happened to the priest of the parish; who, amazed at the relation, repeated it so frequently, that, at last, he told it to a person who was acquainted with that quality peculiar to the asbestos; and, on examination, found the flakes to be that fossil.

The weather is much colder at Solikamsky than at other places situated several degrees nearer to the north pole; perhaps its great distance from any part of the ocean may be partly the cause of the excessive cold which sometimes prevails.

December 10th, the ambassador took post horses, and set out for Tobolsky, leaving the baggage to follow as should be most convenient. About midnight we came to a village called Martinsky; here having changed horses, we soon reached the mountains named Verchatursky-Gory, where we found the snow very deep, and a strong frost still continued. We kept on our journey, ascending and descending these high and steep mountains for the space of fifteen hours. In such of the valleys as are fit for culture, are found Russian villages well peopled. And, where the woods are cut down, there appeared a beautiful land-skip, even at this bleak season.

These mountains divide Russia from Siberia. They run in a ridge from north to south, inclining a little to the east and west of these points. They are quite covered with wood, consisting of tall firs of different kinds, larinxes, birch, and other trees natural to the climate;

and abound with game and various kinds of wild beasts. Their length, from north to south, I cannot ascertain; but compute their breadth, where we passed, to be about forty English miles. But they are not near so high as the mountains I have seen in Persia, and other parts of the world.

Having passed these mountains, we descended, on the 11th, into a country finely varied with plains and rising grounds, interspersed with woods, villages, corn-fields, and pasturage; and, in the evening, reached the town called Verchaturia, from verch which signifies high, and Tura the name of the river on which the town stands. This river is navigable, and runs to the east till it discharges itself into the Tobol. Verchaturia is pleasantly situated upon a rising ground, and fortified with a ditch and palisades. It is governed by a commandant, who has under him a garrison, consisting of some regular troops and cossacks. What makes Verchaturia considerable, is its being a frontier town, and commanding the only entry from Russia into Siberia. Here is a custom-house, where all merchants are obliged to make entry of what sums of money or merchandise they carry into Siberia, or from Siberia into Russia; on all which is charged a duty of ten per cent to his majesty. Though this impost may appear high, it is really very moderate, considering the profits which the trade yields, and it extends only to the money to be employed in traffick; for every merchant is allowed a certain sum for his expences, free of all duty.

The country, adjacent to Verchaturia, is inhabited by a race of people called Vogullitz, who differ in language, dress, and manners, from any nation I ever saw. Their features and persons have a resemblance of the Tzoowashians near Cazan. They have some obscure notions of the Deity; and are very fond of a kind of wizards called Shamans, whom they hold in great esteem. I shall have occasion to speak more fully of these Shamans afterwards. The Vogullitz know nothing of agriculture; but live in huts in the woods, and subsist by hunting and fishing. They are an honest inoffensive people, but not very numerous; arising perhaps from their unsocial and uncomfortable manner of life. The archbishop of Tobolsky hath of late, by his pious labours, converted many of them to Christianity; who now begin to build houses, and cultivate some appearance of society; and, probably, in time, the rest will follow so laudable an example: this however will depend much on the encouragement they meet with, from the clergy and subgovernors of provinces. I visited them as often as any opportunity offered, both in their huts and houses, and endeavoured to procure some information about their original, or from whence they came to settle in these northern parts; but could obtain nothing satisfactory on either of these heads.

Before we enter Siberia, it will not be perhaps improper to give a short account of the singular manner in which this most extensive country was discovered by the Russians.

About the beginning of the last century, a certain Don-Cossack, named Yarmak Timotheovitz,* being obliged, by some accident, to leave his native country, and having no means of subsistence, he, with a few accomplices, betook themselves to robbing on the highways. He soon became famous and powerful; for he robbed only the rich; and, by a generosity uncommon in such a character, liberally bestowed to such as were in want. He never killed, nor even hurt any person, unless compelled to such outrages in his own defence. This behaviour so raised his reputation, that all the idle fellows in the country enlisted themselves in his gang, proud to follow so brave and enterprising a leader. He became at last so troublesome that the governors of the southern provinces sent out troops to apprehend him; but, being previously informed of the design, he withdrew from the land, and procuring boats upon the Volga, commenced pirate on that river. Being attacked here also, he was forced to cross the Caspian sea, and shelter himself on the Persian shore, where he passed some time under the disguise of a merchant. Being again discovered, he was obliged by the Persians, to quit their coast: and now his only refuge was to return to the Volga, where he behaved with great circumspection, often lurking in woods and villages; and, being in no want of money, paid the inhabitants liberally for every thing he needed. Foreseeing however that such a numerous gang could not be long concealed, he took the resolution of leaving the Volga, and steered his course up the river Kama, at that time little frequented by the Russians, or any other nation; here he hoped to find, at least, a safe retreat during the winter. Yarmak, therefore, with his followers, amounting to the number of two hundred, continued their voyage up the Kama, till they were stopped by the ice, at no great distance from a large village, now belonging to Baron Stroganof. The inhabitants were alarmed at the sight of so many armed men, whom they were not able to oppose, and therefore gave them an hospitable reception. Yarmak demanded only provisions, and winter quarters, for his money, promising to leave them unmolested next spring. In consequence of this declaration,

* Bell gives a somewhat glamourised version of the career of the great robber-adventurer Yermak, but rightly brings out his key role in the conquest of Siberia. Bell's dating is wrong, however. Yermak crossed the Urals in 1581.

he and his followers passed the winter very quietly in this remote place; afraid, however, at the approach of summer, of being discovered by the government, and uncertain what course to steer; it was at last determined to cross the mountains of Verchaturia, and go to the eastward, in hopes of finding some inhabited country; or, at least, a safe retreat.

Having passed the mountains, they arrived at the river Tur; and, finding it navigable, soon made a sufficient number of canoes for the whole gang. After rowing for some days down the Tur, they discovered several villages of Mahometan Tartars, who were surprised at the sight of such a number of strangers; of whom they had before never so much as heard. Yarmak having got what intelligence he could procure of the situation and government of the country, pursued his voyage to the river Tobol; where he found the towns populous, and the land well cultivated. His approach alarmed the king of the Tartars, who assembled a numerous body of horse and foot, armed with bows and arrows, lances, and other such weapons with whom our adventurer had many skirmishes, and defeated great multitudes by means of his fire-arms; which had never before been known in these parts. The poor Tartars were as much amazed, and terrified, at the sight of the Russians and their arms, as the inhabitants of Mexico on the arrival of the Spaniards in America; to which Siberia may, in many respects, be compared.

Yarmak, finding his enemies daily more numerous, the nearer he approached the residence of the Tartar king; having also lost many of his men, in continual encounters, and spent the greatest part of his ammunition; knowing, besides, of no place of safety, where he might pass the winter, which is both long and severe in this quarter; at last determined to retreat. He therefore steered his course to the west, up the Tobol and Tur rivers. The furious Tartars gave him no rest, but harassed him perpetually from the banks. He himself and few more escaped, with a considerable booty, and returned to the village where they wintered the preceding year. The inhabitants, on seeing the rich furs and other spoils, gave them a welcome reception. And Yarmak did not forget to dispense his favours liberally, among those who had entertained him in his distress, when he fled from justice.

Our adventurer had now time to reflect on his miserable circumstances. He considered, that his lurking in these parts, though remote from any town, could not be long a secret; to make another attempt against the Tartars with a handful of men, ill provided with arms and ammunition, might perhaps be ruinous, and certainly unsuccessful. He therefore resolved to submit himself to his majesty's clemency, in hopes of obtaining a gracious pardon for himself and his accomplices, on condition of pointing out the way to a rich and easy conquest of a country which he had lately discovered. The proposal was made at court by a friend, and was of too great importance to be neglected. In short, Yarmak was brought to Mosco, under a safe conduct, where he communicated the whole affair. He begged his majesty's pardon, and asked a certain number of troops, which he promised to lead to a glorious conquest. His majesty granted him a pardon, approved of the expedition, and gave immediate orders for the troops to attend him. They marched to Solikamsky, where they passed the winter in making preparations for the enterprize, which was to be undertaken in the spring.

During this interval, Yarmak behaved with surprising prudence and activity, and discovered himself to be a person of uncommon genius. He collected such of his former followers as remained, and formed them into a company, in whom he could confide on all occasions.

At the proper season, the troops set out towards Siberia. On coming into the inhabited part of the country, they found many straggling parties of Tartars in arms, ready to oppose them, and a number of boats upon the rivers, full of armed men: the king of the Tartars himself was on board one of these vessels. This expedition was of short duration; and, in the issue, fully answered the expectations of the Russians. I cannot omit a few particulars of the last action. The Tartars in the boats, being pursued by the Russians, a battle ensued on the river Irtish. Yarmak, observing the king's barge, ordered his crew to board her; which he endeavouring to do at the head of his men, jumped short, fell into the river, and was drowned; to the great grief of all his followers, Thus fell poor Yarmak! Notwithstanding this misfortune, the Russians gained a complete victory. The brave king of the Tartars lost his life in the action. His son and the rest of the royal family were taken prisoners, and sent to Mosco; where they were honourably received by the Czar, and treated according to their quality. The prince had an extensive property granted him in Russia; which the family enjoys to this day, together with the title of Sibirsky Czarevitz, or Prince of Siberia; which, I believe, is a more generous treatment of the conquered than any of the mighty monarchs of Peru or Mexico, or any of their lineage, have experienced.

December 11th, we left Verchaturia, in deep snow. The cold was excessive, and the sky clear.

Next day, we came to a large village, having a few of the Vogullitz

Tartars in the neighbourhood; and, the 13th, arrived at the town of Epantshin. From Verchaturia to this place the country is mostly covered with woods. About the villages there are large plains, for corn or pasturage. The cattle are in good condition. The horses, particularly, being of the Tartar breed, are larger, and better shaped than ordinary, and fit for any use.

Epantshin is but a small place, fortified with a ditch and palisades, and defended by a few soldiers in garrison. This place is sometimes alarmed with incursions of the Tartars, called Kossatshy-Orda, and Kara-Kalpacks; but the Russians have of late so fortified their frontiers, that these rovers appear seldomer than formerly. Both these tribes are Mahometans, live always in tents, and spread themselves, with their flocks, in the great desert; both are very numerous, and own subjection to different chiefs, whom they call Batteer, which signifies a hero. These are chosen by themselves, and are the most famous among them for their abilities in military exploits. They are at continual war with the Kalmucks, who inhabit along the Volga, and with all their other neighbours. They are not able to stand against regular troops; and, when attacked by them, retire into the wide desert, with their families and cattle; whither none, but people accustomed to their manner of life, can follow them.

The country of the Kara-Kalpacks, or Black-Caps, so called from a kind of caps they commonly wear turned up with black lambskins, lies to the south-west, towards the Volga. That of the Kossatshy-Orda extends to the south-east, as far as the river Irtish. The course of this river I shall have occasion to mention afterwards.

The 14th, we came to a pretty large town, called Tumen, situated upon the north bank of the river Tuma, from whence the place takes its name. The banks of the Tuma are high and steep. There is a very convenient wooden-bridge at this place. The Tuma has its source far to the west; and, in its course, is augmented by the Tura, and several other rivers. It continues to run to the east, till, meeting with the Tobol, it loses itself and name.

The country between Epantshin and Tumen begins to be more open, and better peopled, than that westward of these places. For, besides the Russians, who make the greatest part of the inhabitants, we met with several villages inhabited by the descendents of the ancient Mahometans, who were natives of these places. These Tartars subsist by agriculture; and pass their lives without care or disturbance, in the free exercise of their religion and other privileges.

Tumen is a pretty neat place, and well fortified. The streets are spacious, and the houses built in a straight line. The adjacent country is covered with fine woods, interspersed with villages, corn-fields, and pasturage; and provisions of all kinds are very plentiful. The merchants of this place have a considerable trade in furs, particularly the skins of foxes and squirrels; which, indeed, are not so valuable here as they are to the eastward.

Early on the 15th, we left this place, keeping on our course along the banks of the Tuma, till we arrived at the river Tobol, which we crossed, and proceeded along the eastern bank, through a fine country, and well peopled. Though the frost still continued strong, it was not near so violent and piercing as about Solikamsky; which may proceed from the woods being cut down and the country cultivated. On the other side of the river, indeed, the face of the country appeared flat and morassy, abounding with tall and dark woods.

The 16th, about noon, we were in sight of the city of Tobolsky, though distant from us about twenty English miles. It stands upon a very high bank of the Tobol. The walls are white; and the crosses and cupolas of the churches guilded, and make a very fine appearance. About two o'clock, we arrived safe at the city of Tobolsky, the capital of this mighty province, and the residence of the governor. We lodged in the broad-street, leading to the governor's palace and the courts of justice.

We travelled between Tumen and Tobolsky, about two hundred and fifty verst, in the space of thirty hours. Sledges are the most simple and convenient machines for travelling on snow that can be imagined. And the person in the sledge may either sit, or ly along upon the couch according to his inclination.

CHAPTER II

Occurrences at TOBOLSKY; *Observations on the* KALMUCKS, *&c.*
and journey continued to TOMSKY

Tobolsky is situated in latitude fifty eight degrees forty minutes north
at the conflux of the Irtish and Tobol. From this last the city has its
name. Both these rivers are navigable for several hundred miles above
this place. The Irtish, after receiving the Tobol, becomes a noble
stream, and discharges itself into the Oby. This situation was chosen by
the Russians, both for its strength and beauty. Formerly the Tartar
princes had their abode at a place about thirty verst south from
Tobolsky, which is now neglected and ruinous.

Tobolsky is fortified with a strong brick-wall, having square
towers and bastions at proper distances; and is well furnished with
military stores. Within the town stand the governor's palace, courts of
justice, several churches built of brick, particularly a large cathedral,
and the palace of the archbishop. From the walls you have a very
extensive prospect of a fine country, especially to the south. To the
west the land is also flat, and overgrown with tall woods. The inhabitants are chiefly Russians, of different professions; many of them are
merchants, and very rich, by the profitable trade they carry on to the
borders of China, and many places of their own country.

These live mostly upon the hill. Under the hill in the suburbs,
along the banks of the river, are several large streets, called the
Tartar-streets, occupied by the remains of the ancient inhabitants of
these parts. Here, as at other places, these people enjoy the free
exercise of their religion, and the priviledges of trade. They resemble,
in their persons, religion, language, and manners, the Tartars of
Cazan and Astrachan. Their houses are very cleanly. They are very
courteous to strangers, and esteemed honest; on which account they
get great credit in their commercial affairs. Besides the fortification,
formerly mentioned, about the town, the whole suburbs are surrounded
with a ditch and palisades.

When we were at Tobolsky, Siberia was superintended by Mr
Petrof Solovoy, vice governor, a person well acquainted with the business of government, and a captain of the guards. The former governor,
Kneaz Gagarin, had incurred his majesty's displeasure and was recalled; and his successor, Kneaz Alexie Michaylovitz Cherkasky, a
nobleman worthy of such an important trust, was not yet arrived.

As in most other towns, through which we passed, we found here many Swedish officers of distinction; among others, Monsieur Dittmar, formerly secretary to Charles XII king of Sweden. He was a native of Livonia, and equally esteemed for his probity and capacity. He was much respected by the late governor; who, indeed, was a friend to all these unfortunate gentlemen. They were allowed to walk about at large, a hunting or fishing, and even permitted to travel to other places to visit their countrymen. For my part, I think the greatest favour his majesty shewed these prisoners, was the cantoning them in these parts; where they may live well at small expence, and enjoy all the liberty that persons in their circumstances can expect.

I cannot but observe, that the Swedish prisoners, dispersed in most of the towns in this country, contributed not a little to the civilizing the inhabitants of these distant regions; as they were the means of introducing several useful arts, which were almost unknown before their arrival.

Many of the officers, being gentlemen of liberal education, the better to support their tedious captivity, devoted their time to the study of the more agreeable and entertaining parts of science, particularly musick and painting; wherein some of them attained to great perfection. I was present at several of their concerts, and was not a little surprised to find such harmony, and variety of musical instruments, in this part of the world.

They sometimes amused themselves with teaching young gentlemen and ladies the French and German languages, musick, dancing, and other similar accomplishments; whereby they gained many friends among the people of distinction; a circumstance, to men in their situation, both honourable and useful.

In Tobolsky there are always about five or six thousand regular troops, horse and foot, besides a number of irregulars. These troops, added to the natural strength of the place, effectually secure it from any attacks of the neighbouring Tartars.

The woods and fields about Tobolsky are stored with all kinds of game natural to the climate; such as the coq-limoge, coq-bruiere, and gilinots; the last are about the size of a partridge, their flesh is white and very agreeable. There is another kind of these gilinots, somewhat larger, with rough feet; which, in the winter, turn white as a dove. Also the common partridge, which, on the approach of winter, flies off to more temperate climates; wood-cocks, a great variety of snipes, which fly off in autumn, after having hatched their young. As for water-fowl, no country in the world can produce such numbers, and

variety; they are also birds of passage. In my Persian journal I gave
an account of the vast flocks of these fowls on the shores of the
Caspian sea.

Here also you meet with several kinds of small birds, about the size
of a lark, particularly those called snow-birds. They come to Siberia
in vast flocks in autumn, and remain till the spring, when they dis-
appear. Many of them are white as snow, some speckled, and others all
over brown. They are reckoned a very fine and delicious dish.

I observed another very pretty bird, about the size of a thrush, having beautiful red and yellow feathers in the wings and tail, with a tuft
of brown feathers on its head, which it raises at pleasure. These are also
birds of passage; and, as they breed no where in Europe or Asia that
I know of, perhaps both these and the snow-birds may come to
Siberia from the northern parts of America. This conjecture will
appear not improbable, when it is considered, that these birds are of a
hardy nature, and the flight not so far as is generally imagined.

In the woods are various kinds of wild beasts; such as bears, wolves,
lynxes, several sorts of foxes, squirrels, ermins, sables, martins and
rosio-macks, called feel-fress by the Germans. The furs are better of
their kinds than those of any other country. The ermins commonly
burrow in the open fields, and are caught in traps baited with a bit of
flesh; this is done only in the winter, when they are altogether white,
and the fur most valuable. In summer most of these animals turn
brown; when they are not killed, because, at this season, the fur is of
little use. There are also ottars in the rivers and lakes, whose skins
yield a considerable profit. Indeed, furs of all sorts, in this country,
are very profitable. At present, few sables are caught in this neighbourhood; it is said they fly from smoke, which, perhaps, is partly true; yet
I am apt to believe, that these poor animals are chased away towards
the north, to the wild woods, on account of the high value of their
skins.

The woods of Siberia abound also with venison of several sorts; as
elk, rain-deer, roe-buck, together with an incredible number of hares,
which change their colour, from brown in the summer to white in
winter. The hares are generally caught by the country people in toils,
more on account of their skins than their flesh, of which they make
but little use. The skins are bought by the merchants, and sent, in
great quantities, to St Petersburg, and other ports, in order to be
exported to England, Holland, and other countries; where they are
chiefly manufactured into hats.

Having described the land-animals, I shall now give some account of the fish. In my opinion, there are few countries in the world so well watered, with fine navigable rivers and lakes, as Siberia; and few rivers and lakes produce greater quantities, or more variety, of excellent fresh-water fish, than those in this country. For, besides sturgeon, white fish, sterlet, and others, to be found in the Volga, and the rivers in Russia, there are several kinds peculiar to this part of the world; particularly the muchsoon, about the size of a large carp, and much esteemed by persons of delicate taste.

Southward from Tobolsky the soil is fruitful, producing abundance of wheat, rye, barley, oats, and other grain. The cattle also are very numerous, and in winter are fed with hay. In a word, provisions of all kinds are extremely reasonable. From what I have said, it will appear, that Tobolsky is by no means such a disagreeable place as is generally imagined. Whatever the opinions of mankind may be, it is the business of a traveller to describe places and things without prejudice or partiality; and exhibit them fairly, as they really appear. This principle it shall be my study to keep always in view.

Captain Tabar, a Swedish officer, was at this time writing a history of Siberia. He was a gentleman capable for such a performance; and, if it shall ever be published, it cannot fail of giving great satisfaction to the curious.*

Before I leave Tobolsky, it will not be improper to give a short account of the famous river Irtish, that passes this place. It continues its course a little to the eastward of the north, in a strong but smooth current, visiting several small towns and villages, and receiving many lesser streams, and a large river called Konda, running eastward, till it discharges itself into the Oby, at a town called Samariofsky-Yamm about six hundred verst below Tobolsky.

The Irtish takes its rise from a great lake, named Korzan, in a mountainous country, about fifteen hundred verst to the southward of Tobolsky. The country about this lake is inhabited by the Black Kalmucks, a mighty and numerous people, governed by a prince called Kontaysha. From these the Kalmucks on the Volga are descended. After the Irtish hath run for many miles, through a hilly country covered with wood, it passes through a fine fruitful plain, inhabited by the Kalmucks, till it comes to a house called Sedmy-Palaty, or the Seven Rooms, situated to the right in coming down the river.

* I know of no History of Siberia by Captain Tabar. But for an indication of the scope of Swedish studies on the subject see, for example, the anonymous *Relation de la Grande Tartarie, Dressée sur les Mémoires Originaux des Suèdois Prisonniers en Sibérie, pendant la Guerre de la Suède avec la Russie*, Amsterdam, 1737.

It is very surprising to find such a regular edifice in the middle of a desert. Some of the Tartars say it was built by Tamerlane, called by the Tartars Temyr-Ack-Sack or Lame-Temyr; others by Gingeez-Chan. The building, according to the best information I could obtain, is of brick or stone, well finished, and continues still entire. It consists of seven apartments under one roof, from whence it has the name of the Seven Palaces. Several of these rooms are filled with scrolls of glazed paper, fairly wrote, and many of them in gilt characters. Some of the scrolls are black, but the greatest part white. The language in which they are written is that of the Tongusts, or Kalmucks. While I was at Tobolsky, I met with a soldier in the street with a bundle of these papers in his hand. He asked me to buy them; which I did for a small sum. I kept them till my arrival in England, when I distributed them among my friends; particularly to that learned antiquarian Sir Hans Sloane, who valued them at a high rate, and gave them a place in his celebrated museum.*

Two of these scrolls were sent, by order of the Emperor Peter the First, to the Royal Academy at Paris. The Academy returned a translation, which I saw in the rarity-chamber at St Petersburg. One of them contained a commission to a lama or priest; and the other a form of prayer to the Deity. Whether this interpretation may be depended on I shall not determine. The Tartars esteem them all sacred writings, as appears from the care they take to preserve them. Perhaps they may contain some curious pieces of antiquity, particularly of ancient history. Above the Sedmy Palaty, towards the source of the Irtish, upon the hills and valleys, grows the best rhubarb in the world, without the least culture.

Several days journey from the Palaces, down the Irtish, on the western bank, stands an old tower named Kalbazinsha-Bashna, or the tower of Kalbazin. Below this is the lake Yamishoff, to the right, where the Russians have built a small fort, for the conveniency of making and gathering salt from that lake, great quantities whereof are made by the sun; it is brought in barques down the river to Tobolsky, and other places. This fort created some jealousy to the Kontaysha; he sent an ambassador to the governor of Siberia, requesting to have it demolished; but this demand not being granted, the difference came to an open rupture, the event of which time must discover.

---

* Although the British Museum has several references to Bell as the source of various miscellaneous items in Sir Hans Sloane's collections, I have been unable, even with the co-operation of the Museum authorities, which I gratefully acknowledge, to find among them any trace of a scroll or scrolls from John Bell.

Descending farther, you meet with another settlement of the Russians, called Shelezinsky, from a rivulet of that name in its neighbourhood. A little below Shelezinsky stands Omuska, a considerable town, which also derives its name from a river. Both these places are situated on the eastern bank of the Irtish. You now pass some inconsiderable places before you arrive at Tara, a little town situated on the western bank, on the road leading from Tobolsky to Tomsky, through a country called Baraba, of which I shall give some account as we proceed to the east.

Between Tara and Tobolsky are a few small towns, and many villages, inhabited by Mahometan Tartars. And the country abounds with corn, cattle, and fine pasturage.

I have now pointed out the course of the Irtish till it reaches Tobolsky, and from thence till it empties itself into the river Oby. I have nothing further to remark concerning Tobolsky and the country around it, and should therefore now pursue our journey to the eastward; but, before I leave this place, I imagine it will not be improper to subjoin a few more particulars relative to the Kontaysha,* prince of the Kalmucks, whom I formerly mentioned. I am the more inclined to do this, as I can entirely depend on my intelligence; having procured it from persons who have been in that country, and seen this prince; but particularly from an ingenious and penetrating gentleman, who fills a public office in this place, and was employed in several messages to him from the late governor of Siberia.

The territories of this prince are bounded by three of the most potent empires in the world; on the north by Russia, by China on the east, and by the country of the Great Mogul to the south. From the two first he is separated by desert plains, and from the third by almost impassible mountains. To the south-west his frontiers reach near to Bucharia. The Kontaysha is a very powerful prince, and able to bring into the field, at a short warning, an hundred thousand horsemen, who are all of them able-bodied men, well mounted, and armed with bows and arrows, lances and sabres. This is a greater number of horse than any prince that I know can muster, except his Russian Majesty, and the Emperor of China. These Tartars live in tents, all the year, removing from place to place, as called by necessity or inclination. This is the most ancient and pleasant manner of life. It is entertaining to hear them commiserate those who are confined to one place of abode,

---

* On the derivation of this title, see Cahen, *Histoire des Relations de la Russie avec la Chine*, p. 42.

and obliged to support themselves by labour, which they reckon the greatest slavery.

The Kontaysha has always some thousands of his subjects encamped near himself, who treat him with great veneration and respect. And, in justice to him, it must be confessed, that he is as attentive to the interests of his people; and as assiduous in the administration of justice, in particular, as if they were his own children.

The Kalmucks are not such savage people as they are generally represented; for I am informed a person may travel among them with greater safety, both to his person and effects, than in many other countries.

The Kontaysha received the deputies from the governor of Siberia, like ambassadors from foreign princes, and treated them accordingly. This shows what high respect these eastern princes entertain for his Czarish Majesty, when the governor of Siberia is regarded as a sovereign. The ceremony on these occasions was as follows.

The deputy with his servants were admitted into the tent, where the Kontaysha sat, with his queen and several children about him. He desired all of them to sit down on carpets or mats; for the Kalmucks, like most Asiatics, use no chairs. They were entertained with tea before dinner; and, after it, the Kontaysha dismissed the deputy in a friendly manner, telling him, he would send for him next day to receive an answer to the governor's letter, which he punctually performed. This answer was expressed in very plain and concise terms. These Tartars in general write with brevity and perspicuity. I have seen several of their letters translated, which pleased me extremely, as they contained no tedious preambles, nor disgusting repetitions, which serve only to perplex the reader.

The Emperor of China was some time ago* engaged in a war with the Kontaysha, about some frontier towns, of which the latter took possession, and maintained his claim with a strong army. The Emperor sent against him an army of three hundred thousand men,

---

* Bell is here referring to K'ang Hsi's crucial campaign against the Kalmuks in 1696, of which the Jesuit father Gerbillon, who took part in it, has left an eye-witness account. The Kontaysha of that time was the great Galdan, regarded by many as something of a Genghis Khan *manqué*. Whether, left to himself, he could have succeeded in pulling the various Mongolian groupings together into a new Mongol Empire that might again have mastered Asia is an open question – but in any case the Chinese took good care not to leave him to himself. The Kontaysha whom Bell met was Tsewang Araptan, Galdan's nephew and successor, a lesser figure in every way, though the Kalmuks were by no means a spent force. (It was not until the Chinese campaigns of 1755 and 1759 that they were finally humbled.) For the careers of Galdan and Tsewang Araptan see their respective entries in Hummel's *Eminent Chinese of the Ch'ing Period*.

7. A TARTAR KALMUCK

(According to P. Avril, *Voyage en divers états d'Europe et d'Asie, entrepris pour découvrir un nouveau chemin à la Chine*, Paris, 1693)

8. A TARTAR LAMA, A FEMALE KALMUCK, AND A TARTAR KALMUCK

The picture also shows a prayer-wheel and Tartar dwellings (According to A. Kircher *China Monumentis Illustrata*, Amsterdam, 1667)

under the command of his fourteenth son, who is reckoned the best general of all his children. Notwithstanding their superiority in numbers, the Kontaysha defeated the Chinese in several actions. The Emperor at last thought it best to accommodate the difference, and a peace was concluded to the satisfaction of both parties.

It must be observed, that the Chinese, being obliged to undertake a long and difficult march, through a desert and barren country, lying westward of the long wall; being also incumbered with artillery, and heavy carriages containing provisions for the whole army during their march; had their force greatly diminished before they reached the enemy. The Kontaysha, on the other hand, having intelligence of the great army coming against him, waited patiently on his own frontiers, till the enemy was within a few days march of his camp, when he sent out detachments of light horse to set fire to the grass, and lay waste the country. He also distracted them, day and night, with repeated alarms, which, together with want of provisions, obliged them to retire with considerable loss.

This method of carrying on war, by wasting the country, is very ancient among the Tartars, and practised by all of them from the Danube eastward. This circumstance renders them a dreadful enemy to regular troops, who must thereby be deprived of all subsistence, while the Tartars, having always many spare horses to kill and eat, are at no loss for provisions.

I have only to add, that the Kontaysha must be the same prince, who, in our European maps, is generally called the Great Cham of Tartary. As no Europeans travel through that country, these maps must be very erroneous. It is however to be expected, that the Russians will, in time, make a more complete discovery of the eastern parts of Asia.

Our baggage did not arrive at Tobolsky till the 23rd of December. The people refreshed themselves till the 27th, when they again set out, taking the road along the Irtish to Tara. The ambassador and his retinue remained to pass the rest of the holidays.

January 9th 1720, we proceeded towards Tara. We passed through many Tartar villages, and at night lodged in one of their little huts, and warmed ourselves at a good fire on the hearth. These houses consist generally of one or two rooms, according to the ability of the landlord. Near to the hearth is fixed an iron-kettle to dress the victuals. In one end of the apartment is placed a bench, about eighteen inches high, and six feet broad, covered with mats, or skins of wild beasts, upon which all the family sit by day, and sleep in the night. The walls are

E

built of wood and moss, consisting of large beams, laid one above another, with a layer of moss between every two beams. All the roofs are raised. A square-hole is cut for a window, and to supply the want of glass, a piece of ice is formed to fit the place exactly, which lets in a good light. Two or three pieces will last the whole winter. These Tartars are very neat and cleanly, both in their persons and houses. They use no stoves, as the Russians do. Near the house there is commonly a shade for the cattle.

We continued our journey along the banks of the Irtish, having the river to the right or left, as the road lay from one Tartar village to another.

The 15th, we reached Tara, a small town, reckoned about five hundred verst from Tobolsky; in all this road we did not meet with a Russian village, except a small one near Tara. The country abounds with woods, corn-fields, and fine pasturage, which appeared sufficiently from the quantities of hay, and the good condition of the cattle, though the face of the country was covered with deep snow. We found the air at Tara much milder than at any place since we left Kazan.

Tara is situated on the Irtish, and fortified with a deep ditch, strong palisades, and wooden towers, sufficient to defend it against the sudden attacks of the Tartars, called Kossatshy-Orda, who inhabit westward of the Irtish, and are very troublesome neighbours.

Here we laid in provisions for our journey over the Baraba; which signifies, in the Tartar language, a marshy plain. Its inhabitants are a mixture of different Tartar tribes, called Barabintzy, from the name of the country in which they live. They are a poor miserable people, being treated as subjects both by the Emperor and the Kontaysha; and obliged to pay a tribute, in furs and skins of wild beasts, to each. They have no grain nor cattle of any kind, except a few raindeer; and subsist by hunting and fishing. What fish they consume not in the summer, are dried and smoked for their winter provisions. They are partly of the Mahometan and partly of the Kalmuck religion; but this difference causes no disputes.

It is generally reckoned, that more robberies are committed in Baraba, than in any country on the road to China; not by the natives, for they are very honest and hospitable; but by the Kalmucks, who come to collect tribute for the Kontaysha; who sometimes pick up travellers, and carry them off with all their effects. It was said, that a strong party of them, having intelligence that the ambassador was to pass that way, waited to intercept him; on which account he took thirty dragoons and some cossacks, from the garrison of Tobolsky, to escort him to

Tomsky; which was a sufficient guard against any robbers who might attack us: and he knew the Kontaysha was too polite a prince to authorise his subjects to molest any foreign minister who had done him no injury, notwithstanding the differences that subsisted between him and his Czarish Majesty.

Our baggage having waited at Tara till our arrival, we left that place on the 18th; and, next day, came to a large Russian village, sixty verst from Tara, and the last inhabited by Russians, till you pass the Baraba and come to the river Oby.

In the places through which we passed, the ambassador sent for all the hunters and sportsmen, that he might inquire what kinds of game and wild beasts were in their neighbourhood. Hunting is the employment of most of the young fellows in this country; and is very profitable, as they sell the furs to great advantage. We found that this place produced great plenty both of game and wild beasts, but few sables. In the spring, a number of elks and stags come hither, from the south; many of which are killed by the inhabitants, both on account of their flesh and their hides. What of the flesh is not consumed fresh they salt. The hides are very large, and are dressed into excellent buff. The huntsman, having found the track of a stag upon the snow, pursues it upon his snow-shoes, with his bow and arrows, and little dog, till the animal is quite fatigued: for, the snow on the surface, being melted by the heat of the sun, and congealed, at night, by the frost, but not strong enough to bear the weight of such an animal; he sinks deep at every step, and the sharp ice cuts his ancles, and lames him; so that he becomes an easy prey to the hunter.

One of these hunters told me the following story, which was confirmed by several of his neighbours. That, in the year 1713, in the month of March, being out a hunting, he discovered the track of a stag, which he pursued; at overtaking the animal, he was somewhat startled, on observing it had only one horn, stuck in the middle of its forehead. Being near this village he drove it home, and showed it, to the great admiration of the spectators. He afterwards killed it, and eat the flesh; and sold the horn to a comb-maker, in the town of Tara, for ten alteens, about fifteen pence Sterling. I inquired carefully about the shape and size of this unicorn, as I shall call it, and was told it exactly resembled a stag. The horn was of a brownish colour, about one archeen, or twenty eight inches long; and twisted, from the root, till within a finger's length of the top, where it was divided, like a fork, into two points very sharp.

The 19th, we entered the Baraba, and continued travelling through it, for ten days, when we came to a large Russian village called Tzausky Ostrogue, from a rivulet of that name; which discharges itself into the Oby, a little distance eastward from this place. Here is a small fort, surrounded with a ditch and palisades, mounted with a few cannon, and garrisoned by some militia of the country, in order to prevent the incursions of the Kalmucks. We staid a day at this place, to refresh ourselves; and, having changed horses, proceeded towards Tomsky.

Baraba is really what its name signifies, an extensive marshy plain. It is generally full of lakes, and marshy grounds, overgrown with tall woods of aspin, alder, willows, and other aquatics; particularly many large birch-trees, having their bark as white and smooth as paper. The lakes abound with various kinds of fishes; such as pikes, perches, breams, eels; and, particularly, a fish called karrass, of an uncommon bigness, and very fat. These the inhabitants, dry, in summer, for winter provisions; which are all the food to be found among them. I have eat of it often, and thought it not disagreeable. In winter, they use melted snow for water. They are very hospitable; and desire nothing, in return of their civilities, but a little tobacco to smoke, and a dram of brandy, of which they are very fond. The dress, both of men and women, con-sists of long coats of sheep-skins, which they get from the Russians and Kalmucks, in exchange for more valuable furs. As they wear no other apparel, not even shirts, they are very nasty. Their huts are most miserable habitations, and sunk about one half under ground. We were glad, however, to find them, as a baiting-place in such a cold season.

The Barabintzy, like most of the ancient natives of Siberia, have many conjurers among them; whom they call shamans, and some-times priests. Many of the female sex also assume this character. The shamans are held in great esteem by the people; they pretend to correspondence with the shaytan, or devil; by whom, they say, they are informed of all past and future events, at any distance of time or place. Our ambassador resolved to inquire strictly into the truth of many strange stories, generally believed, concerning the shamans; and sent for all of fame, in that way, in the places through which we passed.

In Baraba, we went to visit a famous woman of this character. When we entered her house, she continued busy about her domestic affairs, without almost taking any notice of her guests. However, after she had smoked a pipe of tobacco, and drunk a dram of brandy, she began to be more chearful. Our people asked her some trifling questions about their friends; but she pretended to be quite ignorant, till she got more tobacco, and some inconsiderable presents; when she began to collect her conjuring tools. First, she brought the shaytan; which is nothing but a piece of wood, wherein is cut something resembling a human head, adorned with many silk and woolen rags, of various colours; then, a small drum, about a foot diameter, to which were fixed many brass and iron rings, and hung round also with rags. She now began a dismal tune, keeping time with the drum, which she beat with a stick for that purpose; several of her neighbours, whom she had previously called to her assistance, joined in the chorus. During this scene, which lasted about a quarter of an hour, she kept the shaytan, or image, close by herself, stuck up in a corner. The charm being now finished, she desired us to put our questions. Her answers were delivered very artfully, and with as much obscurity and ambiguity, as they could have been given by any oracle. She was a young woman, and very handsome.

On the 29th of January, we reached the Oby, which we crossed on the ice, and entered a country pretty well inhabited by Russians; where we found provisions, and fresh horses as often as we wanted them. The country is generally covered with woods, except about the villages; where are fine corn-fields, and good pasture grounds. Our course lay a little to the northward of the east from Tzausky Ostrogue.

February 4th, we arrived safe at the town of Tomsky, so called from the noble river Tomm, upon the eastern bank of which it stands.

CHAPTER III

Occurrences at TOMSKY; *Observations on the* TZULIMM TARTARS, *&c.*
and journey continued to ELIMSKY

The citadel of Tomsky is situated on an eminence, and contains the commandant's house, publick offices, and barracks for the garrison. The fortifications, like most others in this country, are of wood. The town stands under the hill, along the banks of the river Tomm. The country about this place is pleasant and fruitful. From the top of the hill you have a very extensive view every way, except to the south, where it is interrupted by hills. Beyond these hills there is a large, dry, and open plain, which stretches a great way southward.

About eight or ten days journey from Tomsky, in this plain, are found many tombs, and burying places of ancient heroes; who, in all probability, fell in battle. These tombs are easily distinguished by the mounds of earth and stones raised upon them. When, or by whom, these battles were fought, so far to the northward, is uncertain. I was informed by the Tartars in the Baraba, that Tamerlane, or Timyr-Ack-Sack, as they call him, had many engagements in that country with the Kalmucks; whom he in vain endeavoured to conquer. Many persons go from Tomsky, and other parts, every summer, to these graves; which they dig up, and find, among the ashes of the dead, considerable quantities of gold, silver, brass, and some precious stones; but particularly hilts of swords and armour. They find also ornaments of saddles and bridles, and other trappings for horses; and even the bones of horses, and sometimes those of elephants. Whence it appears, that when any general or person of distinction was interred, all his arms, his favourite horse and servant, were buried with him in the same grave; this custom prevails to this day among the Kalmucks and other Tartars, and seems to be of great antiquity. It appears from the number of graves, that many thousands must have fallen on these plains; for the people have continued to dig for such treasure many years, and still find it unexhausted. They are, sometimes indeed, interrupted, and robbed of all their booty, by parties of the Kalmucks, who abhor the disturbing the ashes of the dead.

I have seen several pieces of armour, and other curiosities, that were dug out of these tombs; particularly an armed man on horse-back, cast in brass, of no mean design nor workmanship; also figures of deer, cast in pure gold, which were split through the middle, and had some holes in them, as intended for ornaments to a quiver, or the furniture of a horse.

While we were at Tomsky, one of these grave-diggers told me, that once they lighted on an arched vault; where they found the remains of a man, with his bow, arrows, lance, and other arms, lying together on a silver table. On touching the body it fell to dust. The value of the table and arms was very considerable.

The country about the source of the river Tomm, near which these tombs are, is very fruitful and pleasant. At the source of the Tomm the Russians have a small town called Kuznetsky. This river is formed by the Kondoma, and many lesser rivers; all which run to the north.

In the hills above Kuznetsky, there had lately been discovered rich mines of copper, and some of silver; which, since I was in this country have been greatly improved.

On the hills, and in the woods near this place, are many sorts of wild beasts; particularly the urus, or uhr-ox, one of the fiercest animals the world produces, and exceeding, in size and strength, all the horned species. Their force and agility is such, that no wolf, bear, nor tiger, dare to engage with them. These animals are found in the woods of Poland, and some other parts of Europe. As they are well known I need not describe them.

In the same woods is found another species of oxen, called bubul by the Tartars; it is not so big as the urus; its body and limbs are very handsome; it has a high shoulder and a flowing tail, with long hair growing from the rump to the extremity, like that of a horse. Those I saw were tame, and as tractable as other cattle. Here are also wild asses. I have seen many of their skins. They have, in all respects, the head, tail, and hoofs, of an ordinary ass; but their hair is waved, white and brown, like that of a tiger.

There is, besides, a number of wild horses, of a chesnut colour; which cannot be tamed, though they are catched when foals. These horses differ nothing from the common kind in shape, but are the most watchful creatures alive. One of them waits always on the heights, to give warning to the rest; and, upon the least approach of danger, runs to the herd, making all the noise it can; upon which all of them fly away, like so many deer. The stallion drives up the rear, neighing, biting and kicking those who do not run fast enough. Notwithstanding this wonderful sagacity, these animals are often surprized by the Kalmucks; who ride in among them, well mounted on swift horses, and kill them with broad lances. Their flesh they esteem excellent food;

and use their skins to sleep upon, instead of couches. These are the animals peculiar to this part of the country; and, besides these, there are many more, common to this place with the rest of Siberia.

The river Tomm, having passed Kuznetsky, Tomsky, and several other towns of less note, empties itself into the Oby, at a place called Nikolsky, about an hundred verst below Tomsky, in a country overgrown with thick woods. Here the Tomm loses its name, and makes a great addition to the Oby, which now commences a mighty stream.

The Tomm abounds with variety of fine fish; such as sturgeon, sterlet, muchsoon, and the largest and best quabs, called in French guion, that I have any where seen. The method of catching these fish is by planting pales across the river, in which there is left one narrow opening for the fishes to pass through; above this opening, a hole is cut in the ice; and near it is placed a fire, upon some stones laid for that purpose; The fish, on seeing the light of the fire, stops a moment in its passage; and, at this instant, the fisherman strikes it with a spear, through the hole in the ice. This exercise requires great quickness; for the fish is gone in a trice. I killed several of them myself.

Thus, having made a short excursion up and down the Tomm, and given a brief description of the country adjacent, I return again to Tomsky.

Tomsky is a good market for furs of all sorts; but particularly of sables, black and red foxes, ermins, and squirrels. The squirrels called Teleutsky, from the name of the district where they are caught, are reckoned the best of that species. They have a blackish stripe down their back.

Besides the common squirrel, there is another species found here called the flying squirrel. There is little peculiar in its shape or size; only, it has, at the upper joint of the thigh of the fore-leg, a small membrane, stretching to the shoulder, somewhat like the wing of a bat, which it extends at pleasure; and is thereby enabled to spring much farther, from tree to tree, than it could do without the help of these wings. Both the ermins and squirrels are caught only in winter; because in summer their fur is quite brown, short, and of little use.

We waited some days at Tomsky for the arrival of our baggage. Here we found several Swedish officers; who had good quarters in a plentiful, though distant, place. After our people had refreshed themselves for two days, they set out again on the road to Yeniseysky.

During our abode in Tomsky, we diverted ourselves with fishing and hunting. We were present also at several concerts of musick, performed by the Swedish officers, at Mr Kosloff's, commandant of the place. These gentlemen were not less expert in touching their instruments, than their companions at Tobolsky. Mr Kosloff is a good-natured and chearful gentleman, and treats these officers with great humanity. They had along with them a Swedish parson, Mr Vestadius, a man of genius and learning.

The 9th, we were entertained at the commandant's; where were assembled some hundred of his Cossacks, or light horse, armed with bows and arrows. After going through their usual exercise, they showed their dexterity in shooting on horse-back at full speed. They erected a pole, for a mark, in an open field; and, passing it, at full gallop, let fly their arrows; and soon split it all to shivers.

The 12th, about midnight, we went into our sledges, and set out on our journey towards Yeniseysky. For the two following days, we had tolerably good roads, lying through a pretty fine country, inhabited by Russians. The villages are but thinly scattered, yet sufficiently near one another to afford provisions and fresh horses.

On the 14th, we reached a large navigable river, called Tzulimm. We went up this river upon the ice. We met with neither house, nor inhabitant, for the space of six days. We could get no fresh horses, and were obliged to carry both provisions and forage along with us; which made this part of the road very tedious. During all this time, we had no where to warm ourselves, or dress our victuals, but in the thick overgrown woods, which occupy both sides of the river. There is great plenty of fallen trees in these woods, of which we made large fires. The trees are chiefly pitch-fir, rising like a pyramid, with long spreading branches hanging to the ground; which render these woods almost impassible to man or beast. We frequently set fire to the moss and dried fibres of these firs. In the space of a minute the fire mounts to the top of the tree, and has a very pretty effect. The kindling so many fires warmed all the air around.

In summer, the banks of this river are inhabited by a tribe of Tartars, called by the Russians Tzulimmzy, from the name of the river, who live by fishing and hunting. We found several of their empty huts, as we went along. In autumn, these people retire from this inhospitable place, towards the south, near to towns and villages, where they can find subsistence.

The 20th, we arrived at a Russian village, called Meletzky-Ostrogue, where we staid a day to refresh ourselves and horses. In the neighbourhood of this place we found many huts of these Tzulimm-Tartars, who seem to be a different race from all of that name I have yet mentioned. Their complexion indeed is swarthy, like that of most of the other descendents of the ancient natives of Siberia; but I have seen many of them having white spots on their skins, from head to foot, of various figures and sizes. Many imagine these spots natural to the people; but I am rather inclined to believe they proceed from their constant diet of fish and other animal food, without bread. This, of course, creates a scorbutick habit of body, which often breaks out in infants; and the scars falling off, leave that part of the skin as if it had been scalded, which never recovers its natural colour. I have however seen several children with these spots, who seemed healthy.

The Tzulimms, like other Tartars, live in huts half-sunk under ground. They have a fire in the middle, with a hole at the top to let out the smoke, and benches round the fire, to sit or ly upon. This seems to be the common method of living among all the northern nations, from Lapland, eastward, to the Japanese ocean.

The Tzulimms speak a barbarous language, composed of words from many other languages. Some of our people, who spoke Turkish, told me, they had many Arabick words, which they understood. They are poor, miserable, and ignorant heathens. The archbishop of Tobolsky, in person, came lately hither, and baptised some hundreds of them, who were inclined to embrace the Christian faith. As they are a well-disposed and harmless people, probably in a short time they may be all converted.

The river Tzulimm has its source about three hundred verst above Meletsky Ostrogue; from this place it continues its course to the northward, till it meets with the river Oby, at a place called Shabannsky Ostrogue. Ostrogue, in the Russian language, signifies a strong palisade, inclosing a certain piece of ground. On the first settlements made by the Russians in these parts, such inclosures were necessary to prevent any surprise from the inhabitants.

The 21st, early in the morning, we left Meletsky, and travelled through thick woods, along narrow roads. Next day, we came to a small Russian village, called Melay-Keat; where we found our baggage for the first time, since we quitted Tomsky. Near this place the river Keat has its source; and runs towards the west, till it meets with the Oby. Having changed horses at Melay-Keat, we left our baggage, and proceeded on our journey.

On the evening of the 22nd, we came to a zimovey, where we halted a little, to refresh ourselves and bait our horses. A zimovy is a house or two, built in a place at a great distance from any town or village, for the convenience of travellers; and is a sort of inn, where you generally find a warm room, fresh bread, and a wholesome and agreeable liquor, called quass, made of malt, or rye-meal, steeped and fermented; with hay and oats, at easy rates.

From this place we travelled to Beloy, a large village, where we changed horses, and proceeded. From hence to Yeniseysky the country is well cultivated. Upon the road are many Russ villages, where we got fresh horses, as often as we pleased, without halting ten minutes. Thus we continued travelling, day and night, till we arrived, on the 23rd, at the town of Yeniseysky; where we had a friendly reception, and good entertainment, from the commandant, Mr Becklimishof, who had come some miles from town to meet his old friend the ambassador.

Here I found Mr Kanbar Nikititz Aikinfiof, with whom I got acquainted at Cazan, while we wintered there, in the journey to Persia. Some cross accident had been the occasion of his coming to this place. He enjoyed full liberty to walk about at pleasure. He understood several languages, was well acquainted with history, and a chearful good-natured companion.

Here we passed the holidays called Masslapitza, or the Carnaval, which is held on the week before Lent. In the mean time our carriages arrived, which were dispatched again as soon as possible.

The town of Yeniseysky is pleasantly situated in a plain, on the western bank of the river Yenisey, from which the town takes its name. It is a large and populous place, fenced with a ditch, palisades, and wooden towers. Here is a good market for furs of all sorts; particularly of the animals called piessy, which are of two colours, white and dove-colour. These creatures are caught far to the northward of this place. They are nearly of the shape and size of a fox; having a short bushy tail, and a thick soft downy fur, very light and warm, which is much esteemed by the great men in the northern parts of China; and, by them, made chiefly into cushions, on which they sit in winter.

Besides the above, there is here another creature called rossomack in Russ, and feel-fress by the Germans; because they imagine it eats a great deal more in proportion than other animals. I have seen several of them alive. They are very fierce, and about the shape and size of a badger. The neck, back, and tail are black; but about the belly the hair is of a brownish colour, The blacker they are, the more valuable. The skin, being thick, is only used in caps and muffs.* Also elks, rain-deer, and stags. The latter retire to the south on the approach of winter, and return in the spring. Here are likewise an incredible number of white-hares, which perhaps I may mention afterwards.

* Bell is, of course, describing the wolverine or glutton, the skin of which is still valued for making caps. It has the reputation of being the only fur that never freezes.

I must not omit the black foxes, which are in great abundance about Yeniseysky. Their fur is reckoned the most beautiful of any kind; it is even preferred to the sable with respect to lightness and warmness. I saw here one of their skins valued at five hundred crowns, and some of them far exceed this sum.

Before I leave this place I shall give a short description of the course of the famous river Yenisey, according to the best information I could procure. It rises in a hilly country, at a great distance southward from this place. Being joined by many rivers in its course, it grows into a mighty stream; and is, at Yeniseysky, full as large as the Volga. It runs the longest course of any river on this vast continent. The first town, of any note, in coming down this river, is Krassno-Yarr, which stands on the western bank. It is a place of considerable trade, particularly in furs. From this place, along the banks, are many villages, till the Yenisey meets the lower Tongusta, a large river, coming from the east, a few verst above Yeniseysky. Below this place there are many inconsiderable settlements, till you come to Mangaseysky, a town famous for furs, and the shrine of an illustrious saint, called Vassile Mangaseysky, much frequented by the devout people in these parts.

Above this place the Yenisey receives the Podkamena-Tongusta, a large river, running from the south east; and, at Mangaseysky, it meets another river, called Turochansky, coming from the west. The Yenisey now continues its course, almost due north, till it discharges itself into the ocean. This river abounds with variety of excellent fish; such as I have already mentioned, but in lesser quantities.

The 27th, we left Yeniseysky, and travelled about eight or ten verst along the south bank of the river, when we came to thick and tall woods, which obliged us to leave the land and march along the river, on the ice, which was very uneven. This roughness is caused by the frost setting in about autumn, with a strong westerly wind, which drives up great cakes of ice upon one another, in some places four or five feet high. If the frost happens to begin in calm weather, the ice is very smooth, and easy for sledges.

The 28th, we proceeded along the Yenisey, meeting sometimes with villages. The rigour of the cold was much abated; but the face of winter appeared every where, without the least sign of spring. At evening, we entered the river Tongusta, which we found as rough as the former; but, as both the banks were overgrown with thick woods, we were obliged to keep along the ice.

Next day, we still proceeded along the river, in blowing weather and driving snow.

The 1st of March, we overtook our baggage, which we passed; it being thought more convenient, both in order to procure lodging and fresh horses, that the heavy carriages should travel behind.

We continued our journey for several days, along the Tongusta. We found, now and then, little villages, or single houses, on the banks. One day we chanced to meet a prodigious flock of hares, all as white as the snow on which they walked. I speak within compass when I say there were above five or six hundred of them. They were coming down the river, very deliberately, on a small path, of their own making, close to the beaten road. As soon as they saw us, all of them ran into the woods, without seeming much frightened. I am informed that these hares travel to the south, in much greater flocks than this, every spring, and return in autumn, when the rivers are frozen and the snow falls. In most of the villages, we found plenty of this sort of venison; the inhabitants, however, value it but little; for they catch these hares more on account of their skins, of which they make considerable profits, than their flesh.

The Tongusy, so called from the name of the river, who live along its banks, are the posterity of the ancient inhabitants of Siberia, and differ in language, manners, and dress, and even in their persons and stature, from all the other tribes of these people I have had occasion to see. They have no houses, where they remain for any time, but range through the woods, and along rivers, at pleasure; and, wherever they come, they erect a few spars, inclining to one another at the top; these they cover with pieces of birchen bark, sewed together, leaving a hole at the top to let out the smoke. The fire is placed in the middle. They are very civil and tractable, and like to smoke tobacco, and drink brandy. About their huts they have generally a good stock of rain-deer, in which all their wealth consists.

The men are tall and able-bodied, brave, and very honest. The women are of a middle size, and virtuous. I have seen many of the men with oval figures, like wreaths, on their fore-heads and chins; and sometimes a figure, resembling the branch of a tree, reaching from the corner of the eye to the mouth. These are made, in their infancy, by pricking the parts with a needle, and rubbing them with charcoal, the marks whereof remain as long as the person lives. Their complexion is swarthy. Their faces are not so flat as those of the Kalmucks, but their countenances more open. They are altogether unacquainted with any kind of literature, and worship the sun and moon. They have many shamans among them, who differ little from those I formerly described. I was told of others, whose abilities in fortune-telling far exceeded those of the shamans at this place, but they lived far northward. They cannot bear to sleep in a warm room, but retire to their huts, and lie about the fire on skins of wild beasts. It is surprizing how these creatures can suffer the very piercing cold in these parts.

The women are dressed in a fur-gown, reaching below the knee, and tied about the waist with a girdle. This girdle is about three inches broad, made of deer's skin, having the hair curiously stitched down and ornamented; to which is fastened, at each side, an iron-ring, that serves to carry a tobacco-pipe, and other trinkets of small value. Their gowns are also stitched down the breast, and about the neck. Their long black hair is plaited, and tied about their heads, above which they wear a small fur-cap, which is becoming enough. Some of them have small ear-rings. Their feet are dressed in buskins, made of deer-skins, which reach to the knee, and are tied about the ancles with a thong of leather.

The dress of the men is very simple, and fit for action. It consists of a short jacket, with narrow sleeves, made of deer's skin, having the fur outward; trousers and hose of the same kind of skin, both of one piece, and tight to the limbs. They have besides a piece of fur, that covers the breast and stomach, which is hung about the neck with a thong of leather. This, for the most part, is neatly stitched and ornamented by their wives. Round their heads they have a ruff, made of the tails of squirrels, to preserve the tips of the ears from the cold. There is nothing on the crown, but the hair smoothed, which hangs in a long plaited lock behind their backs.

Their arms are a bow and several sorts of arrows, according to the different kinds of game they intend to hunt. The arrows are carried, in a quiver, on their backs, and the bow always in their left hand. Besides these, they have a short lance, and a little hatchet. Thus accoutred, they are not afraid to attack the fiercest creature in the woods, even the strongest bear; for they are stout men, and dexterous archers. In winter, which is the season for hunting wild beasts, they travel on what are called snow shoes, without which it would be impossible to make their way through the deep snow. These are made of a very thin piece of light wood, about five feet long, and five or six inches broad, inclining to a point before, and square behind. In the middle is fixed a thong, through which the feet are put. On these shoes a person may walk safely over the deepest snow; for a man's weight will not sink them above an inch; these however can only be used on plains. They have a different kind for ascending hills, with the skins of seals glued to the boards, having the hair inclined backwards, which prevents the sliding of the shoes; so that they can ascend a hill very easily; and, in descending, they slide downwards at a great rate.

The nation of the Tongusy was very numerous; but is, of late, much diminished by the small pox. It is remarkable, that they knew nothing of this distemper, till the Russians arrived among them. They are so much afraid of this disease, that, if any one of a family is seized with it, the rest immediately make the patient a little hut, and set by him some water and victuals; then, packing up every thing, they march off to the windward, each carrying an earthen pot, with burning coals in it, and making a dreadful lamentation as they go along. They never revisit the sick, till they think the danger past. If the person dies, they place him on a branch of a tree, to which he is tied, with strong wythes, to prevent his falling.

When they go a hunting into the woods, they carry with them no provisions; but depend entirely on what they are to catch. They eat every animal that comes in their way, even a bear, fox, or wolf. The squirrels are reckoned delicate food; but the ermins have such a strong rank taste and smell, that nothing but starving can oblige them to eat their flesh. When a Tonguse kills an elk or deer, he never moves from the place, till he has eat it up, unless he happens to be near his family; in which case, he carries part of it home. He is never at a loss for fire, having always a tinder-box about him; if this should happen to be wanting, he kindles a fire by rubbing two pieces of wood against each other. They eat nothing raw, but in great extremity.

The sables are not caught in the same manner as other animals. The fur is so tender, that the least mark of an arrow, or ruffling of the hair, spoils the sale of the skin. In hunting them they only use a little dog, and a net. When a hunter finds the track of a sable upon the snow, he follows it, perhaps, for two or three days, till the poor animal, quite tired, takes refuge in some tall tree; for it can climb like a cat; the hunter then spreads his net around the tree, and makes a fire; the sable, unable to endure the smoke, immediately descends, and is caught in the net. I have been told, by some of these hunters, that, when hard pinched with hunger, on such long chaces, they take two thin boards, one of which they apply to the pit of the stomach, and the other to the back opposite to it; the extremities of these boards are tied with cords, which are drawn tighter by degrees, and prevent their feeling the cravings of hunger.

Although I have observed, that the Tongusy, in general, worship the sun and moon, there are many exceptions to this observation. I have found intelligent people among them, who believed there was a being superior to both sun and moon; and who created them and all the world.

I shall only remark farther, that from all the accounts I have heard and read of the natives of Canada, there is no nation, in the world, which they so much resemble as the Tongusians. The distance between them is not so great as is commonly imagined.

The 4th of March, we came to a little monastery, called Troytza, dedicated to the Holy Trinity; where we found about half a dozen monks, who gave us an hospitable reception in their cells, and furnished us with provisions and fresh horses. The monastery stands upon the north-side of the river, on a very pleasant though solitary bank, encompassed with woods, corn-fields, and good pasturage. Most of the villages are on the north side of the river, as it is higher than the south side.

The same day, we proceeded on our journey along the river. We met with, daily, great flocks of hares in their progress to the westward, and many Tongusians in their huts. It is to be observed, that, from this river northward to the frozen ocean, there are no inhabitants, except a few Tongusians on the banks of the great rivers; the whole of this most extensive country being overgrown with dark impenetrable woods. The soil, along the banks of this river, is good; and produces wheat, barley, rye, and oats. The method taken by the inhabitants to destroy the large fir-trees, is, to cut off a ring of bark from the trunk, about a foot broad, which prevents the ascending of the sap, and the tree withers in a few years. This prepares it for being burnt in a dry season; by which means, the ground is both cleared of the wood, and manured by the ashes, without much labour.

The Russians observe, that, where the sort of fir, commonly called the Scotch fir, grows, the ground never fails of producing corn; but it is not so where the pitch, or any other kind of fir, prevails.

The 7th, we came to the head of the Tongusky, which is formed by the conflux of two other rivers, the Angara and the Elimm. The first issues from the great Baykall lake; and runs towards the west, till it meets the Tongusky, when it loses its name. We left the Angara and Tongusky on our right hand, and proceeded along the Elimm, which we found much smoother than the Tongusky. The Elimm is a considerably large and navigable river. The banks on the south side are very high, and covered with rugged rocks, overgrown with woods; but, to the north, you meet with several villages, corn-fields, and pasturage.

We kept on our course up the Elimm, a little to the northward of the east, till the 9th, when we arrived at the town of Elimsky, so called from the name of the river, which stands in a narrow valley, on the south side of the river, encompassed with high hills and rocks covered with woods. This place is but small, and is only considerable as it stands on the road to the eastern parts of Siberia; for travellers to China generally take to the south-east, towards Irkutsky; and those who travel to Yakutsky and Kamtzatsky, to the north-east.

F

CHAPTER IV

Observations on YAKUTSKY *and* KAMTZATSKY, *&c. Journey continued to* IRKUTSKY, *and occurrences there, &c.*

At Elimsky I met with general Kanifer. He was adjutant general to Charles XII of Sweden, and much esteemed by that great warrior, for his military exploits. Kanifer was a native of Courland. He was taken prisoner by the Russians in Poland, and sent hither; where he lived in ease and solitude, and was regularly visited by all travellers.

This gentleman had a creature called kaberda, which was brought to him when a fawn, by some of the Tongusy. It is the animal from which the sweet-smelling drug called musk is taken. The musk grows about the navel, in form of an excrescence, which is cut off, and preserved, when the creature is killed. There are many of them in this country; but the musk is not so strong scented as that which comes from China, and more southern climates. The general had bred this creature to be very familiar. He fed it at his table with bread and roots. When dinner was over, it jumped on the table, and picked up the crumbs. It followed him about the streets like a dog. I must confess it was pleasing to see it cut caprioles, and play with children like a kid.

The kaberda is a size less than the fallow-deer, and its colour darker. It is of a pretty shape, having erect horns, without branches; is very swift, and haunts rocks and mountains, of difficult access to men or dogs; and, when hunted, jumps from cliff to cliff with incredible celerity, and firmness of foot. The flesh is esteemed better venison than any of the deer kind, of larger size; whereof there is great variety in these parts.

Before I leave Elimsky, I shall, as usual, give a short account of some of the places adjacent; particularly those to the north-east, towards the river Lena, and Yakutsky, according as I have been informed by travellers, on whose veracity I could entirely depend.

The people who travel in winter, from hence to these places, generally do it in January, or February. It is a very long and difficult journey; and which none but Tongusians, or such hardy people, have abilities to perform. The Russians frequently finish it in six weeks. The common method is as follows: After travelling a few days in sledges, when the road becomes impassable by horses, they set themselves on snow-shoes, and drag after them what is called a nart, containing provisions and other necessaries; which are as few and light as possible.

9. METHODS OF TRAVELLING ON ICE
   (According to Avril, *Voyage en divers états d'Europe*, 1693)

10. DOG-DRAWN SLEDGES IN SIBERIA (see page 71)
(From Ides, *Three Years' Travels*, 1706)

This nart is a kind of sledge, about five feet long, and ten inches broad, which a man may easily draw upon the deepest snow. At night, they make a large fire, and lay themselves down to sleep in these narrow sledges. As soon as they have refreshed themselves, they again proceed on their snow-shoes, as before. This manner of travelling continues about the space of ten days, when they come to a place where they procure dogs to draw both themselves and their narts. The dogs are yoked by pairs; and are more or fewer in number, according to the weight they have to draw. Being trained to the work, they go on with great spirit, barking all the way; and the person, who lies in the sledge, holds a small cord to guide the dog that leads the rest. They are fastened to the sledge by a soft rope, which is tied about their middle, and passes through between their hind legs. I have been surprised to see the weight that these creatures are able to draw; for travellers must carry along with them provisions, both for themselves and the dogs. These watchful animals know the time of setting out in the morning; and make a dismal howling, till they are fed and pursue their journey. This way of travelling would not, I believe, suit every constitution; the very sight of it satisfied my curiosity. Thus, however, these people proceed for near three weeks, till they arrive at some villages on the Lena; where, leaving the dogs, they procure horses, with which they travel to the town of Yakutsky. This place has its name from a rivulet, called Yakut, which empties itself into the Lena.

I have been, perhaps, too particular in describing the method of travelling with snow-shoes and dogs; but, as these things are known to few Europeans, I concluded an account of them would not be disagreeable. I have seen several Swedish officers who have travelled to Yakutsky in this manner. I tried the snow-shoes myself, and found them very fatiguing; but time and practice make them easy and familiar.

There is a more agreeable road, from Elimsky to Yakutsky, than that I have mentioned, which is by water, down the river Lena; but this rout will not agree with the time and circumstances of every traveller. Those who travel from Irkutsky, by this course, go, by land, to a place called Vercholensky Ostrogue, situated near the source of the Lena, where they embark and fall down the stream. Those who go from Elimsky, cross the country directly, about two days journey, to the first convenient place upon the Lena, where they procure vessels, and sail down the river to Yakutsky, or any other place; but in this passage, by water, they are pestered with numbers of large gnats and muskitoes, which lessen the pleasure of the voyage.

Before I proceed to the northward, it will not be improper to give a

short description of the famous river Lena, which, for the length of
its course, and quantity of water, may be compared to any of the largest
rivers in the world.

The Lena rises at a small distance northward from the Baykall lake,
and runs to the north, with little variation, till it discharges itself into
the Northern Ocean. I compute the length of it, from the source to
the ocean, to be about two thousand five hundred English miles,
though it is much more by common report. It is navigable during this
whole course, having no cataracts so great as to prevent the passage of
vessels of considerable burden. It receives many great rivers, most of
which come from the east. It may easily be imagined, that the Lena
cannot fail of being stored with various kinds of excellent fish, when
the other rivers in Siberia afford such plenty and variety. The banks
are generally overgrown with tall thick woods; wherein are abundance
of game, and wild beasts. The country, between its source and the
Baykall lake, is well peopled, abounding with many Russ villages, and
corn-fields, along the banks of the river.

Having formerly mentioned Yakutsky and Kamtzatsky, I shall add
a few observations on these two provinces.

The town of Yakutsky, capital of the province of that name, is
situated on the west bank of the river Lena, and governed by a commandant; whose office is reckoned very lucrative, as many sables, and
other valuable furs, are found in that province.

The winter here is very long, and the frost so violent, that it is never
out of the earth, in the month of June, beyond two feet and an half
below the surface. When the inhabitants bury their dead above three
feet deep, they are laid in frozen earth; for the heat of the sun never
penetrates above two feet, or two feet and an half: so that, I am informed, all the dead bodies remain in the earth, unconsumed; and will
do so till the day of judgment.

The town, and many villages in its neighbourhood, are inhabited
by Russians, who have horses and cows, but no sheep nor corn. They
are plentifully supplied with corn from the southern parts of the country, by water-carriage along the Lena. And, in summer, they make
hay enough to feed their cattle in winter.

The province of Yakutsky is inhabited by a numerous tribe of
Tartars; by which name the Russians call the whole of the natives of
this country, however they differ from one another in religion, language, and manners. Those of this province are named Yakuty. They
occupy a great space of territory round this place, especially to the east,
where they border with the extensive province of Kamtzatsky.

The Yakuty differ little from the Tongusians, either in their persons or way of life. Their occupation, like that of the other natives, is fishing and hunting. They have flattish faces, little black eyes, and long black hair, plaited, and hanging down their backs. Many of the men are marked in the face with charcoal, after the manner of the Tongusians. I have, however, seen many of these people, both men and women, of good complexions. They often sell their children to the Russians, who are very fond of them; as they generally make trusty servants.

These people, though otherwise humane and tractable, have, among them, one very barbarous custom: When any of their people are infirm through age, or seized with distempers reckoned incurable, they make a small hut for the patient, near some river, in which they leave him, with some provisions; and seldom, or never, return to visit him. On such occasions, they have no regard to father or mother; but say, they do them a good office in sending them to a better world. Whereby it appears, that, even these rude ignorant people have a notion of a future state.

Under Kamtzatsky I include all that vast tract of land, reaching from the river Amoor, along the shore of the Eastern, or Japanese ocean, called by the Russians Tikoe More, or the Calm Sea, to the north-east point of the continent. The country, along the shore, is very pleasant and healthy, especially to the south, where the climate is temperate. This part of the country produces grain, and, as I have been informed, even grapes, and other fruits. The inhabitants are very humane and hospitable.

When the Russians first entered this province, the Kamtzedans endeavoured to oppose them. For this purpose they assembled great numbers of men, armed, after the fashion of their country, with bows, arrows, and short lances, headed with bone, sharpened at the point. Whence it appears, that these people knew no more the use of iron, than the Mexicans on the arrival of the Spaniards in America. Their multitudes were soon dispersed by a few Russians with firearms, which, in those days, had rifled barrels, and a small bore, which killed at a great distance. The poor Kamtzedans, seeing their people fall without any visible wound, and astonished with the fire and noise of the gun-powder, left the field in the utmost consternation. Their dispositions now were wholly inclined to peace; and a few of their chief men were sent to the Russians, in order to obtain it. They prostrated themselves, in the most submissive manner, before the leader of the party, and begged of him to grant them peace; which he did, on condition of their paying to his Majesty an annual tribute of sables, or other furs. This condition they have punctually performed ever since.

Many parts of Kamtzatsky are hilly and mountainous, particularly to the north, and covered with tall woods. At Ochotsky is a good harbour, and timber enough to build a royal navy. There are many great and small rivers, that run through the country, and empty, themselves into the Eastern Ocean, among which is a great river called Anadeer. To the north of this river, towards the ocean, lies an extensive tract of land, little known, and inhabited by a fierce and savage people, called by the Russians, Anadeertzy, who continue very untractable.

I have nothing further to add concerning these remote provinces; only, I am persuaded that the islands of Japan can be at no great distance from the southern parts of Kamtzatsky. What confirmed me in this opinion is, that I saw at St Petersburg a young man, a native of Japan, who, I believe, is yet alive in the Academy of Sciences at that place. I asked him, by what accident he was brought so far from his own country; and he gave me the following account. That his father and himself, with a few persons more, being at a noted town called Naggisaky, on the west coast of the island, employed about some affairs of trade, and having finished their business, intended to return to their own habitations, on the north shore, by sailing round the coast. Therefore went they on board a small boat, and begun their voyage homeward; but, meeting with a strong gale off the land, they were unfortunately driven out to sea; and, in a few days, were cast upon the coast of Kamatzatsky, half-starved, and in the greatest distress. In this condition they met with a Russian officer, who afforded them all that assistance which common humanity dictates on such occasions. Notwithstanding all his care, several of the old people died; being quite spent with fatigue, and want of victuals. That he and another youth, who was since dead, were sent to St Petersburg, where his Majesty was pleased to order that they should be provided for in the Academy. This young man could read and write both the Japanese and Russian languages.

We set out from Elimsky on the 12th; and next day, in the evening, came to a small village, upon the north bank of the river Angara, about eighty verst distant from Elimsky. During these two days we saw no house, nor any inhabitants; the whole of the country, through which we passed, being covered with tall and thick woods. There is a narrow road cut for sledges; and the trees on each side, meeting at the top, shade it by day; and in the night make it very dark, and almost dismal.

We passed the night in this village, where we got fresh horses; and, next morning, repeated our journey almost due east, up the river Angara, upon the ice. Along the banks we found many villages well-peopled. The face of the country had now a different aspect, from what I had seen for several months; sometimes we saw a fine champaign country, exhibiting a beautiful and extensive prospect; at other times, the view was agreeably varied with woods, and rising grounds. The north-side of the river is mostly over-grown with woods. There are some openings along the banks; where we found villages, and abundance of cattle and provisions.

The 15th, we arrived at a large village, called Ballagansky; situated on the south-side of the Angara, near a rivulet, running from the south called Unga. The situation of this place is very pleasant, as it stands in a fruitful plain, and has many corn-fields and woods in the neighbourhood.

Here we found another tribe of the natives of Siberia, who differ, in some particulars, from all those I have formerly described. They are called by the Russians Bratsky, but by themselves Buraty. They live in tents all the year; and, having large flocks of sheep, and many cows and horses, they remove from place to place, as the convenience of grazing requires. Their language has a great affinity to that of the Kalmucks; and they have priests among them who can read and write that language. As to their dress, and manner of life, I could observe little difference between them and the Kalmucks on the Volga; and therefore conclude they have both descended from the same original. Their faces, however, are not quite so flat as those of the Kalmucks; their noses being somewhat higher, and their countenances more open.

The Buraty are stout active men, but hate all kind of labour. For, though they have the example of the Russians plowing and sowing their ground, and living plentifully on the produce of this rich and fertile soil, they chuse still to live in their tents, and tend their flocks, on which their subsistence intirely depends.

The chief exercise of the men is hunting and riding. They have a good breed of saddle-horses; and their horned cattle are very large. Their sheep have broad tails, and their mutton is excellent. They have also great abundance of goats. For all these animals they make no provision of fodder; but leave them to feed in the open fields. When the snow falls to a great depth, which seldom happens in these parts, they drive them southward to rising grounds, where little snow lies.

Their arms are bows and arrows, lances and sabres; all of which are used on horse-back; for, like the Kalmucks, they have no infantry. They are dexterous archers, and skilful horsemen.

These people were formerly subject to a prince of the Mongals; but now live very quietly under the Russian government. They are at present a very numerous people, reaching towards the east and south of the Baykall lake; and are generally reckoned very honest and sincere.

As to their dress, the men wear a coat, or rather gown, of sheep-skins, girt about the middle, in all seasons; a small round cap, faced with fur, having a tassel of red silk at the top; which, together with a pair of drawers and boots, makes up the whole of their apparel. The women's dress is nearly the same; only their gowns are plaited about the waist, and hang down like a petticoat. The married women have their hair hanging in two locks, one on each side of the head, drawn through two iron rings to prevent its floating on the breast; and looking very like a tye-wig. Round their fore-head they wear a hoop of polished iron, made fast behind; and on their head a small round cap, faced with fur, and embroidered, in their fashion, to distinguish it from those of the men. The maids are dressed in the same manner; only, their hair is all plaited, hanging in separate locks round their head; and is as black as a raven; some of them have good complexions. Both the men and women are courteous in their behaviour. I should like them much better if they were a little more cleanly. Both their persons and tents are extremely nasty, from their using only skins to preserve them from the cold; on these they sit, or lie, round a little fire, in their tents.

The religion of the Buraty seems to be the same with that of the Kalmucks, which is downright Paganism of the grossest kind. They talk indeed of an almighty and good being, who created all things, whom they call Burchun; but seem bewildered, in obscure and fabulous notions, concerning his nature and government. They have two high priests, to whom they pay great respect; one is called Delay-Lama, the other Kutuchtu. Of these priests I shall have an opportunity to give some account afterwards.

In passing the tents of the Buraty, I often observed a long pole; whereon was hung, by the horns, the head and skin of a sheep. On inquiring the reason of this appearance, I was told that the animal, whose head and skin these were, had been slain, and offered in sacrifice, to the God who protected their flocks and herds. I could observe no images among them, except some relicks given them by their priests, which they had from the Delay-Lama; these are com-monly hung up in a corner of their tents, and sometimes about their necks, by way of an amulet, to preserve them from misfortunes.

The 16th, we came to another large village, called Kamenka,

11. BURATY (see pages 75-76)

12. BURATY HUNTING SCENE (see page 87)
   (Both from Ides, *Three Years' Travels*, 1706)

situated on the north bank of the river, where we found many of the Buraty in their tents. This day we had some rain, which melted much snow, and made it dangerous to travel upon the ice; so that we were obliged to leave the river, and make the best of our way along the banks; for several of our horses broke through the ice, and were got up again with no small difficulty.

The 17th, our route lay to the south-east. The alteration of the weather was now very perceptible; the heat of the sun was very intense, and the snow suddenly disappeared, leaving no marks of winter, except the ice upon the river, which was vanishing very fast. Thus, in the space of a few days, we passed from a cold winter to a warm spring; and one would almost have imagined we had been imperceptibly dropped into another climate. Our sledges, in which we had travelled and lodged, for most part, during the winter, could now be of no use; and we left them to be put on wheel carriages, in order to follow us as should be convenient.

Having procured such horses and furniture as the place afforded, we proceeded along the north bank of the Angara, towards Irkutsky. We were escorted by some Cossacks, and a party of the Buraty, armed with bows and arrows. We hunted all the way as we travelled; and were not a little surprised to see the Buraty kill many hares with their arrows. This exercise was very seasonable, as we had been confined to sledges for more than three months, during our journey from Cazan to this place.

On the 18th of March, we arrived at the town of Irkutsky, so called from the rivulet Irkut, which falls into the Angara near it. It stands on the north bank of the Angara, in a large plain, to the north of which the grounds are very high, and covered with woods. On the south side of the river, towards the Baykall lake, are high hills, rising to the south, and covered with tall trees; among which are many larinxes and Siberian cedars. The larinx, called in Russ lisvinitza, is a well known tree in these parts; near the root of it grows a famous drug, called agarick, in form of a mushroom. It sheds its leaf in autumn, and in summer it looks like a pine; it grows very straight and tall, and is reckoned good timber for ship-building; it bears a cone like the fir-tree, containing the seed, but not half so large.

What is called the cedar is a large tall tree, which never sheds the leaf; it is white and smooth, but has not the least smell of cedar. They use it chiefly in building houses; and it makes the finest white floors, and freest from knots, of any wood I know. The leaves are like those of a pine; but grow in tassels, very beautiful. The cones are large; and, instead of seed like the fir, contain a small nut with a kernel; of which the people in this country are very fond, and eat it by way of a desert, in place of better fruit. It has a pleasant taste, like that of almonds; and is esteemed good for the stomach.

The town of Irkutsky is fortified with a ditch, and strong palisades, having towers at certain distances. The garrison consists of some regular troops, besides a number of cossacks, or the militia of the country. The town contains about two thousand houses; and the inhabitants are plentifully supplied with provisions of all kinds, from the neighbouring villages. The adjacent woods abound with variety of game. The river affords sturgeon, and many other kinds of fish, but no sterlet; because, as I apprehend, they delight in muddy streams; and the water at this place is so clear, that, in two fathoms depth, one may see the pebbles at the bottom.

At Irkutsky is a good market for furs of all sorts, and likewise for many kinds of Chinese goods. All merchandise must be entered at the custom-house, in this place, and pays a duty of ten per cent; which produces a considerable revenue to his majesty.

The 25th of March, our baggage arrived, after surmounting many difficulties on the road. They had been obliged to leave many of the sledges, after taking the baggage off them, and putting it on wheel-carriages.

Our design was to have crossed the Baykall sea upon the ice, and then proceeded, by land, to the town of Selinginsky; but we came too late for that purpose. The season was so far advanced, that, before our carriages arrived, the river was almost free of ice. We were informed, indeed, that the ice, upon the lake, was sufficiently strong to bear horses; but, upon considering the matter, it was thought most advise-able to remain here, till the ice in the sea was also melted, that we might go by water to Selinginsky; and orders were immediately given that vessels should be prepared for this purpose.

April 1st, we crossed the river, accompanied by Mr Rakitin the commandant, in order to take a view of the country towards the south. We rode through fine woods, of stately oaks and other trees, formerly mentioned. We hunted all the way, and found abundance of game. At last, we came to a small Russian village, in a fruitful valley, en-compassed with hills covered with woods, where we lodged. Next day we went ten or a dozen miles farther, in search of wild beasts; but, finding none, we returned to the same village, and the day following to Irkutsky.

The 10th, we were entertained with a famous Buratsky shaman, who was also a lama, or priest, and was brought from a great distance.

As these shamans make a great noise in this part of the world, and are believed, by the ignorant vulgar, to be inspired, I shall give some account of the behaviour of this one, in particular, by which it will appear that the whole is an imposition.

He was introduced to the ambassador by the commandant, accompanied by several chiefs of his own tribe, who treat him with great respect. He was a man of about thirty years of age, of a grave aspect and deportment. At his introduction he had a cup of brandy presented to him, which he drank, but refused any more.

After some conversation, he was desired to exhibit some specimen of his art; but he replied, he could do nothing in a Russian house; because there were some images of saints, which prevented his success. The performance was therefore adjourned to a Buratsky tent in the suburbs. Accordingly, in the evening, we went to the place appointed, where we found the shaman, with several of his companions, round a little fire, smoking tobacco; but no women among them. We placed ourselves on one side of the tent, leaving the other for him and his countrymen. After sitting about half an hour, the shaman placed himself cross-legged upon the floor, close by a few burning coals upon the hearth, with his face towards his companions; then he took two sticks, about four feet long each, one in each hand, and began to sing a dismal tune, beating time with the sticks; all his followers joined in the chorus. During this part of the performance, he turned and distorted his body into many different postures, till, at last, he wrought himself up to such a degree of fury that he foamed at the mouth, and his eyes looked red and staring. He now started up on his legs, and fell a dancing, like one distracted, till he trode out the fire with his bare feet. These unnatural motions were, by the vulgar, attributed to the operations of a divinity; and, in truth, one would almost have imagined him possessed by some demon. After being quite spent with dancing, he retired to the door of the tent, and gave three dreadful shrieks, by which, his companions said, he called the demon to direct him in answering such questions as should be proposed. He then returned, and sat down in great composure, telling he was ready to resolve any question that might be asked. Several of our people put questions in abundance; all which he answered readily, but in such ambiguous terms that nothing could be made of them. He now performed several legerdemain tricks; such as stabbing himself with a knife, and bringing it up at his mouth, running himself through with a sword, and many others too trifling to mention. In short, nothing is more evident than that these shamans are a parcel of jugglers, who impose on the ignorant and credulous vulgar.

The 6th of April, we went to a monastery, about five miles to the westward of this place, where we dined with the archbishop of Tobolsky. This prelate had lately come hither to visit some monasteries; and, in his way, had baptized a number of Osteaks and other heathens. From this time till the 8th of May, little material happened. We waited patiently for the dissolving of the ice on the Baykall lake, of which we expected to receive the most certain knowledge by means of the floating-ice on the Angara; for, when this happens, that river is filled with floating-cakes, which are driven along with great fury by the wind and current.

The 11th, the river was now clear of ice. Our baggage was shipped on board large flat-bottomed boats, and drawn up the stream; the wind being southerly made the progress of the boats very slow. The ambassador therefore resolved to remain at this place, till he heard they had nearly reached the lake, which is about forty verst from Irkutsky.

Before we left this place, Mr Kremensky, our interpreter for the Latin tongue, died of a hectick disorder. He was a Polish gentleman, and had laboured under this distemper for some years.

CHAPTER V

The 15th of May, the weather being very hot, we did not set out till
after dinner, when we left Irkutsky, accompanied by the commandant and some other officers of the place. We rode along the north bank
of the river, through pleasant woods, and some open fields, till we came,
about midnight, to a few fishermen's huts, where we halted for a few
hours, and repeated our journey early next morning.

At noon, we arrived at a small chapel, dedicated to St Nicolas,
where travellers usually pay their devotions, and pray for a prosperous
passage over the lake. About this religious house there are a few fishermen's huts. Two monks constantly attend, to put people in mind of
their duty, and receive a small gratuity from the passengers.

Here we found our boats, waiting for us, below the falls of the
Angara. From hence you can see the lake, bursting out betwixt two
high rocks, and tumbling down over huge stones, that ly quite cross
the river, which I reckon to be about an English mile broad. The
whole channel of the river is covered with these rocks, from the mouth
of the lake down to the chapel of St Nicolas, about the distance of an
English mile. There is no passage for the smallest boats, except along
the east shore, through a narrow strait, between the rocks and the land.
In the most shallow places there is about five or six feet water, and
breadth, all the way, sufficient for any single vessel. But if, by stress
of weather, or any other accident, a boat should have the misfortune
to miss this opening, and be thrown upon the rocks, she must immediately be dashed to pieces, and the whole crew inevitably perish. The
waters, dashing upon the stones, make a noise like the roaring of the
sea; so that people near them can scarce hear one another speak. I cannot express the awfulness with which one is struck, at the sight of such
astonishing scenes of nature as appear round this place, and which, I
believe, are not to be equalled in the known world. The pilots and
sailors, who navigate the lake, speak of it with much reverence; calling
it the Holy Sea, and the mountains about it, the Holy Mountains;
and are highly displeased with any person, who speaks of it with dis-
respect, or calls it a lake. They tell a story of a certain pilot, who
always gave it that appellation, but was severely punished for his contempt. Being on a voyage in autumn, he and his crew were tossed from

side to side of the lake, till they were half-starved, and in great danger of perishing. Necessity, at last, forced this hardy mariner to comply with the prevailing custom, and pray to the Holy Sea and Mountains to have compassion on him in such distress. His prayers were effectual, and he arrived safe to land; but was observed, ever after, to speak of the sea with the greatest respect.

The afternoon was spent in adjusting the tackle, and preparing the barques for being drawn up the strong narrow current.

The 17th, the wind being contrary, and blowing pretty fresh, the pilots would not venture out. I, and three more of our company, took this opportunity of walking up to the top of the mountains, where we had a full view of the sea, and the land to the south, on the other side of it, and also to the west as far as it extends. The land on the south side of the lake rises gradually, till it terminates in hills mostly covered with wood; but, on the western shore, there are very high mountains, several whereof are overspread with deep snow, which we could easily discern, though at a great distance.

The Baykall sea, opposite to the mouth of the Selinga, is reckoned about fifty English miles broad, though it is much broader in some other places; and about three hundred miles in length. It is wholly fresh water, and is supplied by the Selinga and many other rivers, from the south, and by the higher Angara from the east. The course of the sea is from south-west to north-east, and has very few shelves or rocks. There is only one large island, near the middle of it, called Olchon. It is bounded on the north by a ridge of high rocks, which run from one end of it to the other. The only opening, by which it discharges itself, is that into the Angara; which, though it is a natural passage, appears as if cut through the rocks by art. In my opinion, one cannot imagine a more beautiful prospect of nature, than is seen from the top of these mountains; which may easily be perceived from the short and imperfect sketch I have drawn of it. The woods, on the summit of the rocks, are short, and thinly scattered; but, on their declivity towards the north, and in the valleys, the trees become gradually both taller and larger. There is abundance of game and wild beasts in these woods, particularly the wild boar, which was the first of that species we found in this country; a certain sign of a temperate climate; for these animals cannot endure the excessive cold in more northerly parts. The hunting of these animals being a dangerous kind of sport, we carefully avoided their haunts. In the evening we returned to our barques at the chapel of St Nicolas.

The Baykall is abundantly furnished with various kinds of excellent fish; particularly sturgeon, and a fish called omully, in shape and taste resembling a herring, but broader and larger. The sea produces also great numbers of seals, whose skins are preferred, in quality, to those of seals caught in salt-water. I am of opinion, that both the seals and fish in the Baykall came originally from the Northern ocean, as the communication between them is open, though the distance be very great.

The seals are generally caught in winter, by strong nets hung under the ice. The method they use, is, to cut many holes in the ice, at certain distances from one another, so that the fishermen can, with long poles, stretch their nets from one hole to another, and thus continue them to any distance. The seals, not being able to bear long confinement under the ice for want of air, seek these holes for relief; and thus entangle themselves in the nets. These creatures indeed commonly make many holes for themselves, at the setting in of the frost. In this manner they catch not only seals, but fish of all kinds, in winter.

The 18th, the wind being favourable, we put off from St Nicolas's. As we had workmen enough, we left part of them on board to assist the pilot, by setting poles; while the rest were employed on shore, in towing the barques against a strong current. In about the space of three hours we got clear of the current, and all hands came on board. We were now quite becalmed, and obliged to take to our oars. We rowed along shore to the eastward, till about noon; when we had an easy breeze, which soon carried us two-thirds over the sea, under our mainsail. The wind now chopped about to the east, and blew so fresh, that we could not make the river Selinga; which was the port where we intended to land. As these barques cannot turn to windward, we were drove about ten miles to the westward of the Possollsky monastery; which stands about six miles to the westward of the Selinga, in a pleasant and fruitful plain, furnishing an extensive view in all directions; where, endeavouring to get to land at any rate, we steered into a bay, in which, we fancied, we saw the shore covered with cockle-shells or white sand. On a nearer approach our mistake appeared. For what seemed shells or sand, at a distance, was only great and small cakes of ice, beating with the waves against the main body of the ice; which lay firm, and covered the whole bay. Our people, on distinguishing the ice, immediately struck sail, and were in no small confusion. But Mr Ismaeloff ordered the sail to be again set, and to steer directly for the ice. In the mean time, all hands were employed in hanging boards about the bow of the vessel, to prevent the cutting of the planks; and in setting poles to push off the large cakes. At last we came among the ice, which made a terrible rattling at first; but the farther we advanced, the easier our barque lay, till we came to the main body of the ice, where she remained as unmoved, as if she had been in a mill-pond, though it still continued to blow hard. We now quitted the ship, and walked about upon the ice, which was yet strong enough to carry horses. By this time the sun was set, which prevented our design of going ashore; for the distance was, at least, five English miles; and there was a great gap in the ice near the place where we lay.

About midnight the wind turned westerly; and at break of day we left our station, and sailed to the eastward; and, about noon, entered the river Selinga; where we found our other three barques. They, having been two or three miles before us the preceeding night, had time enough to reach anchoring-ground; and, by this means, escaped the ice, so little expected at this season of the year. We ourselves, before entering the bay, had sounded, in order to discover whether we could come to an anchor; but no bottom could be found, though we joined several lead-lines together, amounting to above one hundred and fifty fathoms.

The mouth of the Selinga is surrounded with tall reeds, and contains several islands. The entry into it is very difficult, except the wind be fair, because of many flats and sand-banks, thrown up by the current of the river. Here we found great flocks of all kinds of water-fowl, particularly snipes.

The wind continuing fair, we sailed up the river to a small oratory, dedicated also to St Nicolas, where all hands went ashore to return thanks for their safe passage. The prior of the Possolsky monastery came to this place to salute the ambassador; and brought a present of fish, and such other provisions as these religious houses afford.

In the evening we proceeded up the river, till night overtook us, when we hauled our boats close to the bank, and lay till next morning, which was the 20th of May. This day being calm, the barques were towed up the river; and we walked along the banks, hunting all the way in a very pleasant country. At night we lay by, as formerly.

The 21st, the weather was very hot. We continued our voyage in the same manner as before.

The 22nd, the wind being fair, we hoisted sails, and, in the evening, arrived at a large village, well built and peopled, called Kabbansky Ostrogue. This place is pleasantly situated, on a rising ground upon the west bank of the river, surrounded with many corn-fields and much pasturage. Here we took new hands on board our barques, and dismissed the former to return in open boats to Irkutsky.

The 25th, we reached another large village, called Bolshoy Zaimka, situated in a fertile country. In the neighbourhood is a small monastery, and many lesser villages. Many of the Buraty were encamped, with their flocks and herds, on both sides of the river.

The climate on this side of the Baykall lake is much more temperate than on the north side. The land produces rich crops of wheat, rye, barley, oats, buck-wheat, and pease; besides kitchen roots, and other garden stuff. The inhabitants have not yet begun to plant any kind of fruit-trees; which, I am persuaded, would thrive exceedingly; as the winters are short, and the snow does not ly above six weeks or two months. The banks of the river appeared very pleasant; being finely varied with plains and woods.

The 26th, we came to a large town, called Udinsky, from the rivulet Uda, which runs into the Selinga, on the east bank. This place also stands in a fertile plain, having high hills covered with woods towards the east.

In these hills are found several rich ores, particularly of lead; in digging which many hands are now employed. The miners say it is of too hard a quality; however, they have extracted considerable quantities of silver from it; and I have been informed that they also found some veins of silver ore. As these works are but lately begun, it is not doubted that they are capable of great improvement, at an easy charge, as the metal lies so near the surface. Samples of these ores have been sent to St Petersburg; and, I am informed, his majesty has engaged some German miners to make experiments upon them.

Both here and on the Angara, iron is to be found, in great abundance at the very surface. But, as the distance is too great for exportation, it is not worth the labour. To supply the common consumption of the country, the smith takes his bellows, goes to the mine, and smelts and works as much iron as he needs. I have seen some of this iron of an excellent, soft, and pliable quality.

Besides the above mentioned, there are at this place very rich mines of copper. I have seen some of the ore with large veins of pure copper running through it. I make no doubt but time and future discoveries will bring these mines to perfection, to the great emolument of the Russian empire.

All this country is under the jurisdiction of the commandant of Irkutsky, who sends deputies to all the towns of this extensive province, to administer justice, and take care of his majesty's revenues. The power of nominating sub-governors and commandants, is vested, by his majesty, in the governor of Siberia; which gives him an authority equal to a sovereign prince.

G

The ambassador, finding the progress of the boats, against the stream, very slow and tedious; being besides much pestered with gnats and muskitoes; resolved to go by land, the rest of the way, to Selinginsky. For which purpose, the superintendant of this place ordered horses, and a proper escort, to be got ready against next morning, on the other side of the river; the road on this side being interrupted by thick woods and deep rivers.

The 27th, having sent off our barques, we crossed the river; and, having no baggage, we soon mounted. The road lay through a fine plain, covered with excellent grass. In the evening we came to a fountain of pure water, where we lodged in the tents of the Buraty, and slept on bull-hides.

The 28th, early, we proceeded, travelling over some pretty high hills overgrown with wood. About noon we came to a river called Orongoy, which we crossed on a tall camel; it being too deep for horses. At this place we found a number of the Buraty encamped, with their flocks grazing in the neighbourhood.

Our horses having swum the river, we went into one of the Buratsky tents, till they were dried. The hospitable landlady immediately set her kettle on the fire, to make us some tea; the extraordinary cookery of which I cannot omit describing. After placing a large iron-kettle over the fire, she took care to wipe it very clean with a horse's tail, that hung in a corner of the tent for that purpose; then the water was put into it, and, soon after, some coarse bohea tea, which is got from China, and a little salt. When near boiling, she took a large brass-ladle and tossed the tea, till the liquor turned very brown. It was now taken off the fire, and, after subsiding a little, was poured clear into another vessel. The kettle being wiped clean with the horse's tail, as before, was again set upon the fire. The mistress now prepared a paste, of meal and fresh butter, that hung in a skin near the horse's tail, which was put into the tea-kettle and fried. Upon this paste the tea was again poured; to which was added some good thick cream, taken out of a clean sheep's skin, which hung upon a peg among the other things. The ladle was again employed, for the space of six minutes, when the tea, being removed from the fire, was allowed to stand a while in order to cool. The landlady now took some wooden cups, which held about half a pint each, and served her tea to all the company. The principal advantage of this tea is, that it both satisfies hunger and quenches thirst. I thought it not disagreeable; but should have liked it much better had it been prepared in a manner a little more cleanly. Our bountiful hostess, however, gave us a hearty welcome;

and, as these people know not the use of money, there was nothing to pay for our entertainment. We only made her a present of a little tobacco to smoke, of which these people are very fond. I have given this receipt with a view that some European ladies may improve upon it.*

After this short repast, we mounted again; and, in the evening, came to a neat Russian village, on the front of a pleasant hill covered with wood. This place is surrounded with extensive valleys, and fine pasturage; and our accommodation was better than the preceeding night. Here we met Mr Firsoff, colonel of the cossacks, or militia of Selinginsky, with a squadron of horse, armed with bows and arrows, and some firelocks, who came to escort the ambassador to that place.

The 29th of May, we mounted early, and, by means of our cossacks, hunted and ranged the woods, as we went along, in the manner of this country, called oblave in the Russian language. Their method is to form a semicircle of horsemen, armed with bows and arrows, in order to inclose the game. Within the semicircle a few young men are placed, who give notice when the game is sprung; these only are permitted to pursue, the others being confined to keep their ranks. Our cossacks, with their arrows, killed three deer, and several hares. And, if killing harmless animals can be called diversion, this may properly be reckoned one of the finest. After this fashion they hunt bears, wolves, foxes, and wild boars.

About noon we came to a village on the Selinga, where we halted a few hours, and then crossed the river in boats; which was near a mile broad at this place. Our cossacks, however, sought no boats, except one to transport their arms, cloaths, and saddles; which being done, all of them mounted their horses, and plunged into the river without the least concern. As soon as the horses were set a swimming, for ease to them the men dismounted, and, laying hold of the mane with one hand, guided them gently by the bridle with the other. This is the common method in this country of transporting men and horses; which I look upon to be both safe and easy, provided the horse is managed with a gentle hand, without checking him with sudden jerks of the bridle.

We halted a little, after crossing the river, till the horses were dried;

* Bell is no doubt joking. But this brew, described by many travellers since his day, might have appealed to the Scottish lady, his contemporary, whose recipe was to put a pound of tea in the pot with nearly a gallon of 'burn' water, seasoning the mixture with butter, pepper and salt – and keeping the leaves to use again. This recipe, and other Scottish reactions to the still new-fangled tea, is given in Marjorie Plant's *The Domestic Life of Scotland in the 18th Century.*

after which we mounted, and, in the evening, arrived at the town of Selinginsky; where we intended to wait for our barques, and the rest of our people.

Selinginsky is situated on the east bank of the noble river Selinga, in a deep, barren, sandy soil, that produces almost nothing. The choice of this situation was extremely injudicious; for, had the founders gone but half a mile further down, to the place where now the inhabitants have their gardens, they would have had a situation, in every respect, preferable to the present.

This place consists of about two hundred houses, and two churches, which are all of them built with wood. It is defended by a fortification of strong palisades, on which are mounted some cannon.

About a mile eastward of the town is a ridge of high hills, quite covered with wood. On the other side of the river, the country is open, dry, and somewhat barren; but affords excellent pasture, particularly for sheep, whereof the Buraty, the inhabitants, have large flocks. They are of that kind which hath broad tails, and their mutton is very good. These people have, besides, a large sort of horned cattle, and abundance of horses and camels, wherein all their riches consist. Here ends the tribe of the Buraty, and the nation of the Mongalls begins.

The Mongalls are a numerous people, and occupy a large extent of country, from this place to the Kallgan, which signifies the Everlasting Wall, or the great wall of China. From this wall they stretch themselves northward as far as the river Amoor; and from the Amoor, westward, to the Baykall sea; where they border with the territories of the Kontaysha, or prince of the Black Kalmucks. On the south, they are bounded by a nation called Tonguts, among whom the Delay-Lama has his residence. One may easily imagine, from the vast track of land which the Mongalls occupy, that they must be very numerous; especially, when it is considered, that they live in a healthy climate, and have been engaged in no wars, since they were conquered, partly by the Russians on the west, and partly by the Chinese on the east; to whom all these people are now tributaries. In former times the Mongalls were troublesome neighbours to the Chinese, against whose incursions the great wall was built.

Kamhi, the present Emperor of China, was the first who subdued these hardy Tartars; which he effected more by kind usage and humanity than by his sword; for these people are great lovers of liberty. The same gentle treatment hath been observed by the Russians, towards those of them who are their subjects. And they themselves confess, that, under the protection of these two mighty Emperors, they enjoy more liberty, and live more at ease, than they formerly did under their own princes.

The present Prince of Mongalia is called Tush-du-Chan, and resides about six days journey, to the south-east, from Selinginsky. The place is called Urga, and is near to where the Kutuchtu, or high priest, inhabits. When the Mongalls submitted themselves to the Emperor of China, it was agreed, that the Tush-du-Chan should still maintain the name and authority of a prince over his people; but undertake no war, nor expedition, without consent of the Emperor; which has strictly been observed ever since.

It is very remarkable, that, in all the vast dominions of Mongalia, there is not so much as a single house to be seen, All the people, even the prince and high priest, live constantly in tents; and remove, with their cattle, from place to place, as conveniency requires.

These people do not trouble themselves with ploughing, or digging the ground in any fashion; but are content with the produce of their flocks. Satisfied with necessaries, without aiming at superfluities, they pursue the most ancient and simple manner of life; which, I must confess, I think very pleasant in such a mild and dry climate.

From the river Volga, to the wall of China, there are three great Tartar princes; the Ayuka-Chan,* the Kontaysha, and the Tush-du-Chan. These three mighty nations have almost the same features, religion, and language; and live in the same manner. It will easily be perceived, by casting an eye on the map, what an extent of territory these princes possess, whose subjects go by the general name of Kalmuks. Few languages can carry a traveller over a greater extent of country than that of the Kalmuks. With the Arabic, indeed, a person may travel, through many places of the east, from Egypt to the court of the Great Mogul; but, with the Illyric, he can travel much further than with either of the former; viz. from the Gulf of Venice to the outmost boundaries of Kamtzatsky; for the Russian is a dialect of the Illyric.

The greatest part of Mongalia is one continued waste; except the places along the Amoor, and towards the Russian borders on the west. The soil also, to the south, from Selinginsky, is exceedingly fine; and capable, by proper culture, of producing grain of several sorts.

---

* Ayouka or Ayouki, the leader of the Torguts to whom T'u Li-shen's Embassy had been sent (Introduction, p. 11). He was a distant relative of the Kontaysha Galdan and his successor Tsewang Araptan, and also had married a daughter of his to the latter. But the two groups, Kalmuk and Torgut, were, for all their kinship, rarely consistent allies and more frequently at odds.

Since I have mentioned the Amoor, I presume this will be no improper place to give some account of that river. It is called by the Tartars Shaggalynoulla, or the Black Dragon, I suppose from the colour of its waters, and the windings of its course. It is formed of two large rivers, whose sources are in the desert, far to the eastward of this place. One is called Argun, which issues from a lake named Delay; the other is Ingoda, on the north bank of which stands the famous Russian town Nertzinsky. The conflux of these rivers produces the Amoor, which runs towards the east, augmenting daily by means of the many great and small streams it receives, till it becomes one of the largest rivers in this part of the world; and, after a long course, discharges itself into the Eastern or Chinese ocean. It is remarkable, that, from Cazan to these parts, the Amoor is the only river that runs eastward. Most, if not all, of the great rivers in Siberia have their courses to the north, and north-west.

Our barques arrived at Selinginsky on the 4th of June. After we had taken out of them what necessaries we wanted, they were dispatched with the rest of the baggage, for the greater security, to his Majesty's store-houses at Strealka, about four miles up the river, where the caravan for China then lay.

In the mean time, the ambassador writ a letter to the Allegada, or prime minister, at the imperial court of Pekin, to notify his arrival; and desire his excellency would give orders for his reception on the borders. This letter was sent to the prince of Mongalia, to be by him forwarded to court; for no strangers are allowed to travel through his territories to China, without his permission. The officer, who carried the letter to the prince, was treated with great civility; and his letter immediately sent to court by an express. A few days after, the prince sent two gentlemen, one of whom was a lama, to congratulate the ambassador on his arrival in these parts. They were invited to dine with the ambassador, and behaved very decently.

The same officer, who carried the ambassador's letter to the prince of Mongalia at Urga, was ordered to present his compliments to the Kutuchtu, or high priest, who is a near relation of the prince. He received the officer in a very friendly manner, desired him to sit down in his presence; an honour granted to very few, except ambassadors, and pilgrims from remote countries; and, at his departure, gave him a present of some inconsiderable things; particularly, a few pieces of Chinese silks.

I cannot leave this venerable personage, without taking some notice of him. I shall therefore relate a few things concerning him, among thousands more ridiculous, which the people in this country tell and believe.

This extraordinary man assumes to himself the character of omniscience, which is the interpretation of the word Kutuchtu; and the people are taught to believe that he really knows all things, past, present, and future. As his intelligence, by means of his lamas, is very extensive, he is easily able to impose on the vulgar in this particular. They also believe that he is immortal; not that his body lives always; but that his soul, upon the decay of an old one, immediately transmigrates into some young human body; which, by certain marks, the lamas discover to be animated by the soul of the Kutuchtu, and he is accordingly treated as high priest.

When the spirit of the Kutuchtu has taken possession of a new body, that is, in plain English, when he is dead, the lamas are immediately employed to discover in what part of the world this wonderful person is regenerated, or born again, as they express it. They need, however, go to no great distance to find him; for, the affair being previously concerted among the chief lamas, they soon determine the choice of a successor; who generally happens to be a young boy, that has been well instructed how to behave on that occasion. When a successor is pretended to be found, a company of lamas are sent to examine the matter, who carry along with them many toys, such as small silver bells, and things of that nature, which belonged to the former Kutuchtu, intermixed with others that did not. All these are laid before the child, who picks out such things as belonged to his predecessor, and discovers the greatest fondness for them; but rejects, with disgust, whatever is not genuine. Besides this trial, some questions are put to him, relative to wars, or remarkable events, in his former state; all which are answered to the satisfaction of the conclave. Whereupon he is unanimously declared to be the self-same Kutuchtu, is conducted with great pomp and ceremony to Urga, and lodged in the tent of the high priest.

Till the new Kutuchtu arrives at a certain age, he is entirely under the government of the lamas; and few are permitted to see him, except at a great distance, and even then it is not easy to get access to him. It may seem surprising, that, in so numerous an assembly of lamas, no intrigues should be carried on, nor disputes arise, among the electors. All is conducted without noise or contention. It is however imagined, that the authority of the prince greatly contributes to their unanimity.

The Mongalls relate, that their Kutuchtu has now lived fourteen generations, and renews his age every moon; for, at the new moon, he appears like a youth; when she is full, like a full-grown man; but, when near the change, he is an old man with grey hairs.

What they call the Urga is the court, or the place where the prince and high priest reside; who are always encamped at no great distance from one another. They have several thousand tents about them, which are removed from time to time. The Urga is much frequented by merchants, from China, and Russia, and other places; where all trade is carried on by barter, without money of any kind. The Chinese bring hither ingots of gold, damasks, and other silk and cotton stuffs, tea, and some porcelain; which are generally of an inferior quality, and proper for such a market. The Russian commodities are chiefly furs of all sorts. Rhubarb is the principal article which is exchanged for these goods, great quantities whereof are produced in this country, without any culture. The Mongalls gather and dry it in autumn; and bring it to this market, where it is bought up, at an easy rate, both by the Russian and Chinese merchants.

The Kutuchtu and his lamas are all clothed in yellow, and no layman is allowed to wear this colour, except the Prince. This mark of distinction makes them known and respected everywhere. They also wear about their necks a string of beads, which are used in saying their prayers. The Mongalls believe in, and worship, one Almighty Creator of all things. They hold that the Kutuchtu is God's vicegerent on earth; and that there will be a state of future rewards and punishments.

The following relation, which I had from a Russian merchant, to whom the thing happened, will show the methods taken by these lamas, to maintain the dignity and character of their mighty highpriest. This merchant had gone to the Urga, with an intention to trade with the Chinese. While he was at this place, some pieces of damask were stollen out of his tent. He made a complaint to some of the lamas, with whom he was acquainted; and the matter was soon brought before the Kutuchtu, who immediately ordered proper steps to be taken with a view to find out the thief. The affair was conducted in this uncommon manner; one of the lamas took a bench with four feet, which seems to have been of the conjuring kind; after turning it, several times, in different directions, at last it pointed directly to the tent where the stollen goods lay concealed. The lama now mounted astride on the bench, and soon carried it, or, as was commonly believed, it carried him to the very tent; where he ordered the damask to be produced. The demand was directly complied with; for it is in vain, in such cases, to offer any excuse.

I shall now subjoin a few observations on the Delay-Lama, or priest of the desert, who is reckoned still superior to the Kutuchtu. He lives about a month's journey to the south-east of this place, among a people called the Tonguts, who use a different language from the Kalmucks. I am informed that the religion of the Tonguts is the same with that of the Mongalls: that they hold the same opinions with respect to the transmigration of the Delay-Lama, as the Mongalls do about the Kutuchtu, and that he is elected in the same manner. What appears most surprising is, that these two mighty Lamas keep a good correspondence, and never encroach on one another's priviledges. The word *delay* signifies either the sea, or a great plain, such as this priest inhabits.*

* This paragraph is, I think, the earliest worthwhile English reference to the Dalai Lama by name though earlier English travellers in India had reported something of his functions. Bell was apparently unaware that Mongolia was actually converted to Lamaism from Tibet, but he notes, correctly, that the Dalai Lama owes his title to the Mongolians. (See Richardson, *Tibet and its History*, pp. 40-41.)

CHAPTER VI

Occurrences at SELINGINSKY; *Several parties of hunting; and journey continued to* SARATZYN, *the boundary between the* RUSSIAN *and* CHINESE *territories.*

The Tonguts are a separate people, governed by a Prince whom they call Lazin-Chan. One of their princes was lately killed, in an engagement with the Kontaysha, king of the Black Kalmucks. The Delay-Lama himself narrowly escaped being taken prisoner, notwithstanding all his foresight.* The Lama threatened the Kontaysha with many disasters, as the consequences of such proceedings. The Kontaysha, however, regarded them very little, till he had attained his ends; after which, he generously reinstated both the Prince and the Delay-Lama in their former dignity. The Kontaysha is of the same profession with the Delay-Lama, and acknowledges his authority in religious matters.

I am informed there is a third Lama, called Bogdu-Pantzin, of still greater authority than either of the former.† But, as he lives at a great distance, near the frontiers of the Great Mogul, he is little known in these parts. Though I am unwilling to throw the least reflection on any society of men instituted for the promotion of religion and virtue, from all I can collect concerning these Lamas, they are little better than shamans of superior dignity.

The answer to the letter, which the ambassador had written to Pekin, was not yet arrived. In the mean time we were obliged to remain at Selinginsky, where we entertained ourselves in the best manner we could.

June the 12th, walking along the bank of the river, I was a little surprised at the figure and dress of a man standing among a number of boys who were angling for small fishes. The person bought all the fishes alive, and immediately let them go again into the river, which he

---

* Bell's version of events in this paragraph is rather garbled, but then his informants may well have had good reasons for misleading him. In particular, the Dalai Lama referred to – the VIth – did not escape, but died, murdered perhaps, on his way to China. The whole fascinating episode (which is of basic importance in the history of China's claim to suzerainty over Tibet) is well summarized in Richardson, *Tibet and its History,* pp. 47-50.

† It is most interesting that Bell should have been told this – presumably on purpose and by interested parties. The Panchen Lama (Bogdu-Pantzin) was certainly not of such authority, though the long process by which the Manchus sought to build up his prestige as a counter-weight in Tibet to the immense religious influence of the Dalai Lama had already begun. On the complicated relationship between the Dalai Lama and the Panchen Lama see Richardson, *op. cit.,* pp. 53-56.

did very gently one by one. The boys were very civil to him, though they looked upon him as distracted on account of his behaviour. During this ceremony he took little notice of me, though I spoke to him several times. I soon perceived, by his dress, and the streak of saffron on his fore-head, that he was one of the Brachmans from India.

After setting all the fish a-swimming, he seemed much pleased; and, having learned a little of the Russian language, and a smattering of the Portuguese, began to converse with me. I carried him to my lodgings, and offered to entertain him with a dram; but he would taste nothing; for he said, it was against the rules of his religion to eat or drink with strangers.

I asked him the reason why he bought the fish to let them go again. He told me, that, perhaps the souls of some of his deceased friends, or relations, had taken possession of these fishes; and upon that supposition, it was his duty to relieve them: that according to their law, no animal whatever ought to be killed or eaten; and they always lived on vegetables.

After this interview, we became so familiar that he came every day to visit me. He was a chearful man, about seventy years of age. He had a bush of hair growing on his fore-head, very much matted, and, at least, six feet in length; when it hung loose, it trailed upon the ground behind him; but he commonly wore it wrapped about his head, in form of a turban. The hair was not all his own; but collected as relicks of his friends, and others of his profession, reputed saints; all which he had intermixed, and matted, with his natural hair. Persons of this character are called Faquers, and esteemed sacred every where.

He told me he was a native of Indostan, and had often been at Madrass, which he called Chinpatan, and said it belonged to the English. This circumstance, added to several others, made me believe he was no impostor, but an innocent kind of creature, as are most of that sect. He came to this country, in company with some others of his countrymen, on a pilgrimage, in order to pay their devotions to the Kutuchtu and Delay-Lama. They had been twelve months on their journey, and had travelled all the way on foot, over many high mountains and waste deserts, where they were obliged to carry their provisions, and even water, on their backs. I showed him a map of Asia, whereon he pointed out the course of his journey; but found many errors in the geography; and no wonder; since few Europeans would have had the resolution to undertake such a journey as this man had done.

The 14th, a chief named Taysha, of those Mongalls who are subjects of his majesty, came to pay his respects to the ambassador, who gave him a friendly reception, and kept him to dinner. He was a merry old man, near fourscore, but so vigorous, that he could mount a horse with as much agility as many young men. He was accompanied with five sons, and many attendants, who treated him with equal respect as a king; and even his sons would not sit down in his presence, till he desired them. I confess it gave me great pleasure to see the decency with which they behaved. One of our company, a pretty fat man, asked the Taysha what he should do in order to be as lean as he was. The old man replied in these few words, 'Eat less, and work more': a saying worthy of Hippocrates himself. In his youth he had been engaged in many battles with the Chinese, whom he held in great contempt. As he was a keen sportsman, the ambassador made an appointment with him for a grand hunting match. After which he and his retinue returned to their tents.

The 15th, we dined at Strealka with the commissary, Mr Stepnikoff,* of the caravan going to China. Strealka is situated, as I formerly observed, about three or four miles up the river from Selinginsky, in a fruitful plain of a triangular figure, formed by the conflux of two fine rivers; the Strealka running from the east, and the Selinga from the south. This would have been the strongest and most beautiful situation, of any in this province, for the town of Selinginsky. I am informed that the founders had a view to this delightful place; but the choice was determined against them by superstitious lots, to which it was referred. This method of chusing situations by lot, has hurt many noble cities, and rendered the work of ages ineffectual to remedy the error.

The same evening we returned, by water, to Selinginsky; and, next day, went a hunting to the west of the Selinga. We had about two hundred cossacks along with us, who followed the common method of ranging the woods, mentioned above. We killed six roe-bucks, and many hares. In the evening, we pitched our tents about a fountain, and feasted on venison.

The 16th, early, we left the woods to our right, and descended into a barren plain, where we found great flocks of antelopes. Our people killed about twenty of them. These animals avoid the woods, and frequent the open plains and deserts. They are exceedingly swift and watchful. And so far resemble sheep, that, if one breaks through the circle, the whole flock follows, though an hundred horsemen were in the way; which proves the destruction of many of these creatures.

* i.e. Istopnikov. See Introduction, p. 14.

The noise of the arrows, with which they are hunted, contributes much to their confusion. The heads of these arrows are broad, and fixed in a round bit of bone, with two holes in it; which make them whistle as they fly through the air.

At noon, we set up our tents near a lake of brackish water, called Solonoy-Osera, or the salt lake. Round the edges lies a thick scurf of salt, as white as snow, which the inhabitants gather for use. Here we found great flocks of water-fowl; such as, swans, geese, ducks. The weather being very hot, we remained till next day.

The 17th, we hunted along the same waste plains, directing our course to the south, towards the river Selinga. This day also we had very good sport. In the afternoon, we pitched our tents near a spring of fresh water, which is no small rarity in these parched deserts; and is as much regarded here, as a good inn would be in other parts of the world. I found, at this place, a prickly shrub, about three feet high, with a beautiful smooth bark as yellow as gold.

The 18th, in the morning, we had terrible flashes of lightning, accompanied with thunder, and heavy showers of hail and rain; which determined us to leave the plains, and return, by the shortest road, to Selinginsky. Besides the game already mentioned, we found many large bustards, which haunt the open country. As it is a very large bird, and rises slowly, our light horsemen killed several of them with their arrows.

The 24th, arrived an officer from the court of Pekin, sent on purpose to discover the number and quality of the embassy. This gentleman, whose name was Tulishin,* was a Mantshu Tartar by birth, and a member of the tribunal for western affairs, with which he was very well acquainted. These officers are called Surgutsky by the Mongalls, and by the Europeans Mandarin, a Portuguese word derived from *mando*.† He had formerly been in this country, and had learned the Russian language. He pretended to have been employed on some business with the Tush-du-Chan at Urga; and, hearing of the ambassador's arrival, had come to pay his respects to him. It was however well known that he was sent to enquire whether the ambassador came on a friendly errand. He was received very kindly; and, after he had stayed three days, and made his observations, returned very well satisfied. At his departure, he told the ambassador, that orders would soon be given

---

* i.e. T'u Li-shen. See Introduction, p. 11. For his career as a whole, see Hummel, *Eminent Chinese of the Ch'ing Period.*

† This is popular etymology. For the derivation of *mandarin* see the *Oxford English Dictionary.*

for his reception on the frontiers; but these could not be issued till his arrival at court, because on his report the whole affair depended. This wise and cautious nation, jealous of all the world, suffer none to enter their territories, but such as bring friendly messages. By this circumstance we were confined some time longer at Selinginsky.

I shall now give a description of the course of the Selinga, according to the best information I could procure from those who had been at its source. The Selinga is formed of two other rivers, called the Idyr and the Tzolato, coming from the mountains of Kungay, far to the southward of this place. It is afterwards joined by two inconsiderable rivers, the Orchon from the south-east, and the Tzida from the south-west; and, lastly, by the Strealka from the east, a little above the town of Selinginsky. At this place it is, at least, twice the breadth of the river Thames; and is navigable a great way above it. The course now is due north, till it discharges itself into the Baykall lake. The source of this river is estimated at the distance of ten or twelve days journey above Selinginsky, which is the common method of computation in this country. It is plentifully furnished with variety of excellent fish. The omuly, which I formerly described, come in vast shoals from the Baykall, in autumn, up this river, to spawn; after which, they return to the sea, so weak, that many of them are carried down floating on the surface of the stream. During the progress of the omuly up the river, the inhabitants of the adjacent villages assemble, with their nets, and catch as many of them as they please. On this occasion the poor take what they can use, and the rest are left upon the banks. These fishes advance up the river, about ten miles a day. On their first appearance, the report is soon spread over the country; and, in two or three hours, the people catch as many as they need, either for present use, or winter provisions. This fish is very agreeable food, either fresh or salted. It is observed, they are much better and fatter, the nearer they are caught to the sea; a plain argument, that, were they caught in the sea, they would still be preferable to any caught in the river. I have often thought, what inestimable treasure these omuly would produce, in other parts of the world; whereas, here, the consumption being small, they are little valued. It is remarkable, that the omuly are not to be found, at any season, in the Angara, or other rivers to the north of the Baykall.

July 5th, the Taysha-Batyr arrived, in consequence of his appointment with the ambassador, and brought along with him three hundred men, well mounted, for the chace. This old gentleman had the appellation of Batyr; a title of great respect among the Mongalls. It signifies a hero; and is conferred only on those who have signalized themselves, by their courage and conduct, in the field of battle. Besides these Mongalls, we carried with us fifty of our Cossacks, and our tents, as we proposed to be abroad some days.

Early on the 6th, we took our way to the eastward, over high hills, and through tall woods, having almost no underwood to incommode the horses, or interrupt our view; which made it very pleasant. After riding a few miles, the Taysha, being master of the chace, ordered his men to extend their lines. The Taysha and we were in the center; and often saw the game pass us, pursued by the horsemen, at full speed, without the least noise, but the whistling of arrows. The horses, being accustomed to this kind of sport, follow the game as a greyhound does a hare; so that the riders lay the bridles on their necks, and attend to nothing but their bows and arrows. One may easily imagine the exquisite entertainment, in seeing several of these horsemen in pursuit of an elk or stag through the valleys. When the animal is driven from the woods, it flies, for safety, to the nearest rocks. Some of these creatures are nearly as large, and strong, as the horses that hunt them. The stags are of two kinds; one called zuber, the same with the German crown-hirsh, but somewhat larger. The zuber is large and beautiful, and carries its head almost upright, as it runs; which prevents its horns being entangled with branches of trees. There are none of them in Russia, nor even in Siberia, except about the Baykall lake, and eastward from it; the places farther to the north being too cold for them. The elk is larger than the stag, and stronger made; having also long branchy horns, but a little flat.

Tired with sport, we left the hills in the afternoon, and came down into a fine valley, where we pitched our tents, near a pure brook. The Taysha then ordered all the dead game to be brought before him, and ranged in proper order. We found, that, this day, we had killed no less than five large elks, four stags, a dozen roe-bucks, several wolves and foxes, besides fawns and hares.

The Taysha caused the game to be divided among the huntsmen; who began immediately to dress it, some of them by boiling, others by broiling, and eat it without either bread, or salt. The tails of the stags, which, by these people, are reckoned very delicate, fell to the Taysha's share. He cut them into slices, and eat them raw. I eat a bit of one of them, and thought it very palatable. The taste resembled nothing so much as that of fresh caviare. After we had feasted on variety of excellent venison, for we had no other provisions, we went to rest, well satisfied with the diversion of the day.

July 7th, early in the morning, we left the plains, and directed our course eastward, in the same order we observed the preceeding day. As our sport was much the same, I need not mention the particulars. About noon we pitched our tents, near a spring of fresh water, in a valley where the grass was about two feet long. This circumstance is a proof of the goodness of the soil; which, in my opinion, cannot fail, if properly cultivated, to produce any kind of grain. As the weather was excessively hot, we staid in this place till next day.

July 8th, we continued our sport in the woods till noon; when we came into an extensive plain, in which we set up our tents, near a spring of brackish water. In this place we observed several flocks of antelopes, which we reserved for next day's hunting.

In the morning, our Taysha dispatched some of his horsemen to the tops of the hills, in order to discover where the antelopes were feeding; which, as I formerly observed, are the most watchful, and, at the same time, the swiftest animals in the world. When they returned, we extended our wings to a great distance, that we might surround these creatures with the greater ease; and, before noon, our people killed above twenty of them. After which we returned to our tents, that were left standing in the morning.

July 10th, we took leave of the Taysha, whose tents were to the east of this place, and returned next day to Selinginsky.

During this short excursion, I could not enough admire the beauty of the country through which we passed. The gentle rising of the hills, many of which have their tops only covered with wood, and the fertility of the vales, contribute to form one of the most delightful landskips the world can afford. To this may be added the temperature, and dryness, of the climate; in which respects this far exceeds any country with which I am acquainted. After mid-summer there is almost no rain till December, when the snow falls; and in such moderate quantities that it does not hinder the cattle from lying abroad all the winter.

In surveying these fertile plains and pleasant woods, I have often entertained myself with painting, in my own imagination, the neat villages, country seats, and farm-houses, which, in process of time, may be erected on the banks of the rivers, and brows of the hills. There is here waste land enough to maintain, with easy labour, several European nations, who are, at present, confined to barren and ungrateful soils: and, with regard to the Mongalls, whose honesty and simplicity of manners are not unamiable, I should like them very well for neighbours.

From what I have read of North America, I am of opinion, that this country resembles none so much as some of our colonies in that quarter of the world; particularly the inland parts of Pensylvania and Maryland. Both countries ly nearly in the same latitude; in the one we find great lakes and mighty rivers; in the other, the Baykall sea, and rivers, which, for the length of their course and quantity of water, may be ranked with any in the western world.

Having rested ourselves a few days after our fatigue, on the 16th of July, we set out on another hunting-match, attended by our own cossacks, and a few of the neighbouring Mongalls. We went, on this occasion, farther northward, and nearer to the Baykall lake, than in our former expedition. Our sport was almost of the same kind as already described. I shall only add, that both the stag and elk shed their horns once a year; at which time they retire to thickets, and solitary places, till their horns begin to spring again. It is surprising that animals so large, with such prodigious weight of branchy horns, should run, with almost incredible speed, through the thickest woods, without entangling themselves; but, to avoid this misfortune, they point their noses always parallel to the horizon. When either the elk or stag are closely attacked, they make a vigorous defence both with horns and hoofs. At rutting time, especially, these creatures are so very furious, that it is extremely dangerous for any person to approach their haunts; they will then run at a man full speed, and, if he escapes being wounded by their horns, will trample him to death with their sharp hoofs. As the weather was excessively hot, we kept the field only two days; and then returned to Selinginsky.

July 20th, another Mandarin arrived from Pekin, accompanied by an officer from Urga ; who brought a letter to the ambassador from the Tush-du-chan, acquainting him, that he might soon expect a person, properly authorised, to conduct him to the imperial city. No news could be more agreeable. We hoped now to be soon released from this solitary place, and arrive at the end of our journey. We were indeed well enough lodged, and wanted neither the necessaries nor conveniencies of life. The abundance of rural diversions, which this place afforded, coinciding happily with the genius of most of our gentlemen; and the harmony that subsisted among the retinue, though composed of people from most nations in Europe, and some from Asia, contributed not a little to our passing the time very agreeably. Notwithstanding these advantages, and the affability and courteous behaviour of the ambassador, which heightened them all, we were uneasy at being detained so long on the frontiers. We were apprehensive that

H

some accident might happen to prevent our journey; especially, as it was reported among the Mongalls, that, the Emperor of China, being far advanced in years, was sometimes sick, and not disposed to receive foreign ministers.

The 24th, there fell such a shower of hail-stones as no man then alive had ever seen. It was happy for us we were not then abroad, as the open field affords no kind of shelter. The hail lay some days in the woods, and cooled the air; which, before that time, had been excessively hot. This day the Kutuchtu sent two lamas to compliment the ambassador, to wish him a good journey, and a happy sight of the Emperor, or Boghdoy-chan, as he is called by these people.

August 9th, a courier arrived from Pekin, who told the ambassador, that he had passed our conductor on the road; and that we should now prepare for our journey to the capital, as that gentleman would arrive in a few days.

On the 24th, our conductor, called Lomy, at last arrived. He was, by birth, a Mantshu Tartar, and a member of the court for the western department. After remaining with us for some days, he returned to Yolla, a place upon the border, in order to procure horses and camels for our journey.

September 8th, we sent our baggage by water to Strealka, and next day we followed it. We lived in tents, while we staid at this place, till horses and camels were got ready. In the mean time, our people were employed in packing up the baggage into proper loads for camels. Strealka, I formerly observed, is the place where his majesty's commissary of the caravan has his abode, and the government of Siberia their store-houses. I imagine, therefore, it will not be improper, before we proceed, to give some account of the trade carried on from this place.

Formerly the fur trade was free to all his majesty's subjects, both Russians and Tartars. The merchants repaired to Siberia at the proper seasons, where they bought, at cheap rates, all the rich furs they could find; and disposed of them in Persia, Turkey, and Poland, at a price much below the real value. The government of Siberia perceived a very considerable diminution of the revenue in that country, and soon discovered the true cause of it; which was, that, a great part of the furs belonging to his majesty remained unsold. Upon inquiry, it appeared that this was owing to the foreign markets being supplied with these commodities, at low rates, by the subjects, before the goods belonging to the government could be exposed to sale. The government of Siberia represented to his majesty the loss of so considerable

a branch of his revenue; in consequence of which, an order was immediately issued, prohibiting all private persons, for the future, to
export sables in particular. Since this regulation took place, the
government have sent their own furs, generally once in three years, by
caravans, to China. The value of one of these caravans is reckoned to
amount to four or five hundred thousand roubles, and yields a return
of, at least, double that sum. The Emperor of China, from regard to
the friendship and good neighbourhood of his majesty, gives the caravans free quarters, and liberty to dispose of their goods, and buy
others, without exacting any impost. At first the Emperor not only
gave the caravan free quarters, but also maintained, at his own charge
both men and horses, during their stay in Pekin. This last expression
of his majesty's bounty is, however, now withdrawn.

September 15th, our conductor having acquainted the ambassador
that the horses and camels were ready, our baggage was dispatched to
the frontiers, escorted by our own soldiers and some cossacks; though,
indeed, there was no great occasion for any guard, as the Mongalls
seem to have little use for any thing that belonged to us.

After dining with the commissary of the caravan, at Strealka, on
the 18th, we left that place in the evening, accompanied with the commissary and most of the officers at Selinginsky. After we had travelled
about twenty English miles to the south-east, through fine plains
covered with exceeding long grass, we arrived at the end of the first
stage, called Kolludtzy; where we found our tents, which had been
sent off in the morning, ready for our reception. This day we saw some
scattered tents of Mongalians, with their flocks.

Next day, we travelled about twenty miles farther to a single house,
built by the commissary for a shade to his cattle in winter. We hunted
all the way through a pleasant country, interspersed with little hills
covered with wood; but saw as few inhabitants as the day before.

The 20th, about noon, we reached a place called Saratzyn, or the
New Moon, situated on the bank of a rivulet of the same name. This
rivulet is the boundary between the Russians and Chinese territories,
and separates two of the most mighty monarchies in the world. The
distance between Selinginsky and this place is computed to be about
one hundred and four verst, nearly seventy English miles.

The conductor was encamped on the east side of the rivulet, and we
pitched our tents on the other. The ground, on both sides, rises a little,
and the soil seems to be extremely good. The grass is rank and thick,
and, as the season is very dry, would, with little labour, make excellent
hay. This grass is often set on fire, by the Mongalls, in the spring,

during high winds. At such times it burns, most furiously, running like wild-fire, and spreading its flames to the distance of perhaps ten or twenty miles, till its progress is interrupted by some river or barren hill. The impetuosity of these flames, their smoke and crackling noise, cannot easily be conceived by those who have not seen them. When any person finds himself to the leeward of them, the only method, by which he can save himself from their fury, is to kindle immediately the grass where he stands, and follow his own fire. For this purpose, every person is provided with flints, steel, and tinder. The reason why the Mongalls set fire to the grass is to procure early pasture for their cattle. The ashes, left upon the ground, sink into the earth at the melting of the snow, and prove an excellent manure; so that the grass, in the spring, rises on the lands, which have been prepared in this manner, as thick as a field of wheat. Caravans, travellers with merchandise, but especially armies, never encamp upon this rank grass. And there are several instances of considerable bodies of men being put in confusion, and even defeated, by the enemy's setting fire to the grass.

Before I leave the Russian territories, I shall give some account of the marches between these two famous empires. The frontier, according to the best information I could procure, begins, a great way westward of this place, near the source of the river Dzida; from thence it proceeds to the east, crossing the Selinga, and runs along the tops of the hills, inclining sometimes to the north, and sometimes to the south, till it meets with the rivulet Saratzyn. It runs then in a very irregular line, varying its direction according to the course of the rivers and brooks; or, from the top of one hill to some other remarkable point in view; pointing, in general, towards the north-east, till it ends at the river Argun; which, together with the Ingoda, forms the Amoor. This boundary includes a vast tract of excellent land on the Russian side; and that part of the Mongalls who inhabit it, being stout men, and living much at ease, will, in time, become a numerous people.

The marches were settled upon the present footing about twenty-five years ago, on the following occasion. The Mongalls, on the Chinese side, alledged, that their countrymen, subjects of Russia, encroached on their borders; which created some disputes between the two nations. The causes of this misunderstanding being represented to the two courts, it was agreed to send ministers, with full powers to terminate the affair in an amicable manner. His Majesty's minister, Theodore Alexiovitz Golovin, met the Chinese plenipotentiaries, on the frontiers, in the neighbourhood of Nertshinsky, a considerable town, belonging to Russia, near the river Amoor. All matters were soon accommodated, to the mutual satisfaction of both parties, on the footing of *uti possidetis*; i.e. each of the parties retaining the people and territories that then belonged to them.

This determination kept all quiet for some time. The Chinese, however, soon appeared to be dissatisfied with the decision; and want to have the marches reviewed; to which, in my opinion, the Russians will not easily assent.

The 21st, the conductor came to congratulate the ambassador on his arrival at the borders; and acquainted him, that, the horses and camels being ready, he might proceed when he pleased. I cannot omit an inconsiderable circumstance, that happened at this place, as it strongly represents the caution and prudence of the Chinese. Our conductor, having seen some women walking in the fields, asked the ambassador, who they were? and whither they were going? He was told, they belonged to the retinue, and were going along with it to China.

He replied, they had women enough in Pekin already; and, as there never had been an European woman in China,* he could not be answerable for introducing the first, without a special order from the Emperor. But, if his excellency would wait for an answer, he would dispatch a courier to court for that purpose. The return of this messenger could not be sooner than six weeks; it was therefore thought more expedient to send back the women to Selinginsky, with the waggons that brought our baggage to this place.

* The European merchants trading at Canton were likewise prohibited from bringing their wives and families into that city.

CHAPTER VII

From passing the SARATZYN, *and entering the* CHINESE *territories, to our arrival at the wall of* CHINA

The 22nd of September, having loaded the camels with our baggage, and procured carriages for the boxes that contained his Majesty's presents to the Emperor, which were too large for camels to bear, we mounted, and passed the Saratzyn, and soon entered the Chinese territories. We travelled fifteen miles, when we arrived, about evening, at the river Orchon, running with a smooth stream to the north. The carriages retarded our progress greatly, as the horses were sprightly, and unaccustomed to draught.

This day we commenced guests of the Emperor of China, who entertains all ambassadors, and bears their expences, from the day they enter his dominions, till the time they quit them again. Our retinue consisted of about one hundred persons, who were allowed fifteen sheep every day. The overplus of this large allowance was given to the Mongalls who drove the camels. Besides mutton and beef, there is no other kind of provision to be found, till you come within the wall of China. The mutton is of a middle size; but, I must confess, exceeding fine. The conductor was attended by an officer from the Tush-du-Chan who procured, from the Mongalls encamped nearest our road, what sheep we wanted. The camels were very tractable, and stooped to take on their loads. But the horses were, at first, very unmanageable. Many of them had never before been employed for any use; and were saddled with great difficulty, but mounted with much more; for the very smell of our cloaths, which they perceived to be different from that of the Mongalls, their masters, made them snort and spring with great fury. They were easily managed, notwithstanding, when we got upon their backs.

Our road, this day, lay through fine plains and vallies, covered with rank grass; but not a single tent was to be seen. I inquired why such a fine soil was without inhabitants; and was told, that the Chinese had forbid the Mongalls to encamp so near the Russian borders, for fear of being allured to pass over to their territories, as many had formerly done. These fruitful vallies are surrounded with pleasant hills, of easy ascent, whose summits are covered with tufts of trees. Many of these tufts, being of a circular figure, and having no under-wood, appear as if they had been planted and pruned by art; others are irregular; and, sometimes, a ridge of trees runs from one hill to another. These objects afford a prospect so pleasing to the eye, and so seldom to be found, that one cannot help being charmed. And this pleasure is still heightened by the gentle-flowing rivulets; abounding with fish, and plenty of game, in the vallies, and among the trees.

The 23rd, we set out early, and came to a rivulet, called Ira, running to the north-west, till it falls into the Orchon; which we passed, and pitched our tents on the other side. The rank grass, by accident, took fire; and, had not water been at hand to extinguish it, and the weather very calm, the consequences might have been fatal. We travelled farther this day than the former, as fewer inconveniencies arose from the restifness of the horses.

The 24th, we continued our journey towards the south-east, along smooth roads, through a pleasant country; and, at evening, reached a rivulet called Shara, or the yellow rivulet, on the banks of which we set up our tents. The vallies now were more contracted, and less wood upon the hills, than formerly.

The 25th, we came to a rivulet called Kara, or the black rivulet, from the colour of the water, which is tinged by the richness of the soil.

The 26th, we proceeded. The country retained much the same appearance, and the weather was very fine; but not a single inhabitant was yet to be seen. In the evening, I walked from our tents, with some of our company, to the top of a neighbouring hill, where I found many plants of excellent rhubarb; and, by the help of a stick, dug up as much of it as I wanted.

On these hills are a great number of animals called marmots, of a brownish-colour, having feet like a badger, and nearly of the same size. They make deep burrows on the declivities of the hills; and, it is said, that, in winter, they continue in these holes, for a certain time, even without food. At this season, however, they sit or ly near their burrows, keeping a strict watch; and, at the approach of danger, rear themselves upon their hind-feet, giving a loud whistle, like a man, to call in the stragglers; and then drop into their holes in a moment.

I should not have mentioned an animal so well known as the marmot, had it not been on account of the rhubarb. Wherever you see ten or twenty plants growing, you are sure of finding several burrows under the shades of their broad spreading leaves. Perhaps they may some times eat the leaves and roots of this plant. However, it is probable, the manure they leave about the roots, contributes not a little to its increase; and their casting up the earth makes it shoot out young buds, and multiply. This plant does not run, and spread itself, like docks,

and others of the same species; but grows in tufts, at uncertain distances, as if the seeds had been dropped with design. It appears that
the Mongalls never accounted it worth cultivating; but that the
world is obliged to the marmots for the quantities scattered, at random,
in many parts of this country. For whatever part of the ripe seed happens
to be blown among the thick grass, can very seldom reach the ground,
but must there wither and die; whereas, should it fall among the loose
earth, thrown up by the marmots, it immediately takes root, and produces a new plant.

After digging and gathering the rhubarb, the Mongalls cut the
large roots into small pieces, in order to make them dry more readily.
In the middle of every piece they scoop a hole, through which a cord
is drawn, in order to suspend them in any convenient place. They
hang them, for most part, about their tents, and sometimes on the
horns of their sheep. This is a most pernicious custom, as it destroys
some of the best part of the root; for all about the hole is rotten and
useless; whereas, were people rightly informed how to dig and dry this
plant, there would not be one pound of refuse in an hundred; which
would save a great deal of trouble and expence, that much diminish
the profits on this commodity. At present, the dealers in this article
think these improvements not worthy of their attention, as their gains
are more considerable on this than on any other branch of trade.
Perhaps the government may hereafter think it proper to make some
regulations with regard to this matter.

I have been more particular in describing the growth and management of the rhubarb*; because I never met with an author, or person,
who could give a satisfactory account where, or how, it grows. I am
persuaded, that, in such a dry climate as this, it might easily be so
cultivated as to produce any quantity that could be wanted.

I omit any computation of the distances of places, along this road,

---

* The anonymous author of the *Relation de la Grande Tartarie* commented likewise
(pp. 84-85) on the abundance of rhubarb in this region and the advantage to the Russian
Treasury if the trade were 'fidellement administré'. The maladministration of the rhubarb
trade may be studied in Cahen, *Histoire des Relations de la Russie avec la Chine*, pp. 62-63,
but Bell's interest in the subject should be seen in the light of the enormous demand in his
native land for rhubarb root for medicinal purposes in the eighteenth century. Claudius
Rondeau, the British Minister at St Petersburg, wrote to Lord Harrington on December
31, 1737, that he had been unable to procure seeds or a plant of rhubarb 'even for a bribe
of 200 ducats'. A Scot, Dr James Mounsey, Physician to the Empress Elizabeth, is credited
with having introduced the plant to Great Britain from Russia. According to Marjorie
Plant, *The Domestic Life of Scotland in the 18th Century*, the eminent Edinburgh physician,
Sir Alexander Dick (the acknowledged expert on the subject of rhubarb at the time), was,
as late as 1777, selling his year's crop of $9\frac{1}{2}$ pounds at 1 guinea the pound.

13. RHUBARB (see pages 107-108)
    (According to Kircher *China Monumentis Illustrata*, 1667)

14. NERTZINSKY (see page 109)
    The treaty of 1689 between Russia and China was concluded here. (From Ides, *Three Years' Travels*, 1706)

15. ON THE MONGOLIAN PLAINS
16. A CARAVAN CROSSING THE PLAINS
   (*Photos*: John Massey Stewart, 1964)

17. A MONGOLIAN YURT OF TODAY
    (*Photo*: John Massey Stewart, 1964)

18. INTERIOR OF A YURT
    (*Photo*: Fitzroy Maclean, 1964)

19. INTERIOR OF A YURT
   (*Photo*: John Massey Stewart, 1964)

as the whole of it, from the borders to Pekin, has been measured by a wheel, or machine, given to the caravan, by the governor of Siberia, for that purpose. I shall afterwards subjoin the exact distances taken from this measurement.

The 27th, and 28th, we pursued the same road, over hills and through vallies. For, though few travel this way, the caravans, with their heavy carriages, leave such marks as are not soon effaced. It is only of late that the caravans travelled this road. Formerly they went farther to the north, by a Russian town called Nertzinsky, and thence to a Chinese city called Naun. That road is more convenient than the present, as it lies through places better inhabited; but the present is shorter, and therefore taken by most travellers.

The 29th, we reached a river called Buroy, where we lodged. At this dry season all these rivers are fordable; and they abound with sturgeon, and other fish. Next morning, Mr Venant, our chief cook, dropped down, as he was coming out of his tent, and immediately expired, notwithstanding all possible care was taken for his recovery. We interred him as decently as time and circumstances would admit; and proceeded to a river called Bor-Gualty, where we pitched our tents for this night.

October 1st, after a long day's journey, we reached a rivulet called Koyra. The face of the country appeared nearly the same as formerly.

The 2nd, after another long march, we came to the banks of the river Tola, the largest we had seen since we left the Selinga.

Next day, we crossed the Tola at a pretty deep ford, where the river was in breadth about the flight of an arrow at point blank. It was noon before our camels got over, and too late to proceed. We were therefore obliged to set up our tents on the east banks of the river, which was overgrown with tall oziers.

Here our conductor furnished us with fresh horses and camels. From the borders to this place, our stages were regulated by brooks and rivers; for the conveniency of getting water. And, for the same reason, as there are no rivers nor brooks, from hence to the wall of China, fountains and springs will be our only stages.

On the banks of the Tola we found many Mongalls encamped, with numerous flocks of cattle, being the first inhabitants we had seen since our leaving the border. The Russians, and the Mongalls who are subjects of Russia, claim all the country westward from the Tola; which, they say, is the natural boundary between the two empires. This would indeed be a considerable addition to the dominions of Russia. But, as both these mighty monarchs are abundantly provided with a vast extent of territory, neither party think it worth while to dispute about a few hundred miles of property, which, obtained, would perhaps not balance the cost, or contribute but little to the advantage of either.

The appearance of the country was now greatly altered to the worse. We saw no more pleasant hills and woods; neither could I find one single plant of rhubarb. The soil was dry and barren; and the grass not to be compared to what we had already passed over.

The 4th, after every man had drunk his fill of the pure and wholesome water of Tola, and filled his bottle with it, we departed with some regret, as we could hope for no more rivers, or brooks, till we came to the wall of China. We soon entered the desert commonly named, by the Mongalls, the Hungry Desert. How far it deserves that title, will be seen as we advance.

In the evening, we reached some pits, called Tola-Tologoy, of brackish water, where we pitched our tents. The road still pointed to the south-east, with little variation, over grounds that rose a little at first, but afterwards gradually declined. We saw many Mongalian tents, and cattle, dispersed along the desert.

The 5th, we set out again, and, in the evening came to some fountains, called Chelo-Tologoy, of pretty fresh water. The country was quite level, and appeared to the eye as plain as the sea. The soil was dry, barren, and gravelly; and neither tree nor bush to be seen; a prospect not very agreeable.

The 6th, early in the morning, we proceeded eastward, through the same sort of flat country. The weather was very fine, and the roads excellent. In the evening, we arrived at a pool, called Tylack, of brackish water, where we remained the following night. This day we saw several large flocks of antelopes, and some Mongalls in their tents; which was no disagreeable object in this continued plain. We passed few of these tents without visiting them, where we always found an hospitable reception, and were entertained with some zaturan, a kind of tea which I formerly described. And, if we happened to stay till our baggage was gone out of sight, the landlord conducted us, by the shortest way, to the springs that terminated the next stage.

The next day, we came to the wells called Gachun. Our bisket being now spent, we were reduced to live on mutton only, during the rest of our journey through this desert; which we accounted no great hardship, as it was extremely fine. It is not a little surprising, that, notwithstanding the barren appearance of this unsheltered plain, the cattle are in good condition, but particularly the sheep. The short grass, though in many places thinly scattered, must be of a very nourishing quality. This will naturally proceed from the climate, and the soil, which every where partakes of a nitrous quality, as plainly appears from the scurf of salt round the edges of the lakes and ponds, and the taste of the water, generally brackish in the springs and pits.

The 8th, our conductor furnished us with a fresh set of cattle, which detained us later than our usual time of setting out. This day, the soil was very much inclined to gravel, containing a number of red and yellow pebbles, many of which, being transparent, made a fine appearance while the sun shone. We were informed there were sometimes stones of value found here; which so much excited our curiosity, that each of us, every day, picked up a considerable quantity. On examination, most of them were thrown away, as altogether useless; the few we thought proper to retain were wrought into very good seals. A man might gather a bushel of such stones every day in this desert. One of our people, a Grecian by birth, who understood something of the nature of stones, found one that he called a yellow sapphire, and valued it at fifty crowns. Perhaps these pebbles might be of that kind which the lapidaries call cornelian; for they are sufficiently hard, and take a fine polish.

The 9th, we set out early, and travelled to a pool named Oko-Toulgu. This day, a lama from the Kutuchtu, going to Pekin, joined our company, who, by his habit and equipage, seemed to be a person of eminence. In marching along the tedious desert, the conversation turned on a terrible earthquake which happened, during the month of July last, in China, between the long wall and Pekin; and had laid in ruins several villages, and walled towns, and buried many people in their ruins. The lama inquired what was the opinion of the learned men in Europe concerning the cause of this phaenomenon. We told him, it was commonly reckoned to be subterraneous fire; and then asked, in our turn, to what cause such extraordinary appearances were imputed by his countrymen? He replied, that some of their learned lamas had written, that God, after he had formed the earth, placed it on a golden frog; and, whenever this prodigious frog had occasion to scratch its head, or stretch out its foot, that part of the earth, immediately above, was shaken. There was no reasoning on a notion so fantastical; we therefore left the lama to please himself with his hypothesis, and turned the discourse to some other subject.

The 10th, we came to the springs called Korpartu. The appearances of things this day were almost the same as on the preceding days. The soil appeared so barren, that none of the common methods of improvement could make it bear any kind of grain, or even alter its present condition. The dispositions of its inhabitants, the Mongalls, seem wonderfully suited to their situation; as they appear more contented with their condition than those who possess the most fruitful countries.

In the evening of the 11th, we arrived at Khododu; where we found the water clear, and pretty fresh, bursting, in a strong spring, from the gravelly earth, and running, in a stream, to a considerable distance, till it loses itself in the sand. This was the first running water we had seen since we left the Tola. And we were as happy, while sitting round this fountain, and broiling our mutton chops, as others at a table plentifully furnished with Burgundy and Champaign. Our appetites were, indeed, very keen; to which daily exercise, the coldness of the air, and drinking nothing but water, greatly contributed.

Next morning, being the 12th, there was a little frost upon the ground. Several flocks of gray plovers came to drink at the spring; of which our people killed as many as our present circumstances required. These poor harmless birds seemed insensible of danger; and, perhaps, they had never before heard the report of a gun; for no sooner was the piece fired, than they took a short flight round the fountain, whistling as they flew, and immediately alighted to drink again. The plover is a pretty bird, and pleasant to eat; and the soles of its feet are as hard as so much horn, which prevent its being hurt by the stones or gravel. In the evening, we came to the wells called Bouk-Horlike, without any thing material happening, or any difference on the face of the country.

The 13th, we continued our journey to the wells of Buduruy; where we were again furnished with fresh horses and camels.

The 14th, we came to a place, called Kadan-Kachu, where we were obliged to dig a pit, four feet deep, in order to procure water; which was very bad, having both a disagreeable smell, and bitter taste; but was drinkable, when boiled with some tea. We could, however, get none for our cattle, as the high wind filled the pits with sand as fast as we could dig them. This sand is of a whitish colour, and so light and dry, that it is driven, by the winds, into your face and eyes; and becomes very disagreeable. Most of our people, indeed, were provided with a piece of net-work, made of horse-hair, which covered their eyes; and is very useful in drifts, either of sand or snow.

The 15th, we travelled over deep sands; and, in the evening, arrived at other springs called Tzagan-Teggerick. The wind continuing high, it was with much difficulty we set up our tents. It is to be observed, that, on these deep and light sands, our European tents are of little use, as there is no earth in which the tent-pins can be fastened. The Tartar tents are much preferable; for, their figure being round and taper like a bee-hive, the wind takes but little hold of them; and they stand, equally well, on a sandy, or on any other surface. They are, besides, warmer, more easily erected, taken down, and transported.

The 16th, we left the deep sand, and travelled along the same sort of dry gravelly ground as formerly. In the evening, we pitched our tents at the springs called Sadjin. The variety of objects, in this dreary waste, are so few, that, in this, as well as in other respects, it much resembles the sea. Here one can see no farther than if he was placed on the surface of the water, out of sight of land; the rounding of the globe in both cases, being the same. Sometimes, in the morning, I have been agreeably surprized in fancying I saw, at a small distance, a fine river, having rows of trees growing upon its banks; but this was only a deception of the sight, proceeding from the vapours magnifying some scattered shrubs into great trees.

The 17th, we came to some wells of very bad water, called Oudey, where we found fresh horses and camels waiting for us. Our conductor resolved to lose no time, being apprehensive that we might be over-taken in the desert by the frost and deep snow, which usually happen at this season. Such an event would have retarded our march, and in-commoded us not a little in many respects. We therefore travelled as long stages as the convenience of water, and the strength of our cattle would permit.

The 18th, after a long day's journey, we came to the wells called Ulan-Kala. We found, almost every day, Mongalls in their tents, which stood like so many hives, dispersed through this solitary plain.

The 19th, we mounted again, and travelled to the springs named Tzilan-Teggerick. This day we saw several flocks of antelopes; and, indeed, few days passed in which we did not see some of these animals.

The 20th, we came to a place called Ourandabu. The weather still continued fair, the sky clear, and the mornings frosty. The water, at this place, was tolerable; but we were obliged to dig for it. When it happened that we had a long stage from one spring to another, for fear of coming too late, we usually sent a couple of men before us, in order to gather fewel, and to dig pits, that the water might have time to settle before our arrival.

The 21st, we proceeded; and, in the evening, arrived at a lake of salt water. After digging, however, we found some fresher. Were it not that these lakes and pits are scattered through this desert, it must have been altogether uninhabited, either by man or beast. This consideration, among many others, has often led me to admire the infinite wisdom of almighty God, in the dispensations of his providence, for the support of all his creatures.

In my opinion, these springs are produced by the rains and melted snow in the spring; for the water, sinking in the sand, is thereby prevented from being exhaled, in summer, by the heat of the sun; which must be very scorching in this desert, in which there is not the least shade to be found.

The 22nd, we quitted the salt lake, in a cold frosty morning, and a strong northerly wind; which was very disagreeable. At evening we reached the wells of Kulat. These pits take their names from the quality of the water, as salt, sour, sweet, bitter; or from the different tribes of people who inhabit the country in the neighbourhood.

In the midst of our fatigues, we had the satisfaction to be among a friendly people, who did every thing in their power to lessen our wants.

Next day, we reached the wells of Mingat. The weather, though cold, was not unpleasant. And, the 24th, having got fresh horses and camels, we came, in the evening, to a pond of brackish water, called Korunteer, upon the extremity of a dismal bank of sand, running a-cross our road.

The day following, we entered on the sand-bank, along a narrow and crooked passage between two hillocks. Every one prayed for calm weather while we travelled over the sand; which put me in mind of being at sea. We continued our journey, through deep sand, till about noon; when, all our horses and camels being tired, we halted in a hollow place; where we dug, and found very bad water. We remained here till next morning.

Our cattle being a little refreshed, though they had been very indifferently fed among the sand, where nothing was to be seen but some tufts of withered grass, we set out again. Along this bank there is not the least tract, or path of any kind; for the smallest blast of wind immediately effaces it, and renders all the surface smooth.

We had gone but a few miles when most of our people were obliged to alight, and walk on foot, the horses being quite tired with the deepness of the sand; which made our progress extremely slow. The weather, fortunately, was still very calm. About noon, we pitched our tents in a hollow place, encompassed with high hillocks of sand. I observed, that, in the open desert we had already passed, the prospect was much confined; but here it was quite straitened; for, if you ascended one of these mounts, you could see nothing but mount rising above mount, like so many sugar-loaves, or rather like so many cupolas.

20. THE GOBI DESERT
Bell's Hungry Desert!
(*Photo*: John Massey Stewart, 1964)

In the evening it began to blow a little at north-east, which drove about the light sand like snow; but, about midnight, the wind rose to such an height, that all our tents were overset at once, and our beds filled with sand. As it was near morning, we thought it not worth while to pitch them again. We therefore prepared ourselves to set out at the dawn, in hopes of getting over the sand-bank before night; which, by riding and walking by turns, in order to hasten our progress, we happily effected. And, in the evening, reached the springs of Kochatu.

At the place where we passed the sand, it was not above twenty English miles in breadth, which took us up three days. We could have travelled four times that distance on the plain, with more ease both to ourselves and cattle. I am informed this bank of sand runs a great way southward; and, in some places, is above thirty leagues broad. They, whose business calls them often to cross the sands, have thin leather coats, made on purpose, and round pieces of glass tied before their eyes.

This sand-bank appears like the waves of the sea; for the hillocks, some of which are about twenty feet of perpendicular height, are of so light a nature, that the wind carries them from place to place; levelling one, and forming another. And hence it is easy to conceive, that, a weary traveller, lying down on the lee-side of one of these hillocks, might, in a few hours, be buried in the sand; which is reported to have often happened in this and other sandy deserts.

The 28th, we proceeded along the plain to the springs called Chabertu. I cannot but take notice of the uncommon manner the people here have of killing their sheep. They make a slit with a knife between two ribs, through which they put their hand, and squeeze the heart till the creature expire; by this method all the blood remains in the carcass. When the sheep is dead, and hungry people cannot wait till the flesh is regularly dressed, they generally cut out the brisket and rump, wool and all, and broil them on the coals; then scrape off the singed wool, and eat them. This I have found, by experience, to be no disagreeable morsel, even without any kind of sauce.

The next day, we travelled another stage to the wells of Saminsa; where we found better water than usual. The length and thickness of the grass showed that the soil now began to mend. This day there fell some snow, and the wind was cold and northerly.

The 30th, we got fresh horses, and proceeded to the springs of Krema. From the appearance of the grass one would conclude, that the soil, at this place, was very fine. We saw great numbers of horses, belonging to the Emperor, turned out to graze. Notwithstanding all the haste we had hitherto made, we were, this day, overtaken by a fall of snow, which proved very inconvenient; not so much on account of the cold, but it covered all fewel, so that we could find none to dress our victuals.

The 31st, we came to a place called Naringkarussu, where, to our great satisfaction, we found a small brook of fresh water, and some Mongalian huts. I observed, that, from the sand-bank eastward, the soil becomes gradually better every day. This was now the fortieth day since we left the border; during which time we had not halted one day, nor seen a single house; and the twentieth and eight, from the time we quitted the river Tola, and entered the desert, in which we had neither seen river, tree, bush, nor mountain. Though we were obliged now and then to fetch a compass, on account of the watering places, yet, in general, our course deviated but little from the south-east point.

The 1st of November, we halted at this place, that we might have time to put things in order before we passed the long wall, which was now at no great distance.

Next day we proceeded, and about noon we could perceive the famous wall, running along the tops of the mountains, towards the north-east. One of our people cried out Land, as if we had been all this while at sea. It was now, as nearly as I can compute, about forty English miles from us, and appeared white at this distance. We could not, this night, reach the passage through the mountains; and, therefore, pitched our tents in the open plain as usual. We now began to feel the effects of the cold; for the snow, continuing to ly upon the desert, proved very inconvenient on many accounts; but particularly by retarding the progress of our heavy and cumbersome baggage. But we comforted ourselves with the hopes of soon seeing an end of all our toils, and arriving in a rich and inhabited country; for, though all of our people were in good health, they began to be very weary of the desert; and no wonder, as many of them had lain in the open field ever since we left Selinginsky.

November 3rd, after travelling about an hour, we passed the vestiges of a camp, which seemed to have been regularly designed. I was informed that the Emperor encamped here, when he led his troops against the Mongalls, called, by the missionaries in China, the Western Tartars.

The nearer we came to the mountains, we were the more surprised at the sight of the so much celebrated wall of China, commonly called, for its length, the endless wall. The appearance of it, running from one high rock to another, with square towers at certain intervals, even at this distance, is most magnificent.

About noon, we quitted the plain, and entered an opening between two mountains. To the left, the mountains are very high. On the right, they decline as far as they are within view; but, I am told, they rise again to a great height.

We descended by a narrow path, about eight feet broad, between the mountains, till we came to a small Chinese monastery, situated on the declivity of a steep rock. Curiosity led us to visit this solitary place. But, the road being impassable to horses, we alighted and walked thither. On our arriving near the place, the monks came out to meet us, with the usual friendly salutation of the country; which is performed by laying one of their hands on the other, and then shaking them, and pronouncing these words *Cho-loy-cho*.* The compliment being returned, they conducted us into the apartments of their little chapel, and treated us with a dish of green tea; which was very agreeable. In the chapel was a sort of altar-piece, on which were placed several small brass images; and, in one of the corners, I observed a sack filled with wheat. The habit of the monks, was a long gown with wide sleeves. On their heads was a small cap, and their long lank hair hung down over their shoulders. They had very few hairs in their beards. This being the first Chinese house we met with, I have, on that account, been more particular in describing it. Every thing now appeared to us as if we had arrived in another world. We felt, especially, a sensible alteration in the weather; for, instead of the cold bleak wind in the desert, we had here a warm and pleasant air.

We again proceeded along the narrow path; but of breadth sufficient for a wheel-carriage. The road being steep, and in many places rugged, we walked down the hill; and, in half an hour, came to the foot of it, where we found ourselves surrounded, on all sides, by high rocky mountains. Our route now lay along the south side of a rivulet, full of great stones, which had fallen from the rocks in rainy weather. In the cliffs of the rocks you see little scattered cottages, with spots of cultivated ground, much resembling those romantick figures of landskips which are painted on the China-ware and other manufactures of this country. These are accounted fanciful by most Europeans, but are really natural.

After we had travelled about seven or eight miles, along the bank of the brook, we came, in the evening, to a Chinese village, at the foot

---

* In considering Bell's transcriptions of Chinese and Mongolian it should be remembered that as a Scot he uses *ch* as the strong aspirate. Even so, the present rendering is not quite right. The Embassy was, I am sure, greeted with the words that in Giles's romanization would be written '*Hao lai-lo*' – literally 'Welcome'.

I

of a high mountain, where we lodged in clean rooms with warm fires of charcoal. There were no chimneys in the rooms; but, instead of these, the charcoal was put into a portable grate of brass or iron, and allowed to burn clear in the open air; after which it was brought into the apartment. Though the desert is one continued plain, it lies much higher than the plains and villages of China; for, when we entered the defile, the ascent was very inconsiderable when compared with the descent on the other side.

Here we began to taste of the fine fruits of China; for, soon after our arrival in the village, our conductor sent a present to the ambassador of some baskets of fruits; consisting of water-melons, musk-melons, sweet and bitter oranges, peaches, apples, wall-nuts, chess-nuts, and several other sorts which I never saw before; together with a jar of Chinese arrack, provisions of several sorts, and some Chinese bread, called bobon, made of wheaten flour, and baked over a pot with the steam of boiling-water. It is very light, and not disagreeable in taste; at least it seemed so to us, who had seen no bread for a month before.

Next day, we halted to refresh ourselves after our long fatigue. I took this opportunity to walk up to the top of the mountain, in order to view the adjacent country; but could only see a continuation of the chain of mountains, rising one above another, and, to the northward, some glimpses of the long wall, as it runs along them.

The 5th, we proceeded eastward, down the south bank of a river, whose channel was covered with great stones. The road is cut out of the rock, for a considerable length, at those places where there is no natural passage between the rocks and the river; which must have been a work of great labour. This river cannot fail to be a complete torrent in time of great rains.

Having travelled about six or eight miles, we arrived at the famous wall of China. We entered at a great gate, which is shut every night, and always guarded by a thousand men, under the command of two officers of distinction, one a Chinese, and the other a Mantzur Tartar; for, it is an established custom in China, and has prevailed ever since the conquest of the Tartars, that, in all places of publick trust, there must be a Chinese and a Tartar invested with equal power. This rule is observed both in civil and military affairs. The Chinese pretend, that, two in an office are a sort of spies upon one another's actions, and thereby many fraudulent practices are either prevented or detected.

CHAPTER VIII

From the wall of CHINA *to* PEKIN ; *Our entry into that city*

As soon as we had entered the gate, these two officers, and many subalterns, came to compliment the ambassador on his safe arrival; and asked the favour of him to walk into the guard-room and drink a dish of tea. We accordingly dismounted, and went into a spacious hall on the south side of the gate. This apartment was very clean, having benches all around; and is kept on purpose for the reception of persons of distinction. We were entertained with variety of fruits and confections, and several sorts of tea. After staying about half an hour, the ambassador took leave of the gentlemen, and we proceeded on our journey. We travelled about four miles farther, and came to a considerable town named Kalgan. At some distance from the place, we were met by the commandant, and the Mandarin Tulishin, who had paid us a visit at Selinginsky. They accompanied the ambassador to his lodgings; which were in houses a-part from the rest of the town; and provisions were sent us in great plenty.

From the wall to this place, the country, to the north, begins to open; and contains some villages, corn-fields, and gardens.

The same evening, the ambassador and the gentlemen of the retinue were invited to sup at the commandant's house; and horses were sent to carry us thither. We alighted in the outer-court, where the commandant in person waited for us; and conducted us, through a neat inner-court, into a hall, in the middle of which stood a large brass chaffing-dish, in shape of an urn, with a fire of charcoal in it. The floor was covered with mats, and the room quite set round with chairs, and little square japanned tables. The ambassador sat at a table by himself, and the rest of the company at separate tables, by two and two. We were first entertained with tea, and a dram of hot arrack; after which supper was brought, and placed on the tables, without either table-cloth, napkins, knives, or forks. Instead of forks, were laid down, to every person, a couple of ivory-sticks, with which the Chinese take up their meat. The dishes were small, and placed upon the table in the most regular manner; the vacancies being filled with saucers, containing pickles and bitter herbs. The entertainment consisted of pork, mutton, fowls, and two roasted pigs. The carver sits upon the floor, and executes his office with great dexterity. He cuts the flesh into such small bits, as may easily be taken up by the guests, without further trouble. The meat being cut up, is given to the footmen, who supply the empty dishes on the tables. The whole is served in China-ware; and neither gold nor silver is to be seen. All the servants perform their duty with the utmost regularity, and without the least noise. I must confess, I was never better pleased with any entertainment.

The victuals being removed, the desert was placed on the tables in the same order; and consisted of a variety of fruits and confections. In the mean time a band of musick was called in, which consisted of ten or twelve performers, on various, but chiefly wind-instruments, so different from those of that class in Europe, that I shall not pretend to describe them. The musick was accompanied with dancing, which was very entertaining. The dancers were nearly as numerous as the musicians. Their performances were only a kind of gesticulation, consisting of many ridiculous postures; for they seldom moved from the same place. The evening being pretty far spent, we took leave, and returned to our lodgings.

The 6th, a great fall of snow, and a cold frosty wind, obliged us to halt at this place.

Next day, the frost and snow still continued; notwithstanding, we set out, and passed over a stone-bridge, near this place, paved, not with small stones, but, with large, square, free stones, neatly joined. After travelling eastward about thirty English miles, we reached a large and populous city called Siang-Fu. We were met, without the gate, by some of the principal inhabitants, and conducted to our lodgings.

When we arrived, the governor was out a-hunting with one of the Emperor's sons. As soon as he returned in the evening, he waited on the ambassador, and complimented him in a very polite manner; excusing himself for not waiting on him sooner. At the same time, he gave his excellency a formal invitation to supper; for it is appointed, by the court, that foreign ambassadors should be magnificently entertained in all the towns through which they pass. But the ambassador, being somewhat indisposed, desired to be excused.

Our route, this day, was through a fine champaign country, well cultivated, but containing very few trees. We passed several small towns, and many villages, well built, and inclosed with walls. The roads were well made, and in good order; running always in straight lines, where the ground will allow. I had heard a great deal of the order and oeconomy of these people; but found my information far short of what I daily saw in all their works and actions. The streets of every village run in straight lines.

Upon the road we met with many turrets, called post-houses, erected at certain distances from one another, with a flag-staff, on which is hoisted the imperial pendant. These places are guarded by a few soldiers, who run a-foot, from one post to another, with great speed; carrying letters or dispatches that concern the Emperor. The turrets are so contrived, as to be in sight of one another; and, by signals, they can convey intelligence of any remarkable event. By this means the court is informed, in the speediest manner imaginable, of whatever disturbance may happen in the most remote provinces of the empire. These posts are also very useful, by keeping the country free from highwaymen; for should a person escape at one house, on a signal being made, he would certainly be stopped at the next. The distance of one post-house from another is usually five Chinese li, or miles; each li consisting of five hundred bow-lengths. I compute five of their miles to be about two and an half English.

The 8th, we halted at this place. As we could not be present at the entertainment to which we were invited, last night, by the governor, he had resolved that the delicacies, prepared on that occasion, should not be lost; and therefore sent into our court twelve tables, whereon were placed, by a number of people, all the victuals that were dressed the preceding night, with the desert, and several sorts of tea. The whole was afterwards brought into the hall; and there placed, in form, upon the tables. When this was done, an officer of distinction came to desire the ambassador to taste of his Imperial Majesty's bounty. We accordingly sat down at the tables in great order. Every thing was very good, but mostly cold; having been carried through the streets to some distance. After we had removed from the table, the person, who had the direction of the entertainment, called our servants, and ordered them to sit down at the tables, and eat. This produced a very diverting scene; but, had it not been complied with, the governor would have thought himself highly affronted.

In the evening, the Emperor's third son went through this city, on his way towards the capital. He was carried, upon men's shoulders, in a palankin; a vehicle very easy for the traveller, and well known in European settlements in India. The Emperor's sons have no other names than those of first, second, third, &c. This prince had only a small retinue of a few horsemen.

Our new conductor, Tulishin, invited the ambassador and his retinue to pass the evening at his lodgings. His excellency excused himself, as he had not been at the governor's. All the gentlemen, however, accepted the invitation. The entertainment was elegant, and something like that I formerly described, accompanied with dancing and musick, and quail-fighting. It is surprising to see how these little birds fly at one another, as soon as they are set upon the table; and fight, like game-cocks, to death. The Chinese are very fond of this diversion; and bet as high on their quails, as the English do on cocks. They are also great lovers of cock-fighting; but it is reckoned among the vulgar sports. The quails are generally parted before they hurt one another too much; and reserved, in cages, till another occasion.

The 9th, having sent off the baggage in the morning, the ambassador returned the governor's visit. We only staid to drink tea; after which we immediately mounted, and pursued our journey to a small town called Juny; where we arrived in the evening. Near this place is a steep rock, standing on a plain, inaccessible on all sides, except to the west; where a narrow winding path is cut in the rock, which leads to a Pagan temple and nunnery, built upon the top of it. These edifices make a pretty appearance from the plain; and, as the story goes, were built, from the foundation, in one night, by a lady, on the following occasion. This lady was very beautiful, virtuous, and rich; and had many powerful princes for her suitors. She told them, she intended to build a temple and a monastery, of certain dimensions, with her own hands, in one night, on the top of this rock; and whoever would undertake to build a stone-bridge, over a river in the neighbourhood, in the same space of time, him she promised to accept for a husband. All the lovers, having heard the difficult task imposed on them, returned to their respective dominions; except one stranger, who undertook to perform the hard condition. The lover and the lady began their labour at the same time; and the lady completed her part before the light appeared; but, as soon as the sun was risen, she saw, from the top of the rock, that her lover had not half-finished his bridge; having raised only the pillars for the arches. Failing, therefore, in his part of the performance, he also was obliged to depart to his own country; and the lady passed the remainder of her days in her own monastery.

The river is about a quarter of a mile from the rock, and the pillars still remain about five or six feet above the water; they are six or eight in number, and good substantial work. This tale I relate as a specimen of many fabulous stories, which I heard every day, and the people firmly believe. In the monastery there are, at present, many monks and nuns.

The chain of mountains running to the north, which bound this plain to the west, are very high, rugged, and barren. Their breadth, from the desert to the plain habitable country of China, I compute not to exceed fifteen or twenty miles, and in many places it is much less. But their length, I am informed, is above one thousand English miles. They encompass all, or the greatest part of the empire of China, to the north and west. These impregnable bulwarks, together with the almost impassable deserts, have, in my opinion, so long preserved this nation from being over-run by the western heroes. One would imagine, that a country, so fortified by nature, had little need of such a strong wall for its defence; for, if all the passes of the mountains are as narrow and difficult as that where we entered, a small number of men might defend it against a mighty army.

Juny is but a small place; it suffered greatly by the earthquake that happened in the month of July the preceding year; above one half of it being thereby laid in ruins. Indeed more than one half of the towns and villages, through which we travelled this day, had suffered much on the same occasion; and vast numbers of people had been buried in the ruins. I must confess, it was a dismal scene to see, every where, such heaps of rubbish.

All the best houses being thrown down by the earthquake, we were lodged in the priests apartments of a temple, which had escaped the general devastation. Our conductor treated the monks with very little ceremony, and desired them to seek other lodgings for themselves. These priests were not at all superstitious, as appeared sufficiently from the little reverence they paid to their idols, and statues of reputed saints. They conducted us into the temple, and several apartments adjoining, where stood many images of saints, some of which were monstrous figures of stone and plaister. One of the priests gave us the history of some of them; which I thought too absurd to be inserted. We then returned into the temple, which was a small but neat building. In one end of it we saw an altar, rising by steps to the cieling, on which were placed a number of small images, cast chiefly in brass, resembling men and women, birds and beasts. We were entertained in the temple with tea, till the priests had removed their beds. At the entrance is hung a large bell, attended by a priest, who tolls it on seeing passengers, in order to invite them to say their prayers; which having done, they generally leave a small gratuity to the temple.

In the night, we were a little alarmed with the shock of an earthquake, which awakened all our people, but did no damage.

Next day, our conductor notified to the ambassador, that he could proceed no farther till he received an answer to some dispatches he had sent to court. These news were not altogether agreeable, as we apprehended another shock of an earthquake. Nothing, however, of that kind happened during the two days we were obliged to remain at this place.

The 12th, we continued our journey to a little town, where we lodged. This, and most of the towns, and villages, through which we passed to day, had suffered greatly by the earthquake; particularly one considerable walled town, where very few houses remained, and the walls were levelled with the ground.

About noon, next day, we came to a large, populous, and well built city, with broad streets, as straight as a line. Near this place runs a fine river, which appears navigable; having a-cross it a noble stone bridge, of several arches, and paved with large square stones. In the evening, we arrived at a small town, after passing through a very pleasant and fruitful country.

On the 14th, we halted at this little town. But our baggage, and his majesty's presents, advanced a stage farther. These, by order of the Mandarin, our conductor, were carried on men's shoulders, covered with pieces of yellow silk; as every thing is which hath any connexion with the court. Whatever is distinguished by this badge is looked on as sacred. And he who has the care of any thing belonging to the Emperor needs no other protection: such is the reverence paid him all over the empire. The yellow colour is chosen by the Emperor, because, among the Chinese, it is the emblem of the sun, to which he is compared.

The following day, our road, lying over some rocks, was very rugged. In some places it was cut, for a considerable length, above twenty feet deep, through the solid rock; which appears to have been a work of great labour and expence. But no people, I ever saw, take such pains to make their streets, and high-ways, easy to travellers, as the Chinese. In some places of the rocks were cut out images of Chinese saints; but the workmanship very mean.

Near this place, we passed through six or eight strong semicircular walls, within one another, which have the endless wall for their common diameter, and take in a great compass. In all these walls there are large well built gates, guarded by a constant watch, both in times of peace and war. At one of them, the ambassador was saluted with three great guns, from a tower over the gate-way. These walls seem to be of the same materials and architecture with the long wall; having square towers at the distance of a bow-shot from each other. While we stopped at one of the gates to refresh ourselves, I took the opportunity to walk into one of these towers, where I saw some hundreds of old iron cannon thrown together as useless. On examination, I found them to be composed of three or four pieces of hammered iron, joined, and fastened together with hoops of the same metal. The Chinese have,

21. A GATE IN THE GREAT WALL
    (According to Kircher, *China Monumentis Illustrata*, 1667)
22. KALGAN. The first Chinese town within the Great Wall
    (From Ides, *Three Years' Travels*, 1706)

23. ARRIVAL AT THE GREAT WALL, 1692
    Peter the Great's envoy Isbrandt Ides and his retinue arriving at the Great Wall (see page 11)
    (From Ides, *Three Years' Travels*, 1706)

however, now learned to cast as fine brass cannon as are any where to be found. From this tower I was led, by a broad stone-stair, to the top of the wall, which is above twenty feet in breadth, and paved with large square stones, closely joined, and cemented with strong mortar. I walked along this flat, till I came to a rock, where I found a high stair of above a thousand steps, the whole breadth of the wall, which led to a tower on the summit, from whence I could see a like stair, on the other side, forming a descent to a narrow passage between two rocks. I observed also, that the wall was neither so high nor broad where it was carried over another rock, to the south-west, as at the place where I stood. But time not allowing me to go farther, I returned, by the same way, to our company; and, after staying a few hours, we proceeded, this afternoon, to the town of Zulinguang, where we lodged.

The next day, after travelling about two hours, we came to the last semicircular wall. Here ended all the hills and mountains. Our road now lay through a fine champaign country, interspersed with many small towns and villages. In the evening, we reached a large neat city called Zang-Ping-Jew. In the market place, stood a triumphal arch, whereon were hung a number of streamers, and silken pendants, of various colours. The streets were clean, straight, and broad; in some places covered with gravel, in others paved with flat square stones.

As soon as we had reached our lodgings, the governor of the place came to salute the ambassador, and invited him to an entertainment, prepared by order of his majesty.

The invitation was accepted, and we immediately went to the governor's palace. The entertainment was very magnificent, somewhat of the same kind with that I formerly described, and accompanied with musick and dancing. This place is situated in a fruitful plain, about thirty English miles northward of Pekin.

The 17th, after travelling about a dozen of miles, we came to a small town called Shach. The weather being very fine and warm, the governor came to meet the ambassador, and desired him to refresh himself a little by drinking tea. Here we halted about an hour, and then proceeded six or eight miles farther, to a small village, about four miles from the capital; where we lodged.

Next morning, two Mandarins came from court to congratulate the ambassador on his arrival, and brought some horses, on which he and his retinue were to make their entry. The furniture of the horses was very simple, and far inferior to the costly trappings of the Persians.

My lodgings, in this village, happened to be at a cook's house; which gave me an opportunity of observing the ingenuity of these people, even on trifling occasions. My landlord being in his shop, I paid him a visit; where I found six kettles, placed in a row on furnaces, having a separate opening under each of them, for receiving the fewel, which consisted of a few small sticks and straw. On his pulling a thong, he blew a pair of bellows, which made all his kettles boil in a very short time. They are indeed very thin, and made of cast iron, being extremely smooth both within and without. The scarcity of fewel, near such a populous city, prompts people to contrive the easiest methods of dressing their victuals, and keeping themselves warm during the winter, which is severe for two months.

About ten of the clock, we mounted, and proceeded towards the city, in the following order.

An officer, with his sword drawn.

Three soldiers.

One kettle-drummer.

Twenty four soldiers, three in a rank.

The steward.

Twelve footmen.

Two pages.

Three interpreters.

The ambassador, and a Mandarin of distinction.

Two secretaries.

Six gentlemen, two and two.

Servants and attendants.

The whole retinue was drest in their best apparel. The soldiers in uniform, carrying their muskets like horsemen standing centry; drawn swords being refused by our conductor, the officer only had that priviledge.

We travelled from the village, along a fine road, through a cloud of dust and multitudes of spectators; and, in two hours, entered the city at the great north gate; which opened into a spacious street, perfectly straight, as far as the eye-sight could reach. We found it all sprinkled with water, which was very refreshing after the dust we had passed through.

A guard of five hundred Chinese horsemen was appointed to clear the way; notwithstanding which, we found it very difficult to get through the crowd. One would have imagined all the people in Pekin were assembled to see us; though I was informed that only a small part of the inhabitants of the city were present. I observed also great crowds of women unveiled; but they kept in the windows, doors, and in corners of the street. The soldiers did not behave with roughness to the people, as in some other places of the east; but treated them with great mildness and humanity. Indeed the people, of themselves, made as much way as was possible for them, considering their numbers. After a march of two hours from the gate where we entered; we, at last, came to our lodgings, in that part of the city called the Tartar's town; which is near the center of Pekin, and not far from the Emperor's palace.

We lodged in what is called the Russia-house. It was allotted, by the present Emperor, for the accommodation of the caravans from Moscovy; and is surrounded with a high wall of brick, which incloses three courts. The first, from the street, is appointed for the guard of Chinese soldiers. The second is a spacious square, on the sides where-of are apartments for servants. The third is divided from the second by a high brick-wall, through which you enter by a great gate. Opposite to this gate is the great hall, which rises a few steps above the level of the court. The floor is neatly paved with white and black marble; and, on the same floor, to the right and left of the hall, are two small bed-chambers. This hall was occupied by the ambassador. In the same court are two large houses, divided into apartments, in which the retinue was lodged. All these structures are but of one story, with large windows of lettice-work, on which is pasted white paper. The cielings are very slight and airy; consisting only of strong laths, with reeds laid a-cross them, and done over on the in-side with paper. The roofs pro-ject considerably over the walls, and are covered with fine, light, glazed tiles; which, as far as I could learn, are of a quality to last ages. The bed-chambers only of the hall are neatly finished with lath and plaister.

The same evening, the master of the ceremonies came to compliment the ambassador. He, in the Emperor's name, enquired into the chief subject of his commission; and, having received a satisfactory answer, retired.

This gentleman, named Aloy,* was, by birth, a Mongall Tartar; and a great favourite of the Emperor. He was a person of great politeness; and a good friend to the Christians, especially the missionaries, who received fresh marks of his kindness every day. In his youth he con-versed much with the Jesuits, who taught him geography, and some other branches of science; which contributed not a little to raise his character among the Chinese, and recommend him to the notice and favour of the Emperor.

Thus we happily arrived at the famous and long wished for city of

* 'Aloy' was an official title (= Master of Ceremonies), not a personal name.

Pekin, the capital of this mighty empire, after a tedious journey of exactly sixteen months. It is, indeed, very long; yet may be performed in much less time. I am of opinion that travellers might go from St Petersburg to Pekin, and return, in the space of six months; which, were it necessary, I think I could easily demonstrate.*

After the departure of the master of the ceremonies, the aleggada, or prime minister, sent an officer to salute the ambassador, and excuse himself for not paying him a visit immediately, as it was then late in the night; but promised to see him next day. At the same time he sent great variety of fruits and provisions, as a mark of respect, notwithstanding we were abundantly supplied with these things by those appointed for that purpose.

At ten of the clock at night, the officer on guard, in the outer-court, locked our gate, and sealed it with the Emperor's seal; that no person might go out, or come in, during the night. The ambassador, not approving of this proceeding, as soon as the gate was opened in the morning, sent his secretary, and an interpreter, to the prime minister, to complain of his being confined. The aleggada said he was altogether ignorant of what had happened; but expressly forbid any such behaviour for the future. In Persia, indeed, and some other nations of the east, it is the custom to restrain foreign ministers from conversing with the inhabitants, till they have had an audience of the prince.

---

* The Jesuit Father Avril, who made two unsuccessful attempts to open up for his Order an overland route through Siberia to China, would have accepted this conclusion. He noted in 1692 that the Russian merchants 'font presentement ce voyage si surement & en si peu de tems, qu'il ne leur faut ordinairement que quatre mois pour aller à Pekin & pour revenir à Moskou . . .'. I think Father Avril must mean four months each way. His reasoning – based on careful interrogations, not on personal experience – may be studied in his *Voyage en divers états d'Europe et d'Asie, Entrepris pour découvrir un nouveau chemin à la Chine*, Paris, 1692.

CHAPTER IX

Occurrences at PEKIN, *audience of the ambassador, &c.*

The 19th, the prime minister, accompanied with the master of the ceremonies and five Jesuits, came to compliment the ambassador. As soon as they entered the gate, two of their attendants walked before them, at some distance, making a humming noise; the usual sign that some person of distinction is coming. Aloy desired the ambassador would give him a copy of his credentials; which was not easily complied with, till these ministers absolutely insisted on it; alledging that the Emperor never received any letters from his best friends, among whom he reckoned his Czarish Majesty the chief, without knowing the contents. The Latin copy was at last produced, the original being in the Russian language; and the master of the ceremonies and the missionaries having translated it into Chinese, took their leave. But the aleggada remained for the space of three hours, talking on different subjects. This minister, it seems, was a great sportsman. He asked to see the ambassador's dogs, which were a few grey-hounds, and some French buck-hounds. He was desired to receive, in a present, any of them which pleased him best; but he would accept only of a couple of grey-hounds.

In the mean time, the Emperor sent an officer to enquire after the ambassador's health; who brought along with him a table, carried by four men, and covered with yellow silk, on which was placed variety of fruits and confections; and, in the middle, a large piece of excellent mutton. The officer acquainted the ambassador that these provisions were brought from the Emperor's own table; and therefore hoped he would eat of them. This circumstance was accounted a singular mark of the Emperor's favour.

The day following, the ambassador had a visit from the president of the council for western affairs, called Asschinoma, accompanied by four missionaries, two of which were messieurs Paranim and Fridelii.* The conversation turned chiefly on the ceremonial of the ambassador's introduction to the Emperor, which was a matter not easily settled. The principal points, insisted on by the ambassador,

---

* Father D. Parrenin was also to play a key role in the next Russian Embassy to Peking after Izmailov's. Both he and Father E. X. Fridelli had been prominent among the Jesuit map-makers whose astonishing labours in this field had done so much to win for their order the Emperor's favours. See Baddeley, *Russia, Mongolia, China*, p. clxxxvi *et. seq.*

畅春园

24. CH'ANG-CH'UN YÜAN

The pleasure garden of the Emperor K'ang Hsi, where the Russian Ambassador Ismailov was gi
his first ceremonial reception. (A contemporary drawing from the *Wan-shou Gheng-tien Ch'u-chi*, rep
duced from Fu Lo-shu, *A Documentary Chronicle*)

were, that he might deliver his credentials into the Emperor's own hands, and be excused from bowing thrice three times on entering his Majesty's presence; to which custom all must submit who appear before the Emperor. The president, on the contrary, asserted, that the constant practice in China, for many ages past, was directly opposite to these demands; that their Emperors never received letters of credence with their own hands; that the custom was for the ambassador to lay them on a table, at some distance from the throne, or the place where the Emperor may happen to sit; after which they were delivered to the Emperor by the officer appointed for that purpose.

At the same time, the president invited the ambassador to an entertainment, to be given at a palace in the city, where, he said, the Emperor would be present, and speak with him. His excellency replied, he would accept of the invitation, provided he might, on that occasion, deliver the Czar his master's letter. He was told this was neither a proper place nor time for that purpose; but that the Emperor intended to give him a publick audience very soon, and receive his credentials in form.

The ambassador was apprehensive, that, the Emperor having already seen a copy of his credentials, should he also see himself at the entertainment, his publick audience might thereby be retarded; and therefore declined the invitation. It appeared, however, afterwards, that this suspicion was without foundation; and that the Emperor intended nothing more than to do honour to the ambassador.

The 21st, the aleggada paid a second visit. His servants brought tea ready made, some jars of arrack, with fruits and confections. From this day little material happened, except daily messages from court relating to the ceremonial, till the 27th; when this affair was, at last, adjusted on the following terms. 'That the ambassador should comply with the established customs of the court of China; and, when the Emperor sent a minister to Russia, he should have instructions to conform himself, in every respect, to the ceremonies in use at that court.' This affair gave the ministry at Pekin much trouble; and, I must confess, the missionaries took great pains to soften matters on both sides.

On the 28th, the day appointed for the ambassador's publick audience of the Emperor, horses were brought to our lodgings for the ambassador and his retinue; the Emperor being then at a country house, called Tzan-Shu-Yang,* about six miles westward from

---

* i.e. the *Ch'ang-ch'un Yüan*, the garden and palace which K'ang Hsi built (or restored) to the west of Peking in 1687, and where it was his practice when possible to spend several months every year. The Jesuit missionaries were granted a residence near by, and K'ang

Pekin. We mounted at eight in the morning, and about ten arrived at court; where we alighted, at the gate, which was guarded by a strong party of soldiers. The commanding officers conducted us into a large room, where we drank tea, and staid about half an hour till the Emperor was ready to receive us. We then entered a spacious court, enclosed with high brick-walls, and regularly planted with several rows of forest-trees, about eight inches diameter, which I took to be limes. The walks are spread with small gravel; and the great walk is terminated by the hall of audience, behind which are the Emperor's private apartments. On each side of the great walk are fine flower-pots and canals. As we advanced, we found all the ministers of state, and officers belonging to the court, seated upon fur cushions, cross legged, before the hall, in the open air; among these, places were appointed for the ambassador and his retinue; and in this situation we remained, in a cold frosty morning, till the Emperor came into the hall. During this interval, there were only two or three servants in the hall, and not the least noise was heard from any quarter. The entry to the hall is by seven marble steps, the whole length of the building. The floor is finely paved with a neat checker-work of white and black marble. The edifice is quite open to the south; and the roof supported by a row of handsome wooden pillars, octangular, and finely polished; before which is hung a large canvass, as a shelter from the heat of the sun, or inclemencies of the weather.

After we had waited about a quarter of an hour, the Emperor entered the hall at a back-door, and seated himself upon the throne; upon which all the company stood. The master of the ceremonies now desired the ambassador, who was at some distance from the rest, to walk into the hall; and conducted him by one hand, while he held his credentials in the other. Having ascended the steps, the letter was laid on a table placed for that purpose, as had been previously agreed; but the Emperor beckoned to the ambassador, and directed him to approach; which he no sooner perceived, than he took up the credentials, and, attended by Aloy, walked up to the throne, and, kneeling, laid them before the Emperor; who touched them with his hand, and inquired after his Czarish Majesty's health. He then told the ambassador, that the love and friendship he entertained for his majesty were

---

Hsi is said to have studied mathematics with them there. On the relationship between the *Ch'ang-ch'un Yüan* and later Imperial retreats to the west of Peking (including the present-day 'Summer Palace') see C. B. Malone, *History of the Peking Summer Palaces under the Ch'ing Dynasty*.

K

such, that he had even dispensed with an established custom of the empire in receiving his letter.*

During this part of the ceremony, which was not long, the retinue continued standing without the hall; and we imagined, the letter being delivered, all was over. But the master of the ceremonies brought back the ambassador; and then ordered all the company to kneel, and make obeisance nine times to the Emperor. At every third time we stood up, and kneeled again. Great pains were taken to avoid this piece of homage, but without success. The master of the ceremonies stood by, and delivered his orders in the Tartar language, by pronouncing the words *morgu* and *boss*; the first meaning to bow, and the other to stand; two words which I cannot soon forget.

This piece of formality being ended, the master of the ceremonies conducted the ambassador, and the six gentlemen of the retinue, with one interpreter, into the hall. Our clerks, inferior officers, and servants, remained still without; together with many courtiers and officers of distinction. We were seated on our own cushions, in a row upon the floor, to the right of the throne, about six yards distance. And immediately behind us sat three missionaries, dressed in Chinese habits, who constantly attend the court. On this occasion, they served, by turns, as interpreters.

Soon after we were admitted, the Emperor called the ambassador to him, took him by the hand, and talked very familiarly on various subjects. Among other things, he told him, that, he was informed his Czarish Majesty exposed his person to many dangers, particularly by water; at which he was much surprised; but desired he would take the advice of an old man; and not hazard his life, by committing himself to the rage of the merciless waves and winds, where no valour could avail. We were near enough to hear this piece of friendly and wholesome advice.

This conversation being finished, the Emperor gave the ambassador, with his own hand, a gold cup full of warm tarassun; a sweet fermented

* According to the Jesuit de Mailla, the text of Izmailov's letter (written 'en langue Russe, en Latin & en Mongou') was as follows. '*A l'Empereur des vastes contrées de l'Asie, au souverain monarque de Bogdo, a la Suprème Majesté de Kitai; amitié et salut.* Dans le dessein où je suis d'entretenir & d'augmenter l'amitié & les liaisons étroites qui ont été etablies depuis long temps entre Votre Majesté, mes prédécesseurs & moi, j'ai jugé à propos d'envoyer à votre Cour, en qualité d'ambassadeur extraordinaire, Léon Ismailof, capitaine de mes gardes. Je vous prie de le recevoir d'une manière conforme au caractère dont il est revêtu; d'avoir égard & d'ajouter foi à ce qu'il vous dira par rapport aux affaires qu'il a à traiter comme si je vous parlois moi-même, & de lui permettre de demeurer à votre cour de Pe-king jusqu'à ce que je le rappelle. De Votre Majesté, le bon ami, *Pierre*' (*Histoire Générale de la Chine*, XI, p. 335).

liquor, made of various sorts of grain, as pure and strong as Canary wine, of a disagreeable smell, though not unpleasant to the taste. This cup was brought about to the gentlemen; and all of us drank the Emperor's health; who observed, that this liquor would warm us that cold morning. His Majesty also found many faults with our dress, as improper for a cold climate; and, I must confess, I thought him in the right.

On the left side of the throne sat five Princes, sons to the Emperor; together with all the ministers and grandees of the court. The tarassun, however, was handed about to none but ourselves, and the Jesuits behind us. Eight or ten of the Emperor's grandsons now entered the hall. They were very handsome, and plainly dressed; having nothing to distinguish them, but the dragon with five claws, woven into their outer garments, and a yellow tunic of sattin, bearing the same device, with little caps on their heads faced with sable. After them came the musicians carrying their instruments. By this time the hall was pretty full; and, what is surprising, there was not the least noise, hurry, or confusion. Every one perfectly knows his own business; and the thick paper soles of the Chinese boots prevent any noise from their walking on the floor. By these means every thing goes on with great regularity; but at the same time with wonderful quickness. In short, the characteristic of the court of Pekin is order and decency, rather than grandeur and magnificence.

The Emperor sat cross-legged on his throne. He was dressed in a short loose coat of sable, having the fur outward, lined with lamb-skin; under which he wore a long tunic of yellow silk, interwoven with figures of golden dragons with five claws; which device no person is allowed to bear except the imperial family. On his head was a little round cap, faced with black fox-skin; on the top of which I observed a large beautiful pearl in the shape of a pear, which, together with a tassel of red-silk tied below the pearl, was all the ornament I saw about this mighty monarch. The throne also was very simple, being made of wood; but of neat workmanship. It is raised five easy steps from the floor, is open towards the company; but has a large japanned screen on each side to defend it from the wind.

The master of the ceremonies, and a few officers of the household, were dressed in robes of state, of gold and silver stuffs, with monstrous dragons on their backs and breasts. Most of the ministers of state were dressed very plain, having nothing like ornaments about them; a few only had large rubies, sapphires, and emeralds. These precious stones are cut into the shape of pears, through which a hole is drilled, to fix them on the top of their bonnets. These holes diminish the value of the stones, one half at least, at an European market. I once saw, however, one of these rubies, with a hole drilled through it, which was bought at Pekin for a trifle, valued at ten thousand pounds Sterling in Europe.* But such bargains are rarely to be met with; this being a stone of the first class, for bigness and purity. As for diamonds, the Chinese, it seems, do not much esteem them; for few diamonds are found in China, and these very rudely cut and shaped; and so, indeed, are all their coloured stones.

It was now about noon; at which time our entertainment began to be served up; (of which I shall also give some account.) There were first brought neat little tables, covered with variety of fruits and confections, and placed before all the company. It seems to be the fashion in this country to bring the desert first; at least that was the case at all the entertainments where I was present. In this, as in many other things, the behaviour of the Chinese is quite contrary to that of the Europeans. Soon after the fruits, the victuals were served in the same manner, and placed on small tables before the guests. They consisted of fowls, mutton, and pork, all very good of their kinds; and the whole was either boiled, or stewed with pickles; but nothing roasted. The Emperor sent several dishes from his own table to the ambassador, particularly some boiled pheasants; which were very agreeable.

The musick played all the time of dinner. The chief instruments were flutes, harps, and lutes, all tuned to the Chinese taste. There was also some vocal musick; an old Tartar, in particular, sung a warlike song, to which he beat time, by striking, with two ivory rods, upon a chime of little bells that hung before him. A young Tartar sung a call to war, dancing at the same time, and keeping time by drawing the head of an arrow a-cross his shield. Then entered two little girls, who danced and sung while the instruments played. After them came tumblers, who performed various feats of activity, in the court before the hall. These were succeeded by wrestlers, fencers, and other performers of the same species. The Emperor sent frequently to the ambassador, to ask how he liked the musick, dancing, and other entertainments. He also inquired about several princes and states of Europe, with whose power, by sea and land, he was not unacquainted.

* Baddeley, *Russia, Mongolia, China*, p. 431, identifies this ruby as one which Istopnikov brought back from Peking from the caravan of 1706 which he led, and which became one of the greatest gems of the Russian Crown. But if Istopnikov really got it 'for a trifle' there was something odd about the transaction. The Chinese were not ignorant of the value of rubies.

But, above all, he wondered how the kingdom of Sweden could hold out so long against so great a power as that of Russia. After this conversation, the Emperor informed the ambassador that he would soon send for him again; but, as the night was cold, he would detain him no longer at present; and immediately stept from his throne, and returned to his private apartments by the same passage he left them. We also mounted, and repaired to our lodgings in the city, so well satisfied with the gracious and friendly reception of the Emperor, that all our former hardships were almost forgot.

The 29th, the Mandarin Tulishin came to our lodgings, with two clerks, and took a list of the presents, sent by the Czar to the Emperor. These consisted of various rich furs, clocks, repeating watches set in diamonds, mirrors; and the battle of Poltava, nicely turned in ivory, done by his Czarish Majesty's own hands, and set in a curious frame. The ambassador, at the same time, delivered to the Mandarin, as a present from himself to the Emperor, several toys of value, a fine managed horse, some grey-hounds, and large buckhounds.

Every thing was entered in a book, very exactly, even the names and qualities of each particular dog. There was also tied about the neck of each dog, a yellow silk-cord, drawn through a hole in a little bit of wood, which hung from the dogs neck, as a mark of its belonging to the court. The Chinese, in general, are very fond of little harlequin dogs that play monkey tricks. A servant of ours had one of that kind, which he sold for an hundred ounces of silver.

The same day, all the fruits and confections of the entertainment given at the audience, which remained, were sent to the ambassador's lodgings. They were carried in great state through the streets, covered with yellow silk; and an officer of the court walked before the procession.

Next day, the Emperor sent to our lodgings several large dishes of massive gold, containing a kind of delicate fish, called mu, already dressed; but in such a manner that I did not know to what to compare it. Also some bowls filled with excellent vermicelli; and a sort of pastrypuffs, baked over the steam of boiling water, exceeding, in whiteness, any thing of that kind I ever saw. All these things were sent from his Majesty's own table; an honour which he grants but seldom. It seems he was resolved we should have provisions in abundance; for, besides all these, we received our daily allowance, in which we were by no means stinted.

After dinner, the master of the ceremonies, accompanied with the captain of the eunuchs, and three Jesuits, came to visit the ambassador.

This eunuch was a great favourite of the Emperor, on account of the knowledge he had acquired in mathematics and mechanics. He made the ambassador a present of a small enamelled gold-watch, and a wind-gun, both of his own making. The Emperor himself is a great lover of the arts, so far, that, whoever distinguishes himself, in any useful branch of them, is sure to meet with proper encouragement. The eunuch also made a present, to the ambassador, of a steel to strike fire; and then desired to see the presents; which was granted. At taking leave, Aloy told the ambassador, that the Emperor intended to give him a Chinese dress, which was more convenient and warmer than the European.

December the first, Merin-Sanguin, a general officer, and brother to the first minister of state, came to visit the ambassador. Notwithstanding the high rank of this military gentleman, he had no sword about him; for, at Pekin, no person, not even officers and soldiers, except when on duty, wears a sword, or any other weapon, in the city.

The day following, the ambassador had a second audience of the Emperor, at the same palace. On this occasion the Czar's presents were carried to court, by a number of people sent for that purpose. The Emperor viewed them all at a distance; after which they were delivered to an officer appointed by his majesty to receive them. This audience was held in a private hall within the inner-court, where only the officers of the houshold, and the gentlemen of the retinue, were present. We were entertained in the same manner as before. The Emperor conversed very familiarly with the ambassador, on various subjects; and talked of peace and war, in particular, in the style of a philosopher. In the evening, we returned to the city, in a cold north wind, which blew the dust about in clouds. Scarcely had we arrived, when the fruits and confections, according to custom, were sent to our lodgings.

This evening, one of the Emperor's grandsons came to visit the ambassador. He was a genteel youth, about fourteen years of age, and had not above half a dozen of attendants.

Next day, the weather continued cold and frosty. The sky was clear, and a strong wind at north-west, blowing the dust about. I observed that the north-west winds are the coldest in this place; as they come over the vast tracts of ice and snow in Siberia.

The 4th, there was a fall of snow, to the deepness of seven or eight inches; which was immediately thrown into heaps, and the streets clean swept. This day the missionaries sent a present to the ambassador, consisting of several sorts of venison, and wild-fowl, and a greater variety of fine fruits, and confections, than I ever saw in any country; together

25. A CHINESE SCHOLAR AT HOME
(From Du Halde, *Description de la Chine*, 1735)

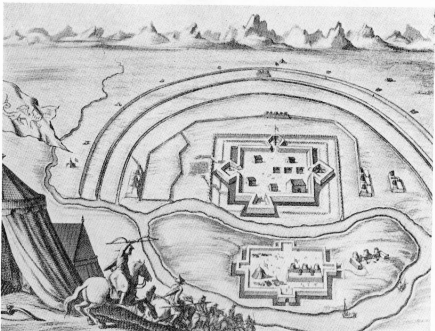

26. THE FRUIT LI-CHI (see page 139)
   (From Du Halde, *Description de la Chine*, Paris, 1735)

27. THE SIEGE OF ALBAZIN (see page 139)

with a couple of jars of wine made by themselves. Among the fruits there were some species which I had never before seen; particularly a sort of apple, about the size of a common orange, with a smooth skin of a yellowish colour, very soft and sweet, or rather luscious; also a fruit about the bigness of a walnut, but quite round, resembling in taste a prune, but far more delicious; it contains a smooth hard stone; and the whole is covered with a thin brownish shell, so brittle that it is easily broken between the finger and thumb. Some of these shells are rough, and others smooth. They serve to prevent the tender fruit from being devoured by birds, and from flying dust; and, what is something uncommon, the fruit does not adhere to the shell, but a small vacuity is left between them. It is not only pleasant to the taste, but is accounted very wholesome.

The 5th, the ambassador had a third audience of the Emperor, in the palace at Pekin. As some affairs relating to the two empires were to be discussed, the secretary only, M. de Lange, accompanied the ambassador. After he was introduced, the Emperor told him, he had given orders to the tribunal for western affairs to hear the subject of his commission; and then retired to his own apartments, leaving his ministers to transact the business; which was soon finished on this occasion; and the ambassador returned to his lodgings.

The 6th, being St Nicolas' day, a great festival in the Greek church, the ambassador went to the Russian chapel in Pekin to hear divine service. This house stands within the city, under the east wall; and was built, by the bounty of the present Emperor Kamhi, on the following occasion.

About the year 1688, there happened a difference betwixt the government of Siberia and the Chinese, about a small fort, called Albazin, which the Russians had built upon the banks of the river Amoor. The Chinese alledged the fort was erected on their territories; and, jealous of the approach of such powerful neighbours, made several fruitless representations to the governor of Siberia to have it demolished. The Emperor, at last, impatient of longer delay, sent an army of above one hundred thousand men, to do by force what could not be accomplished by negotiation. They invested the place on all sides, and raised batteries against it. After a vigorous defence, the garrison, consisting of about three or four hundred Cossacks, was obliged to surrender for want of provisions. No terms could be obtained; and all the Russians were made prisoners of war. In consequence of which they were carried to Pekin, where the Emperor generously assigned them houses apart from the rest of the inhabitants, permitted the free exercise of their religion, and gave them a daily allowance equal with his own soldiers. By this mild treatment they were enabled to build the little chapel, which they still possess. The descendents of these prisoners are pretty numerous, and useful to their countrymen the Russians as interpreters. I formerly mentioned that these disputes were ended on the following terms; the prisoners on both sides were to remain unexchanged, and the fort of Albazin to be destroyed; since which time the two empires have continued in good correspondence. The inhabitants of Siberia, indeed, regret much the loss of their fort; as it stood in a fine climate, gave them possession of a large extent of country northward from the Amoor; and, besides, opened a passage down that river to the Japanese ocean. It was, however, the occasion of establishing the Greek church in China; which still continues to flourish, though its members are not very numerous. As one priest dies, another from Siberia succeeds him; who minds chiefly his own small flock, and thinks very little of making converts. This circumstance prevents their being obnoxious to the Roman missionaries, who can have no suspicion of their interfering with the interests of their church. These missionaries are constantly employed in making proselytes, and their endeavours have been attended with some success.

The 7th, we dined at the aleggada's, where we were magnificently entertained. There was no other company but ourselves, and we staid the whole day. This was the most elegant and complete entertainment of any I saw in China.

About ten o'clock in the morning, chairs were sent for the ambassador and gentlemen of the retinue, and horses for the servants, though the prime minister's house was very near our lodgings. The chairs were carried through two courts, and set down at the entry into a hall, where the aleggada waited to receive the ambassador. After entering the hall, we were seated on neat cane chairs, with japanned frames, inlaid with mother of pearl. The apartment itself was very simple, open to the south, and the roof supported, on that side, by a row of well turned wooden pillars. It had no cieling; but the rafters appeared finely polished, and perfectly clean. The floor was paved with a checker-work of white and black marble; and in the middle of it stood a large brass chafing-dish, in shape of an urn, full of charcoal. At the entry were placed two large China-cisterns, filled with pure water, in which played some scores of small fishes, catching at crumbs of bread thrown into the water. These fishes are about the size of a minnow, but of a different shape, and beautifully varied with red, white, and yellow spots; and therefore called the gold and silver fish.* I never saw any of them out of this country; though, I imagine, they might easily be brought to Europe, as they are by no means of the tender kind. I had about twenty of them standing in a window at my lodgings; in a morning, after a frosty night, I found all the water frozen, most of the fishes stiff, and seemingly dead; but, on putting them into cold fresh water, they all recovered, except two or three.

After we had drunk a dish of tea, a collation of broths and victuals was placed on the tables, intermixed with variety of fruits and confections. Every person had a table a-part, and all were served in the same manner. This repast, it seems, was only breakfast, though it might well have passed for dinner.

After this entertainment the aleggada carried us first to see his dogs, of which he had great variety. I formerly observed that this gentleman was a great sportsman. He took greater pleasure in talking of hounds than politicks; though, at the same time, he had the character of a very able minister, and an honest man.

We were now conducted through all the different apartments of his house, excepting only those of the ladies, to which none have access but himself, and the eunuchs who attend them. We saw a noble collection of many curiosities, both natural and artificial; particularly a large quantity of old porcelain or China-ware, made in China and Japan; and, at present, to be found only in the cabinets of the curious. They consisted chiefly of a great number of jars of different sizes. He took much pleasure in telling when and where they were manufactured; and, as far as I can remember, many of them were above two thousand years old. He added, that, both in China and Japan, they had lost the art of making porcelain in that perfection they did in former times;† and the fault, in his opinion, lay in the preparation of the materials. These curiosities were piled up on shelves to the very roof of the house, and in such order and symmetry as had a pretty effect.

From the house we went into a little garden, enclosed with a high brick-wall. In the middle of it stood a small basin, full of water, surrounded with several old crooked trees and shrubs; among which I saw that which produces the famous tea. The climate about Pekin being too cold for this shrub, there are only a few bushes of it to be

---

* The Chinese had been artificially rearing gold-fish since at least the eleventh century, and large tubs with many strange varieties in them are still to be seen in the public parks of Peking today.

† This observation will fall strangely on the eyes of modern readers who share the widely held view that the K'ang Hsi era was the golden age of Chinese porcelain.

found in the gardens of the curious. I shall not at present enlarge on
this useful plant, which appeared like a currant-bush, as an opportunity
will occur of giving a fuller account of it before I leave this place. There
was a walk round the garden, which, together with that in the middle,
was covered with small gravel. At each end of the middle-walk was a
piece of artificial rock-work, with water running under it, through holes
so natural they looked as if made by the current of the stream. The
rocks were about seven feet high, and shaded with some old bended
trees. This garden, and many other things in China, display the taste
of the inhabitants for imitating nature.

From the garden we were called to dinner, where we found a plentiful and elegant entertainment, set out in the finest order, far exceeding
any thing of that kind we had seen before. We had no musick nor
dancing, and the whole was conducted with surprising decency and
regularity. The entertainment lasted about two hours, after which we
returned to our lodgings.

This day, our gates were opened to people of all characters, and
merchants and others allowed to go in and out at pleasure. Though all
communication was not prohibited before this time; it was, however,
difficult; and not to be obtained without permission of the proper
officer.

The 8th, we dined at the south convent, where the Italian missionaries generally reside. Here all the Jesuits in the place, to the number
of ten or twelve, were assembled. We met with a friendly reception,
and a most splendid entertainment.

This convent stands within the city, upon a piece of ground given
to the fathers by the Emperor. He gave also ten thousand ounces of
silver towards building and adorning the chapel; which is, indeed, very
neat; and handsomely decorated with pictures of saints, and scripture-
pieces, by the best hands. An account of this remarkable benefaction
of the Emperor Kamhi is cut out, in the Chinese language, in letters
of gold, and fixed above the great gate; which makes the place more
respected. When we arrived, one of the priests was officiating in the
chapel, where were assembled about one hundred Chinese converts. At
dinner we had a few bottles of wine, made in the convent; but I cannot
say it was good; though the grapes were fine, and of an agreeable taste.

After dinner, we were conducted to the Emperor's stables, where
the elephants are kept. The keeper asked the ambassador to walk into
his apartments, till they were equipped; then we went into the court,
and saw these huge animals richly caparisoned in gold and silver stuffs.
Each had a rider on his back, who held in their hands small battle-

axes, with a sharp pike at one end, to drive and guide them. We stood about an hour admiring those sagacious animals; some of them were very large, who, passing before us at equal distances, returned again behind the stables; and so on round and round, till there seemed to be no end of the procession. The plot, however, was at last discovered, by the features and dress of the riders; and the chief keeper told us there were only sixty of them. The climate about Pekin is too cold for them to breed; and all these were brought from warmer countries. The Emperor keeps them only for show, and makes no use of them, at least in these northern parts. Some of them were brought near to the place where we sat, and made obeisance to us, by kneeling and making a dreadful noise; others sucked up water from vessels, and spouted it through their trunks, among the mob, or wherever the rider directed. The sagacity of these animals is most surprising, and approaches so near to reason, that, in this respect, they surpass all the brute creation. After this show, we took leave of the Jesuits, who had accompanied us hither, and returned to our lodgings.

Next day, all the gentlemen dined at the palace of the Emperor's ninth son, in consequence of an invitation from his chief eunuch, who is a great friend to the Russia-house. As the invitation was not from the Prince, the ambassador would not accept of it. Our entertainment was very magnificent, and accompanied with musick, dancing, and a kind of comedy, which lasted most part of the day. The comedians were of both sexes; if the women's parts were not performed by boys dressed like actresses. As the play was in the Chinese language, I could understand nothing of it, except from the gesture and action of the performers. It seemed to be a parcel of detached dissimilar inter-ludes, without any principal end, or unity of design. I shall, therefore, only mention one scene, which appeared to me the most extraordinary. There entered, on the stage, seven warriors, all in armour, with different weapons in their hands, and terrible vizards on their faces. After they had taken a few turns about the stage, and surveyed each others armour, they, at last, fell a quarrelling; and, in the encounter, one of the heroes was slain. Then an angel descended from the clouds, in a flash of lightning, with a monstrous sword in his hand, and soon parted the combatants, by driving them all off the stage; which done, he ascended in the same manner he came down, in a cloud of fire and smoke. This scene was succeeded by several comical farces, which, to me, seemed very diverting, though in a language I did not understand. The last character that appeared on the stage, was a European gentle-man, completely dressed, having all his cloaths bedawbed with gold and silver lace. He pulled off his hat, and made a profound reverence to all that passed him. I shall leave it to any one to imagine, what an aukward figure a Chinese must make in this ridiculous habit. This scene was interrupted, and the performers dismissed, by the master of the feast, from a suspicion that his guests might take offence. The play being finished, we were entertained with jugglers, who exhibited a variety of legerdemain tricks with great dexterity.

The banquet was prolonged the whole day, excepting the time spent in these interludes. No sooner was one course carried off, than another was instantly placed upon the tables; and the whole concluded with deserts of fruits and sweetmeats. One would scarce have imagined, that luxury had made such progress among the sober and industrious Chinese. It must, indeed, be observed, that, there is almost no drinking at their entertainments, as they use no liquor, on these occasions, but tea, and, now and then, a dram of hot arrack. The Chinese handle the two ivory or wooden pins, which they use instead of forks, with such dexterity, that they can even take up needles with them. In place of napkins they sometimes employ a few square pieces of paper.

CHAPTER X

Continuation of occurrences at PEKIN, *&c.*

The day following, the ambassador had a fourth audience of the Emperor, at the palace in the city. This interview was also private, and the ambassador was attended only by his secretary. The Emperor repeated the assurances of his friendship for his Czarish Majesty, talked strongly on the vanity and uncertainty of all human affairs; adding, that he was now an old man, and, by the course of nature, could not live long, and desired to die in peace with God and all mankind. At taking leave, each of them was presented with a complete Chinese suit of cloaths, made of strong silk, interwoven with dragons' claws, and lined with sable.

The 12th, we dined at the French or western convent, where we again found all the missionaries. The chapel, and other edifices, are handsome; but not so grand as the Italian convent. Father Paranim is president of this convent; he is a man of parts and address, and in great favour with the Emperor. I was informed this entertainment was given at the expence of the court, and had some reason to believe it was so, as it far exceeded what might reasonably be expected from the Jesuits. The Emperor's band of musick played all the time of dinner; after which we had jugglers and tumblers of great activity. Among the many feats and tricks performed by these people, I shall only mention two or three, which seemed most uncommon. The roof of the room where we sat, was supported by wooden pillars. The juggler took a gimlet, with which he bored one of the pillars, and asked, whether we chose red or white wine? the question being answered, he pulled out the gimlet, and put a quill in the hole, through which run, as from a cask, the wine demanded. After the same manner, he extracted several sorts of liquors, all which I had the curiosity to taste, and found them good of their kinds.

Another of these expert youths took three long sharp-pointed knives, and, throwing them up by turns, kept one always in each hand, and the third in the air. This he continued to perform for a considerable time, catching constantly the falling knife by the handle, without ever allowing it to touch the floor. The knives were exceeding sharp, so that, had he missed laying hold of the handles, he must infallibly have lost some of his fingers.

The same person took a wooden ball, somewhat less than those commonly used in bowling greens, with a hole through the middle of it, and a rod, two feet long, about the size of a walking staff, pointed at the extremity, to fit the hole in the ball. He then tossed the ball above a yard high, and caught it again upon the point of the rod; not in the hole of the ball, but wherever it happened to meet the point; and, in this manner, he continued to throw up and catch the ball for a considerable time. He now placed the ball upon the point of the rod, taking no notice of the hole, and twirled it round like a top, so quickly, that the motion could not be observed. This seemed extremely dextrous; for, all the while, he played with the ball in appearance; and, when the motion began to slacken, gave it a fresh twirl with his hand, as if the rod and ball had been fastened to each other.

This person also placed a large earthen dish, above eighteen inches diameter, upon the point of the same rod, and twirled it round in the same manner as he did the ball; during this swift motion, he did not always keep the point in the centre of the vessel; on the contrary, he often held it within three inches of the brim. I shall only mention one instance more.

There were placed erect, upon the pavement of the room, two bambos, which are a kind of cane. The length of them was about twenty five feet; at the lower end I reckon them to be near five inches diameter, and, at the top, about the breadth of a crown piece. They were straight, light, and smooth; and each supported by two men. Two boys then climbed up the poles, without the least assistance; and, having reached the top, stood upright, sometimes on one foot and sometimes on the other, and then upon their heads. This being done, they laid one hand on the top of the pole, and stretched out their bodies almost at right angles to it. In this posture they continued for a considerable time, and even shifted hands. I observed that much depended on the men who held the poles; one of the two at each pole having it fixed to his girdle; and they kept a steady eye on the motions of the boys. There were about twenty or thirty of these performers, who all belong to the Emperor, and never display their art without his permission. I am fully persuaded, that, in tricks and feats of dexterity, few nations can equal, and none excel, the Chinese.

After these diversions, we were conducted to the Emperor's glass-house, which his Imperial Majesty often visits with pleasure. It was erected by himself, and is the first manufactory of the kind that ever was in China. The person employed to superintend and carry on this design was Kilian Stumpff,* a German father, lately deceased; a man in great favour with the Emperor, and well known, in China, for his ingenuity and literature. His Majesty is so fond of this glasswork, that he sent several of the most curious of its productions in a present to his Czarish Majesty. It is surprising, that the Chinese, who have been constantly employed, for so many ages, in the manufacture of China-ware, should never have stumbled upon that of glass. This shows evidently, that the degree of heat necessary in their ovens must not be very great, or their materials free from sand; for it is certain they had no knowledge of glass, of any kind, till this house was erected. I was informed, that, not long ago, some Europeans brought to Canton a parcel of prisms, or triangular glasses, which the Chinese took for natural productions of rock-chrystal; and bought them at the rate of one hundred ounces of silver a-piece. But, from the great quantity imported, they soon discovered their mistake.

On the evening of the 14th, an officer came from court, desiring the ambassador to wait on the Emperor at his palace of Tzangsuang and bring his musicians along with him. These consisted of performers on violins, trumpets, and kettle-drums.

Next day, we arrived at the palace, about ten of the clock; and had immediate admittance to the Emperor's private apartments, few being present but the officers of the houshold and Father Paranim. After a short conference the musick was ordered to play. There were in the room ten or twelve of the Emperor's grandsons, who seemed much entertained with the instruments. I asked an elderly gentleman, who stood by me, how he liked the musick; he said it was very good, but their own was better. No ladies were to be seen; though, I believe, several of them were behind a screen at the other end of the room.

The musick being over, the Emperor ordered one of the princes to conduct the ambassador into the gardens belonging to the palace; into which we entered, along a draw bridge, over a canal of pure water. They abounded with shaded walks, arbours, and fish-ponds, in the Chinese taste. The young princes entertained themselves by shooting with bows and arrows. Some of them displayed great dexterity, being accustomed from their infancy to this exercise, which is accounted both genteel and healthy; as the drawing of the bow extends and

---

* Father Bernard-Kilian Stumpf (1655-1720) was, like all the Jesuits, a man of many parts. In 1715, when he was in charge of the Board of Astronomy, he incurred the displeasure of native scholars by melting down several valuable old Chinese astronomical instruments to make a new quadrant from their bronze. See Hummel, *Eminent Chinese of the Ch'ing Period*, under the entry of Mei K'u-ch'eng.

28. THE FORBIDDEN CITY

A ceremonial banquet for Mongol chiefs in the Pao Ho Tien
(Reproduced from Arlington & Lewisohn, *In Search of Old Peking*)

除日保
和球外
殿藩
宴蒙

L

strengthens the muscles both of the breast and arms. One of the princes shewed us a bow and arrows, used by the Emperor when young; by which it appeared that he had been a person of extraordinary bodily strength. After we had surveyed the gardens in every quarter, we took leave of the princes, and returned to the city.

This day, arrived in Pekin Signior Mezzobarba, ambassador from his Holiness the Pope to the Emperor. This gentleman was a cardinal and patriarch of Alexandria. His retinue was composed of ecclesiasticks of different orders, and a few servants, who were all lodged in the Italian convent. They came from Europe to Macao in a Portuguese ship; from thence to Canton; and then, by land, to this place.

The design of this embassy was to enquire into the disputes and misunderstanding, that had lately arisen in this country, betwixt the Jesuits and Dominicans; relating to certain rites annually performed by the Chinese Christians, at the tombs of their deceased parents or other relations. This custom seems to be the same with that of the parentalia anciently in use among the Greeks and Romans. It is universal in China, from the emperor to the meanest peasant. It seems the Jesuits permitted their converts to visit the tombs of their relations; alledging, that, without such indulgence, no person would embrace Christianity; and, that time would wean them from such superstitious ceremonies. The Dominicans, on the other hand, affirmed that it was next to idolatry, and declared it unlawful to allow any such custom; strictly prohibiting all conformity in their converts. These differences, in all probability, will not soon be determined. The Emperor himself tried to make the parties compromise matters; but, finding his endeavours ineffectual, he left them to agree or dispute according to their pleasure. He inclined, indeed, to favour the opinion of the Jesuits, which he thought most reasonable. At any rate, it must be acknowledged an instance of uncommon condescension, for an heathen Emperor to interest himself so much in the peace of a Christian church.*

* There was more to the celebrated 'Rites Controversy' – of which this paragraph so far as it goes is an admirable summary – than just the question of whether ancestor worship and Christianity were compatible. The mainstay of the Jesuit campaign to Christianize China was, however, that they *were*. Pope Clement XI ruled otherwise in the Bull *Ex Illa Die* of March 1715 – a decision which so displeased K'ang Hsi that when he heard of it in 1717 he ordered the Board of Rites in Peking to proscribe the practice of the Christian religion throughout the Empire. Persecutions followed in the provinces, though not in Peking, where the Jesuits remained under Imperial protection, though no longer so highly regarded as before. The mission of Mezzobarba to which Bell refers was an attempt to reconcile the irreconcilable by offering to allow certain mitigations to converts while maintaining the Papal principle. The eight 'permissions' granted by Mezzobarba in fact led to further doctrinal controversy among Christians, and the dispensations were also in them-

The 16th, Mr de Lange and I paid a visit to the Fathers Fridelly and Keaggler, at the oriental or German convent. This place is large enough; but neither the chapel nor buildings are near so magnificent as those of the two other convents. It is called oriental, because situated in the eastern district of the city. Both these fathers, and several other ecclesiasticks of inferior rank in this convent, are Germans. One of the fathers was a clock-maker; and, by such means, they frequently insinuate themselves into acquaintance with people of distinction, who protect them in times of danger. For, in China, they have still a great number of enemies, who would gladly see both them and their religion extirpated; but the favour of the present Emperor hath hitherto prevented, or disappointed, the design of such persons.

The 17th, I sent to inform the captain of the Chinese guard, that I intended to take a turn through the city; who immediately gave orders for a soldier to attend me. When we passed through the gate, the clerk marked our names in his book, and dashed them out at our return. I went into several shops, where were sold different kinds of merchandise; particularly those of the goldsmiths, whose business it is to exchange gold for silver, or silver for gold. In these shops are found vast quantities of those valuable metals, cast into bars of different sizes, and piled up one upon another; which are sold only by weight, as there is no current coin in this country; except one small round piece of brass, with a square hole in the middle, through which may be run a string, for the convenience of carrying them to market. This coin, called joss by the Chinese, is about the value of one tenth of a penny sterling; and is extremely useful among the common people. With one of them, a man can buy a dish of hot tea, a pipe of tobacco, or a dram of brandy, in the streets; and a beggar may dine for three of them. There are, indeed, few beggars to be seen in the city; but, notwithstanding the labour and industry of the inhabitants, they are so numerous, that it is hardly possible to prevent many from being reduced to the utmost necessity. There are cooks shops, where dogs and cats, and such other creatures, are dressed for the entertainment of these people. These coins have Kamhi, the name of the Emperor, on one side; and the words Tum Pao, or the universal price, on the other.

When the Chinese have occasion to buy any thing, above the value

---

selves insufficient to restore the Jesuit position vis-à-vis the Chinese which had been fatally damaged once Clement XI's decision was known. Ancestor worship was, after all, one of the bases on which the whole of Chinese society — and Governmental administration — rested, and the Chinese could not allow that basis to be threatened. See Couling, *Encyclopaedia Sinica*, for a useful account of the Rites Controversy as a whole.

of sixpence, they cut off a piece of silver, and weigh it; which is done in a trice.

Although the want of current coin seems ill calculated for the dispatch of business, the Chinese find no inconvenience on that account. It is so far preferable to money, that it loses little by wearing in the circulation; which coin does, perhaps, more than is generally imagined.

In most of the shops I found both men, and women, unveiled. They were extremely complaisant, and gave me a dish of tea in every shop. These people expose their gold and silver, and other goods of value, with as much freedom and security, as the merchants do in London or Amsterdam.

The 19th, Lange and I went to the French convent, but not one of the ecclesiasticks were at home; having all gone to attend Signor Mezzobarba at an audience of the Emperor; except an old gentleman, Monsieur Bouvett, who had formerly written a small treatise, entitled, "Le portrait de l'Empereur de la Chine"; which he had printed in Europe.*

The 20th, cold and windy.

The 21st, frost and snow, which softened the air, and laid the dust.

Next day, the ambassador, with secretary Lange, went to the council appointed for western affairs, and had a conference on the subject of his embassy.

The winter here lasts only about two months; but is very sharp and piercing while the wind is northerly. If the wind, indeed, is southerly, the air is mild and pleasant, and the sky clear. I mentioned above, that the Chinese have a method of keeping themselves warm during the cold, which I shall now describe as distinctly as I can.

In building a house, they make two stove-holes, one in each side-wall, about three feet from the gable-end. The holes are a foot square; one serves for receiving the fewel, and the other to let out the smoke, when the stove is finished. There is a partition of brick, which runs from one side of the house to the other, about five or six feet from the gable, and only eighteen inches high; which I shall call the front of the stove-bench. Between this and the gable, are built several other thin partitions of brick, in a direction at right angles to the first, having a small opening at the extremity of each. For example, suppose the passage in the first partition to the right hand, and in the second to the left; and so on, alternately, to the last, which communicates with the

* Paris, 1696. Father Bouvet also published in Paris *L'Estat Present de la Chine,* a collection of drawings of Chinese costume. He was one of the six Jesuit mathematicians sent to China by Louis XIV in 1685.

hole, on the other side of the room, for letting out the smoke. These divisions being made, the whole is arched, or otherwise covered with brick; above which is laid a layer of clay, or plaister, to prevent the smoke from rising through the surface. It is plain, that below this bench there will be a winding channel for the smoke, from one side of the room to the other. A few handfuls of brush-wood, straw, or any kind of fewel, will warm the bench, as much as is necessary, to work or sleep without feeling cold. It is generally covered with mats, felts, or other thick stuffs, according to the ability of the owner.

The 22nd, Father Keaggler came to visit us. This gentleman had been long in China, and was well acquainted with the language, customs, and manners, of the country. In talking of the extent of Pekin, he said, that Nankin is at least three times as large. At this rate, Nankin must be one of the largest cities in the world. He added, that it was somewhat diminished, since the court had left that place to reside at Pekin. Nankin is a place of the most extensive commerce, and contains the greatest manufactories, of all sorts of silk and cotton stuffs, of any city in the country; besides those of China-ware. It is watered by a fine navigable river, on which are employed an incredible number of boats, in carrying merchandise and passengers.

The 23rd, cold northerly wind, and strong frost.

The 24th, Christmas-Eve; the ambassador heard divine service in the Russ church.

The 25th, the ambassador and the whole retinue went to church.

The Emperor sent Father Fridelly, accompanied by several Mandarins, with a present, to his Czarish Majesty, of six large boxes of tiles, made of China-ware, fit for such stoves as are used, in Russia, for warming rooms. They were very pretty, blue and white; and, with due care, may last for ages.

January 1st, 1721, the Emperor's general of the artillery, together with Father Fridelly, and a gentleman, called Stadlin, an old German, and a watchmaker, dined at the ambassador's. He was, by birth, a Tartar; and, by his conversation, it appeared he was by no means ignorant in his profession, particularly with respect to the various compositions of gunpowder used in artificial fire-works. I asked him, how long the Chinese had known the use of gun-powder? He replied, above two thousand years, in fire-works, according to their records; but that it's application to the purposes of war, was only a late introduction. As the veracity and candour of this gentleman were well known, there was no room to question the truth of what he advanced on this subject.

The conversation then turned on printing. He said, he could not then ascertain, precisely, the antiquity of this invention; but, was absolutely certain, it was much ancienter than that of gun-powder. It is to be observed, that the Chinese print with stamps, in the manner that cards are made in Europe. Indeed, the connection, between stamping and printing, is so close and obvious, that, it is surprising the ingenious Greeks and Romans, so famous for their medals, never discovered the art of printing.

On this occasion, Father Fridelly told me, that several of the missionaries, who had the good fortune to be in favour with the Emperor, had often solicited that prince to become Christian, and allow himself to be baptized; but he always excused himself, by saying, he worshipped the same God with the Christians; and that such a change of religion might occasion some disturbance in the empire, which by all means he would endeavour to prevent. However this be, it is certain, that, on Christmas day, he sent one of his chief eunuchs to the Italian convent, with orders, that prayers should be offered for him; which was accordingly done, and the eunuch remained in church all the time of divine service.

Next day, the ambassador had another private audience of the Emperor, at the palace of Tzan-Shu-Yang. The weather being very cold, the hall was warmed with several large chafing-dishes, filled with charcoal. We staid above two hours; during which time his Majesty talked very familiarly, on various subjects, particularly history; wherein he discovered himself well acquainted with that of the holy scriptures, as well as of his own country. He said, that the chronology of the Chinese was far more ancient than that of the holy scriptures; but observed, that it ended back in fabulous accounts, concerning which nothing certain could be determined.

As to Noah's flood, he affirmed, that, at or near the same time, there was a great deluge in China, which destroyed all the inhabitants of the plains; but that such as escaped to the mountains were saved.

He then discoursed of the invention of the loadstone, which, he said, was known in China above two thousand years ago; for, it appeared from their records, that, a certain ambassador, from some distant island, to the court of China, missing his course, in a storm, was cast on the Chinese coast, in the utmost distress. The then Emperor, whose name I have forgot, after entertaining him hospitably, sent him back to his own country. And, to prevent the like misfortunes, in his voyage homeward, gave him a compass to direct his course.

The Emperor also confirmed most of the particulars, mentioned above, concerning printing and gun-powder. It is from the holy scriptures, most part of which have been translated by the missionaries, that the learned men, in China, have acquired any knowledge of the western ancient history. And their own records, they say, contain accounts of transactions of much greater antiquity.

At taking leave, the Emperor told the ambassador that he liked his conversation. He desired to be excused for sending for him in such cold weather, and smiling said, he knew the Russians were not afraid of cold.

I cannot omit taking notice of the good nature and affability of this ancient monarch, on all occasions. Though he was near the seventieth year of his age, and sixtieth of his reign, he still retained a sound judgment, and senses intire; and, to me, seemed more sprightly than many of the Princes his sons.

The 3rd, Mr Secretary Lange and I dined at the French convent, where we found Signor Mezzobarba. I never had an opportunity of seeing that gentleman at our lodgings; as nothing passed between him and our ambassador, but messages of common civility and complement.

The 4th, I rode, from our lodgings, through the city, and went out at the north gate, at which we entered on our arrival at Pekin. I proceeded eastward to the end of the north wall, and then along the east wall to the south gate, at which I entered, and returned to our lodgings. This tour took me up about two hours and an half, at a pretty round trot; and, at the same rate, I reckon I could have rode quite round the city in less than five hours; whence a judgment may be formed of the circumference of the walls. The suburbs also are very extensive, especially to the east and south, and, being interspersed with many burying places, all inclosed with brick-walls, and planted with cypress and other ever-greens, contribute much to beautify the neighbourhood of this great city. The Chinese are extremely attentive to the fencing and ornamenting these groves, or burying places; a natural consequence of their uncommon respect for their parents and relations while living, and of their extraordinary veneration for them when dead. Annually, on certain days, they resort to these groves, carrying provisions along with them, and celebrate a kind of feast, in commemoration of their deceased relations.

I shall give an example of the filial duty of the Chinese, in a story I have often heard affirmed for true. A youth, finding his parents reduced to extreme poverty, and knowing of no means for their relief, went and sold himself as a slave; and, having received the price from his master, immediately brought it to his aged parents. When this was spent, the boy had no other resource than to run away from his master, and sell himself again to another; and this he practised for several times, with the same view, although he knew the severity of the law in such cases.

The 6th, while walking through the street, I observed an old beggar picking vermin from his tattered cloaths, and putting them into his mouth; a practice, which, it seems, is very common among this class of people. When a Chinese and Tartar are angry at one another, the Tartar, in reproach, calls the Chinese louse-eater; and the latter, in return, calls the other fish-skin coat; because the Mantzur Tartars, who live near the river Amoor, subsist by fishing, and, in summer, wear coats made of the skins of fishes. But this habit is used only in summer; for, in winter, they wear furs.

The 7th, the Emperor sent us a present of various sorts of fine fruits, particularly some excellent oranges. On this occasion, Father Fridelly told me, that the tree was still standing at Canton, from which the seed was taken that the missionaries first sent to Portugal, where it has prospered so wonderfully; and, from the place whence it was brought, bears the name of the China-orange. I doubt not, that, with due care, some others of the rare fruits and plants in this country, even tea itself, might be propagated in Europe, or in some of the American colonies.

I cannot tell whether the coffee-tree is to be found in China; but am certain that none of its seeds are prepared and drunk there, as among the Persians, Turks, and Europeans.

The 8th, the weather was much milder, the wind southerly, with a small mizzling rain, enough to lay the disagreeable dust.

Next day, secretary Lange and I rode through the streets, to the eastern convent, to visit our friend Fridelly. As we passed, we observed a juggler diverting a crowd. On our coming near he played several tricks with great dexterity. He took an handful of small pence, formerly mentioned, with holes in the middle of them, and laid them on a table. He then thrust them into his nostril, one by one, with his finger; and this he continued to perform, till the whole was exhausted. After this, he suspended an iron-chain, of round links, about four feet long. He then took a mouse out of a box, and made it dance upon the table, quite loose. Then the mouse, at his order, went in at one link of the chain, and out at another, till it ascended to the top; from whence it came down again, the contrary way, without missing so much as one single ring.

The 12th, the Emperor came from Tzan-Shu-Yang, to his palace in the city.

The 13th, the master of the ceremonies came to invite the ambassador to court on the 15th, the first day of the new moon; and, according to the Chinese computation, the first day of the new year. This is one of their highest festivals; and what added to the solemnity of the present, was its being the beginning of a new seculum, or space of sixty years, observed by the Chinese; besides, the Emperor had reigned all the last seculum, and was now going to enter on the second. On this occasion were to be assembled several Tartar princes; particularly, the Kutuchtu and the Tush-du-Chan, together with many persons of distinction from Korea, and all the dominions of China. This feast begins on the first day, and continues during the increase of the moon.

The 15th, we went early to court; and found most of the grandees assembled in the court-yard, sitting on their cushions, and a few of them in the great hall. We entered the court at the great gates, which are seldom opened, except on such extraordinary occasions. The Emperor soon came, and seated himself upon his throne, which was more magnificent than that at Tzan-Shu-Yang; but, like it, plain and unornamented. His Majesty was dressed in the same manner as at our first audience. We were placed, within the hall, on the right of the throne; and Signior Mezzobarba, with the missionaries, at no great distance from us. In the mean time, all the people of distinction, who came from distant places, made their nine bows, to the ground, without the hall. And, as there was not room in the hall to contain one half of the company, many of them remained in the court during the whole time of the audience. Our entertainment was almost the same as at our first audience; which, therefore, I shall not describe.

The Emperor was very chearful, and sent for several of his old acquaintance to speak with him. The Tush-du-Chan and some other Tartar princes were placed on the left of the throne, with the Emperor's sons and grandsons. In a word, this assembly exceeded in number and quality, any thing of the kind I ever saw. I was in hopes to have seen the Kutuchtu on this occasion; but was informed that the Emperor, who shows great respect to this venerable priest, detained him in his private apartments.

This palace occupies a large space of ground, encompassed with an high brick-wall. There are several streets for servants and officers of the houshold. Many of the houses are high, and covered with yellow varnished tiles, which appear like gold in the sun. Northward from the palace is a large canal, of an irregular figure, where the imperial family divert themselves by fishing. This canal is artificial; and the earth dug out of it has raised an high bank, from whence you have a full view of the city, and the country adjacent, to a considerable distance. This mount rises to a ridge, which is planted with trees; resembling the wild and irregular scenes of nature that frequently present themselves in this country. The canal and mount are of an equal length, which I compute to be about an English mile. This must have been a work of vast expence and labour; and, it must be confessed, contributes greatly to the beauty of the place.

The 16th was spent in receiving visits of compliment, from the ministers and officers of the court, on occasion of the new year.

Next day, the visits were returned by Mr secretary Lange and Glazunoff, in name of the ambassador.

The 18th, some of the retinue, accompanied with a Chinese friend, went to a great market, held in the suburbs, about a mile without the city to the southwest. Here we found a number of toys, and things of value, both new and second-hand, exposed to sale in the open street.

Near this place stood a magnificent temple, the doors of which being open, we walked into it; and saw, standing at the south end, a monstrous image, about twenty-five feet high, carved and gilt, having twelve arms and hands, a frightful visage, and great goggling eyes. By the touch it seemed to be made of a kind of plaister. This image is called Fo, which signifies God in the Chinese language. Whilst we walked about in the temple, many people entered, who kneeled and bowed several times to the image; after which they retired, without taking notice of us, or of any body else. In all the lesser temples, I had formerly seen, I found a great number of images of inferior deities, or reputed saints; but this was occupied by Fo only, without any rival.

From the temple we went to a publick tea-house, where we saw many people drinking tea and smoking tobacco; from thence to a tavern, where we dined; and, in the evening, returned to the city.

Next day, I was present at the representation of a kind of farce, in the publick street, not far from our lodgings. There were about twenty strollers assembled on this occasion, who entertained the crowd with many legerdemain tricks, and unnatural gestures. The stage was covered with silk-stuff of various colours.

During the festival there are many such stage-plays performed in all the publick streets. You also find often high crosses erected, on which are hoisted a number of pendents and streamers of party-coloured silks, that make a pretty appearance. At this season all the shops are shut; almost no business is done; and the people go about, dressed in their best cloaths, as on holidays in Europe.

The 20th, the ambassador and all the gentlemen of the retinue were invited to dine, at a publick house in the city, by a young Chinese gentleman. And all of us accepted the invitation, except the ambassador. Our friend was so polite as to send chairs for his guests, about ten of the clock; and, at eleven, we reached the house, which was the largest of that sort I ever saw; and could easily contain six or eight hundred people. The roof was supported by two rows of wooden pillars. This tavern consisted only of one apartment, great part of which was filled with long tables, having benches, on each side, for the accommodation of the company. During the time of dinner we were entertained with musick; and, after it, by a company of players, maintained by the house, who daily act plays on a stage erected at one side of the room. None but people of fashion come to this place.

When a person intends to treat his friends at one of these houses, he sends previous notice of his design, with a note of the company, and the sum to be laid out on each of them; agreeably to these orders, things are executed with the greatest punctuality. The expence on each of our company could not be less than three or four ounces of silver, as we staid the whole day, and had a splendid entertainment, consisting of many courses and deserts, prepared and served in the best fashion of the country. I cannot but observe, on this occasion also, the order and dexterity with which the servants performed their parts in such a numerous assembly. I shall not pretend to give any account of the play; only, that the company seemed highly pleased; and the performers consisted of both men and women, well dressed, and of decent behaviour.

At several tables the people were employed in gaming; some playing at cards, others at dice and draughts. I saw no money among them; though I was informed some of the Chinese play very high. In the evening, we took leave of our hospitable friend, and returned to our lodgings.

The day following, Father Paranim sent us a present of a large sturgeon, and some other fresh fish, brought from the river Amoor. These can only be carried, to such a distance, in the coldest season; when they are preserved fresh, by being kept frozen among the snow. This method is practised, with success, in northern countries; for, provided the fish is immediately exposed to the frost, after being caught, it may be carried, in snow, for many miles, almost as fresh as when taken out of the water.

The 22nd, I went along with our new Chinese friend, named Siasiey, to see a manufactory of China-ware,* standing on the bank of

---

* Bell's enquiries into how porcelain was made must be seen in the light of the fact that in the early eighteenth century the technique was being sought with the same avidity that earlier generations had devoted to the Philosopher's Stone. In fact, by the time of Bell's visit to Peking Meissen was already beginning to turn out true porcelain, but the secret was for long jealously guarded. See Hugh Honour, *Chinoiserie*, pp. 102 *et seq*.

the river Yu, about twelve English miles eastward of the city. After arriving at the place, we passed through several shades and houses, where I saw a number of people at work. The ovens, in particular, seemed very curious. But my view was so cursory and superficial, that I could form no judgment of the materials, or manner of making these cleanly and beautiful vessels, which still remain unrivalled by the similar productions of any other nation. I inquired into the truth of the opinion which the Europeans entertain, "that the clay must ly a century, to digest, before it is fit for use"; and was told, by a master workman, that a few months preparation was sufficient. So far as I could observe, they made no secret, at this place, of what they were employed about. I was, however, told, that, to the south, the Chinese are more cautious, and carefully conceal their art from strangers. One thing I firmly believe, that, although the Europeans understood the art of making porcelain, the Chinese would undersell them at every market in the world. This valuable manufacture is carried on in most of the towns in China; and, as it is sold but a little above the rate of common earthen-ware in Europe, the materials of which it is composed can neither be rare nor costly. This important branch of trade brings an immense treasure into the country, and affords employment to vast numbers of poor, who, otherwise, would be useless and burdensome to the publick. Besides china, they also make a kind of delf, or earthen-ware, for the use of the lower class of people.

Next day, I happened to meet two gentlemen from the peninsula of Korea. Their physiognomies were nearly the same with those of the Chinese; but their dress different. What surprised me most was, that they were as ignorant of the spoken Chinese language as I was, and delivered themselves by an interpreter. When they have any thing material to communicate they put it in writing, which is easily understood by the Chinese. They write in the same manner as the Chinese, from the top of the page, in straight lines, to the bottom, and with a pencil, like those commonly used by painters.

Korea is a fine country, subject to China, situated betwixt the long wall and the river Amoor; and runs out into a point, towards the island of Japan, and the Eastern ocean. The country is very plentiful, and abounds with corn and cattle.

CHAPTER XI

Occurrences at PEKIN *continued; the festival held at court on
the new year, &c.*

The 24th, the master of the ceremonies came to invite the ambassador
to the festival of the new year, which is always when the moon is at the
full, to be held, at the imperial palace of Tzang-Shu-Yang, on the 29th.

In the mean time, the cold continued very piercing; so that I saw
horses, with loaded carriages, cross the ditches, without the walls of
the city, upon the ice.

The 29th, chairs were sent from court to carry the ambassador, and
gentlemen of the retinue; we arrived there in the evening, and lodged
in a house near the palace. Near our lodgings was a pretty garden, with
a canal, on which was a small pleasure-boat. In the middle of the canal,
was raised an artificial mount, planted with some barren trees, in
imitation of nature. We ascended, by a winding path, to the top of the
mount, from whence we had a fine view of all the country around.

The 30th, being the first day of the festival, we went to court. We
were met at the gate by the master of the ceremonies, who conducted
us to the bottom of the stairs of the great hall, where we took our places,
in the open court yard, among a numerous assembly of grandees, whom
we found sitting cross-legged on their cushions. After waiting about a
quarter of an hour, his Majesty appeared, and seated himself upon the
throne; upon which all the company stood. The Chinese made their
bows, as is usual on such occasions; but we were permitted to make our
compliments in our own fashion. It seemed somewhat strange to a
Briton, to see some thousands of people upon their knees, and bowing their heads to the ground, in most humble posture, to a mortal like
themselves.

We were immediately brought into the hall; and the ambassador
was conducted to the throne, in order to congratulate his Imperial
Majesty on the anniversary of the new year. Our station, on this
occasion, as at the first audience, was to the right of the throne. All the
princes, the Emperor's sons and grandsons, together with the Tush-
du-chan, and some other persons of high distinction, were placed to the
left, opposite to us. As the customs of the Chinese are, in many
instances, quite contrary to those of the Europeans; so, I have been
informed, that, among them, the left hand is the place of greatest
honour. After we had drunk a dish of tea, the Emperor beckoned to

the ambassador to come to him again; and inquired into the customs and ceremonies, at the courts of Europe, on festivals of this nature; adding, at the same time, 'he had been informed, that, after drinking the king's health, on such occasions, the Europeans broke the glasses. He approved, he said, of the drinking-part; but did not comprehend the meaning of breaking the glasses'; and laughed heartily at the joke.

The great hall was, by this time, almost full of company; and a number of people of distinction still remained in the area, who could not find room in the hall.

The entertainment now began to be served up. The victuals were carried about in great order; and placed, before the company, on large tables. All the dishes were cold, except those set before his Majesty; who supplied us plentifully with hot provisions, from the throne.

Dinner being ended, the sports were begun by a company of wrestlers, composed of Chinese and Tartars. Many of them were almost naked, having no cloaths but tight canvass drawers. They performed their parts in the area before the hall. When any of them was severely bruised by his antagonist, or much hurt by a fall, which frequently happened, the Emperor sent him a cordial, and ordered him to be properly taken care of. Sometimes also, when he perceived the combatants too eager and warm, a sign was given to part them. These instances of humanity were very amiable in the old monarch, and rendered the sight of such shocking spectacles more tolerable; for many of these wrestlers received such blows and falls, as were sufficient to have knocked the breath out of their bodies.

To the wrestling succeeded many other games, and mock-fights; in which, the performers, armed, some with lances, others with battle-axes, quarter-staffs, flails, or cudgels, acted their parts with great dexterity.

Then appeared two troops of Tartars, clothed in coats of tiger-skins armed with bows and arrows, and mounted on hobby-horses. At first, they behaved as enemies; but, after some skirmishes with their arrows, the parties were reconciled, and began a dance to a dismal tune of vocal and instrumental musick. The dance was interrupted by a person in a frightful mask, of a tall stature, dressed and mounted like the Tartars, who, they said, represented the devil. After making several unsuccessful attacks, on the united body of the Tartars, this formidable hero was at length killed by an arrow, and carried off in triumph. During the dance, each Tartar had a small basket in one hand, and an arrow in the other, wherewith they scraped on the basket, keeping time to the musick. This scraping sounded a little harsh to an Italian ear; for I could observe Signor Mezzobarba, and his retinue, smiling at the performance.

While the Tartars performed in the court, one of the Emperors' sons, a Prince of about twenty years of age, danced alone in the hall, and attracted the eyes of the whole company. His motions were, at first, very slow, so that he seemed scarcely to move at all; but, afterwards, became more brisk and lively. The Emperor was chearful, and seemed well pleased with the different performers; but particularly with an old Tartar, who played on a chime of little bells, with two short ivory rods. The instruments of musick were very various, and all tuned to the Chinese taste. The Emperor told the ambassador, that he knew well their musick would not please an European ear; but that every nation liked their own best.

The dancing being over, there was hoisted up a large vessel, resembling a tub, between two posts erected in the area for that purpose. In the vessel were placed three boys, who performed many dexterous tricks, both in the vessel and on the posts, too tedious to mention. By this time the sun was set, and the company were soon after dismissed for the night.

Next day, the rejoicings were renewed. We did not, however, go to court before the evening; because the fire-works would not begin till the sun was set. On our arrival, we were conducted through a garden, westward from the palace, in the middle of which stood a large building, with covered galleries all around. Before the house was a canal, having over it a draw-bridge. We took our places on the gravel-walk, just under the gallery, where the Emperor sat with his wives and family. Hard by us was the Kutuchtu, in his tent, having one of his lamas standing at the door. This priest never once appeared out of his tent, during the whole show. All the grandees and officers of state were seated on their cushions, along the bank of the canal. The machinery, for the fire-works, was placed on the other side of the canal; and nobody was permitted to go thither, except the people who managed it.

About five of the clock a signal was given, for beginning to play off the fire-works, by a rocket let fly from the gallery where the Emperor sat; and, in the space of a few minutes, many thousand lanterns were lighted. These lanterns were made of paper of different colours, red, blue, green, and yellow; and hung on posts about six feet high, scattered over all the garden; which exhibited a very pleasant prospect to the eye.

Another signal was then given, for playing off the rockets. They sprung upwards to a prodigious height, and fell down in figures of stars, displaying a great variety of beautiful colours. The rockets were accompanied with what I shall call crackers, for want of a more proper name. Their explosion resembled the reports of many great guns, fired at certain intervals, and exhibited a view of many charming colours, and forms of fire. These, with a few fire-works of different kinds, inter-mixed, continued for the space of three hours.

Opposite to the gallery where the Emperor sat, was suspended a large round vessel, about twenty feet in diameter, between two posts about thirty feet high. A rocket sent from the gallery lighted a match, hanging from the vessel, which immediately caused the bottom of it to drop down with a loud noise. Then fell out a lettice, or grate-work, all on fire, and hung between the vessel and the ground, burning furiously, in various colours. This continued for ten minutes, and really exhibited a most curious sight. It seems, this lettice-work was composed of materials that immediately kindled, on being exposed to the air; for no person was seen near the machine.

The grate-work being extinguished, there appeared a lighted match, hanging from the middle of the vessel, and burning up to it. As soon as the fire reached the vessel, thirty fair paper-lanterns, of various colours, dropped from it; and hung, in a straight line, below one another, between it and the ground; which immediately catched fire of themselves, and formed a beautiful and well-proportioned column of parti-coloured light. After this, fell out about ten or twelve pillars of the same form, but of a lesser size; these also took fire as soon as they dropped. This scene continued till the number of one thousand lanterns fell from the vessel, which diminished, every time, till the last were very small. I must confess this presented a delightful object to the spectators.

I could not help being surprized at the ingenuity of the artist, in crowding such a number of lanterns into so small and simple a machine as this seemed to be; and, at the same time, with so much order, that all of them dropped and kindled of themselves, with equal regularity, as if he had let them fall from his hand; for not even one of them was extinguished by accident, or in the least entangled by another. This concluded the first day's entertainment.

The 31st, in the evening, we returned to court; where was opened a new scene of fire-works, which continued, with great variety, till ten o'clock at night.

The 1st of February, we went again to court; where the fire-works were resumed in many different, well-executed, designs. What pleased me most, was a small mount, raised in the middle of the garden, from which sprung a stream of white and blue fire, in imitation of water. The top of the mount contained a cavity, in shape of a large urn, from which the fire rose to a prodigious height.

Opposite to the gallery, where the Emperor sat, were erected three large frames, about thirty feet high each. On one was a monstrous figure of a dragon; on the second, a man on horseback; and the third represented an elephant, with a human figure on his back. All these were composed of a deep blue fire; and were interwoven with vines and grapes, hanging about on all sides, of white, red, and blue fire.

Besides these, there were exhibited, on this occasion, many other ingenious designs of fire-works; which far surpassed any thing of the kind, I ever saw, though I have been present at performances of this nature, exhibited, at St Petersburg, by the best artists in Europe. Besides the art displayed in the contrivance and figure, these works furnished, in particular, a wonderful variety of most beautiful colours, far exceeding my ability to describe. I must confess, they far out-did my expectations, and even common fame, which seldom lessens things of this nature.

The following day, the Emperor gave the ambassador a private audience, and inquired how he liked the diversions and fire-works. On this occasion, the Emperor repeated what has been already observed concerning the antiquity of illuminations composed of gun-powder; and added, that, although fire-works had been known in China for more than two thousand years, he himself had made many improvements upon them, and brought them to their present perfection.

The 3rd, we returned to the city, in a cold frosty day, and the wind at north-west. We found the rejoicings still going on at Pekin; for stages were erected, and plays represented, in all the principal streets through which we passed.

The affairs relating to the embassy being nearly finished, we began now to prepare for our journey to the westward; which was to take place as soon as the extremity of the cold was abated.

The 9th, three missionaries, Paranim, Demail, and Moran, came to pay their respects to the ambassador, and beg the favour of him, that Signior Nicolai, one of their society, might be permitted to accompany him in his journey to Europe; which was granted, provided it was agreeable to the Emperor. The reason of this request was supposed to be, that, Signior Mezzobarba having returned to Rome, without accomplishing the ends of his embassy; the Emperor, who favoured the cause of the Jesuits, had concerted with them, to send Nicolai to

M

the court of Rome, in order to represent the state of this affair, before Mezzobarba could arrive.

Next day, the Emperor sent three officers with presents to his Czarish Majesty; the chief of which were, tapistry for two rooms, neatly wrought on a rich silk-stuff; a set of small enamelled gold cups; some japanned cups, set with mother of pearl; three flower-pieces, curiously embroidered on taffety; two chests of rockets, prepared in the Chinese fashion; about twenty or thirty pieces of silk, in most of which was interwoven the dragon with five claws; a parcel of different sorts of curious fans for ladies; also, a box containing some rolls of white Chinese paper, the sheets of which were of a size much larger than common; besides several other toys, scarce worth mentioning. From these particulars it appears, that these two mighty monarchs were not very lavish in their presents to each other; preferring curiosities to things of real value.

The 11th, several officers came, from court, with presents to the ambassador, and every person of the retinue, corresponding to their different stations and characters; and, so minutely and exactly was this matter managed, that even the meanest of our servants was not neglected. The presents, consisting of a complete Chinese dress, some pieces of damasks, and other stuffs, were, indeed, of no great value. They were, however, carried along the streets, wrapped up in yellow silk, with the usual parade of things belonging to the court; a circumstance which is reckoned one of the greatest honours that can be conferred on a foreign minister.

Next day, the Emperor sent to ask the ambassador, whether he inclined to accompany him to a hunting-match, in a forest not far distant from Pekin ; to which his excellency readily agreed.

The 13th, I dined with one of my Chinese friends, called Fang-fung. In going thither, I met, in the street, two men riding upon asses, with their servants leading them by the bridle. I soon perceived they were Kawlees; which is the name given, by the Chinese and Tartars, to the people of Korea; whom I have mentioned above.

The 14th, the weather was very fine and warm.

The 15th, we went to a fair in the suburbs, which is held the first day of every new moon, where we found many things exposed to sale, not commonly found in shops.

The 16th, the weather being favourable, I took a ride round the walls of the city; which I performed, at an easy trot, in the space of four hours; whereby the compass of Pekin may be nearly computed. The suburbs, especially to the east and south, are very extensive; and, in many places of them, the buildings are equal to those within the walls.

The 17th, being now on the point of our departure, in order to make the most of the short time we had to stay, I rode about twelve miles eastward from Pekin, accompanied with a Chinese friend, to the banks of the river; which I found crowded with a number of barques, of different sizes, which are constantly employed in carrying provisions, and other stores, to the city, from distant parts of the country. I saw many vessels sailing down the stream, towards the south-east. And I was informed, there are nine thousand nine hundred and ninety-nine vessels constantly employed on this river; but why confined to such an odd number I could neither learn, nor comprehend. During a month, or six weeks, in winter, this river is frozen over; at which season, provisions are conveyed by land-carriage, or along the ice.

On this occasion also I revisited the China-manufactory, in order to try whether I could learn any thing of that curious art. But, though the people were very complaisant, and showed me every thing I desired them, I returned as ignorant as I went thither; and, I am persuaded, that, before a person can get any knowledge of the affair, he must be bred a potter, and have time to inspect its whole progress; of which these people seem to make no secret.

The fields, along the banks of the river, are well cultivated; producing fine wheat, and other sorts of grain. I saw also great plantations of tobacco, which they call tharr, and which yields very considerable profits; as it is universally used in smoking, by persons of all ranks, of both sexes, in China; and, besides, great quantities are sent to the Mongalls, who prefer the Chinese manner of preparing it before every other. They make it into a gross powder, like saw dust, which they keep in a small bag, and fill their little brass-pipes out of it, without touching the tobacco with their fingers. The smoke is very mild, and has quite a different smell from ours. It is reported the Chinese have had the use of tobacco for many ages.

I observed, that, in cold weather, the Chinese chewed a kind of nut, about the bigness of a nutmeg, which they called beetle; it is of an astringent quality. They say, it both keeps them warm and cleans their teeth.

Next day was spent in preparing for our journey.

On the 18th, all our gentlemen dined with my Chinese friend, named Siasiey, where we met with a friendly reception, and a sumptuous feast. After dinner, our hospitable landlord put about his cups very freely. At last, he took me by the hand, and desired I would let the ambassador return and remain with him; and he would give me my choice of which of his wives or daughters I liked best. I could not but return my friend hearty thanks for his obliging offer; which, however, I thought it not proper to accept.

Next day, I went to see the market where provisions were sold. It was a spacious oblong, spread with gravel, very neat and clean. The butchers had their shops in a shade, running quite round the place. I saw little beef, but a great deal of mutton. In the middle, was great store of poultry, wild-fowl, and venison; but, what surprised me not a little, was, to find about a dozen of dead badgers exposed to sale. The Chinese, it seems, are very fond of these animals; which are accounted unclean in other parts of the world. All the Chinese merchants have the art of exposing their goods to sale dressed up in the most advantageous manner; and, even in purchasing any trifling thing, whatever the case be that holds it, it is half the cost, and often exceeds it in value.

The 21st, being the day appointed for hunting with the Emperor, at one of the clock in the morning, horses were brought to our lodgings, for the ambassador and those who attended him. We immediately mounted, and, after riding about six miles, to the south-west of the city, at break of day, we reached the gates of the park called Chayza; where we were received by an officer, and conducted, through the forest, to a summer-house, about a mile from the gate, in which the Emperor had slept the preceding night. This was a small but neat building, having a double row of galleries, open to the forest, on all sides, and an avenue leading to it from the gate, planted with several rows of trees. At some distance from the house, we dismounted, and were met by the master of the ceremonies, who conducted us into a gallery. As soon as we entered, the good old Emperor, who had risen long before our arrival, sent one of his eunuchs to salute the ambassador, and ordered us tea and other victuals. On the south side of the house is a canal, filled with clear water, and several large fish-ponds, which make a great addition to the beauties of this charming place. At a convenient distance from the house, stood about a thousand tents, where the courtiers and grandees had lodged the night before. Breakfast being over, the Emperor, who was very fond of arms, sent to desire a sight of the ambassador's fowling-piece. He returned it, with several of his own to be shown us. They had all match-locks. The Chinese are possessed with a notion, that flints, in their climate, acquire a moisture which hinders their firing. But, as far as I could perceive, the air had little effect upon our flints.

A signal was then given that the Emperor was coming; upon which all the great men drew up in lines, from the bottom of the stairs to the road leading to the forest, all on foot, dressed in their hunting habits, the same with those used by the officers and cavalry of the army, when in the field, and armed with bows and arrows. We had a proper place assigned us, and made our bows to his Majesty, who returned a gracious smile, with signs to follow him. He was seated, cross-legged, in an open machine, carried by four men, with long poles rested on their shoulders. Before him lay a fowling-piece, a bow, and sheaf of arrows. This has been his hunting equipage for some years, since he left off riding; but, in his youth, he went usually, every summer, several days-journey without the long wall, and carried along with him all the Princes his sons, and many persons of distinction, to the number frequently of some thousands, in order to hunt in the woods and deserts; where he continued for the space of two or three months. Their provisions were restricted to bare necessaries, and often to what they caught in the woods of Tartary. This piece of policy he practised chiefly with a view to harden the officers of his army, and prevent their falling into idleness and effeminacy among the Chinese; and, at the same time, to set a good example of the austerities he recommended, by living on the same hard fare he prescribed to others.

As soon as the Emperor had passed, the company mounted and followed him, at some distance, till we came into the open forest, where all formed into a semicircle, in the centre of which was the Emperor, having on his left hand about eight or ten of his sons and grandsons, and the ambassador on his right, about fifty paces distant; close by him, were the master of the chace, with some grey-hounds, and the grand falconer with his hawks. I could not but admire the beauty of these fine birds. Many of them were as white as doves; having one or two black feathers in their wings or tails. They are brought from Siberia, or places to the north of the river Amoor.

Our wings being extended, there were many hares started, which the company endeavoured to drive towards the Emperor, who killed many of them with arrows as they passed; those he missed, he made a sign to some of the Princes to pursue, who also killed several of them with arrows; but no other person was permitted to draw a bow, or stir from the line. The same rules of hunting, I formerly observed, are practised by the Mongalls.

From the open field, we continued our route westward, to a place among thickets and tall reeds, where we sprung a number of pheasants, partridges, and quails. His Majesty then laid aside his bow and arrows, and carried a hawk on his hand; which he flew as occasion offered. The hawks generally raked in the pheasants while flying; but, if they took the reeds or bushes, they soon caught them.

After proceeding about two or three miles farther into the forest, we came to a tall wood, where we found several sorts of deer. The young men went in and beat the woods, whilst the rest of the company remained without. We saw much game pass us; but nobody drew a bow, till the Emperor had killed a stag, which he did very dexterously, with a broad-headed arrow; after which the Princes had leave to kill several bucks; among which was one of that species, that bears the musk, called *kaberda* in Siberia, of which I have formerly given a description. The Chinese musk is stronger, and therefore preferable to that from northern parts.

We had now been six hours on horse-back, and, I reckon, had travelled about fifteen English miles; but no end of the forest yet appeared. We turned short from this wood southwards, till, coming to some marshes, overgrown with tall reeds, we roused a great many wild boars; but, as it was not the season for killing them, they all escaped. The hunting these fierce animals is reckoned the most dangerous of all kinds of sport, except the chace of lions and tigers. Every one endeavoured to avoid them, and several of them run furiously through the thickest troops of horse. The Emperor was so cautious as to have a company of men, armed with lances, to guard his machine.

We continued the sport till about four o'clock, when we came to a high artificial mount, of a square figure, raised in the middle of a plain, on the top of which were pitched about ten or twelve tents, for the imperial family. This mount had several winding paths leading to the top, planted, on each side, with rows of trees, in imitation of nature. To the south was a large bason of water, with a boat upon it; from whence, I suppose, the earth has been taken that formed this mount. At some distance from the mount, tents were erected for the people of distinction, and officers of the court. About two hundred yards from it, we were lodged in some clean huts, covered with reeds. The Emperor, from his situation, had a view of all the tents, and a great way farther into the forest. The whole scene made a very pretty appearance.

As soon as we alighted, the master of the ceremonies was sent, by the Emperor, to ask the ambassador how he liked their manner of hunting. He made a suitable return, acknowledging, at the same time, the great honour done him on this occasion.

The Emperor then sent us great plenty of dressed provisions of all kinds; and the officer, who brought them, pointed out several dishes, which his Majesty sent from his own table, consisting of mutton, venison, pheasants, and other sorts of wild fowl.

After dinner, the Emperor sent two of his chief eunuchs to compliment the ambassador; and inform him, that he intended to entertain him with the baiting of three tigers, which had been kept some time, cooped up in a strong grate-work, for that purpose. The hill, where the Emperor's tent stood, was surrounded with several ranks of guards, armed with long spears. A guard, also, was placed before the ambassador's, and the rest of the tents, to secure the whole encampment from the fury of these fierce animals. The first was let out by a person mounted on a fleet horse, who opened the door of the coop by means of a rope tied to it. The tiger immediately left his cage, and seemed much pleased to find himself at liberty. The horseman rode off at full speed; while the tiger was rolling himself upon the grass. At last he rose, and growled, and walked about. The Emperor fired twice at him with bullets; but, the distance being considerable, missed him, though the pieces were well pointed. Upon which his Majesty sent to the ambassador, to try his piece upon him; which being charged with a single ball, he walked towards the animal, accompanied by ten men, armed with spears, in case of accidents; till, being at a convenient distance, he took his aim, and killed him on the spot.

The second was let out in the same manner. The horseman, retiring a little, left the creature rolling upon the grass, like the first. He then returned, and shot at him with a blunted arrow; which roused the animal to such a pitch, and made him pursue so closely, that the horseman narrowly escaped within the ranks, where the furious tiger, endeavouring to leap over the men's heads, was killed at the foot of the mount.

The third, as soon as he was set at liberty, run directly towards the Emperor's tent; and was, in like manner, killed with the spears. A man must be well mounted and armed, who hunts this kind of animals in the woods; where they must be much stronger and swifter than these we saw, which had been confined for many months, and whose limbs, by want of exercise, were become stiff and unwieldy; but, notwithstanding this disadvantage, the courage and nimbleness even of these animals was very surprising. I have seen four sorts of them, the tiger, panther, leopard, and lynx, which are all very fierce; but the first is the largest and strongest.

The Emperor, in his youth, was very fond of hunting these creatures in the woods of Tartary ; but, now, he confines himself within the limits of the forest, where there is game sufficient to gratify any sportsman.

The killing of the tigers finished the diversion of the day; after which we retired to our huts, where we were entertained with a plentiful supper, sent us by the Emperor. After supper, an officer was sent from his Majesty to the ambassador, who brought the tiger's skin he had shot; telling him, that, by the laws of hunting, he had a right to it.

Next morning, the sport was resumed, and varied little from that of the preceding day. About three o'clock, afternoon, we came to another summer-house, in the middle of the forest, where the Emperor lodged the following night; while we lay in a small neat temple in the neighbourhood; and were entertained, by his Majesty, in the same manner as before.

The 23rd, about eight of the clock in the morning, the master of the ceremonies waited on the ambassador, in order to conduct him into his Majesty's presence, to receive his audience of leave. The Emperor received him, in a most friendly manner, in his bed-chamber. He repeated his assurances of the great friendship he entertained for his Czarish Majesty; and expressed great respect for the personal merit of the ambassador. After which the ambassador took leave; and we returned to our lodgings in the city.

I shall only observe further, that this forest is really a most delightful place; is well stored with variety of game; and is of great extent, as will easily be conceived from the account I have given of our two days hunting. It is all inclosed with a high wall of brick. The value of this park, so near the capital, shows the magnificence of this powerful monarch.

The 24th, the ambassador was invited, by the president of the college of mathematicks, to see the observatory; which is situated immediately within the east wall, and commands an extensive prospect. The building is not magnificent; but is furnished with a fine armillary sphere, globes, telescopes, an orrery in good order, and other mathematical instruments of the best European workmanship. This college was erected by the present Emperor, who spares no cost to bring it to perfection; and the meanest of his subjects, who discover a genius for science, or any useful art, are sure to meet with due encouragement.

The Chinese are indebted to the present Emperor for what progress they have made in astronomy. He chiefly promoted this study by countenancing the Jesuits and other missionaries; for I have been informed, that, before their arrival in this country, the inhabitants could scarcely calculate an eclipse. The Chinese, it is indeed pretended, understood astronomy previous to that period; but the know-

29. BUDDHA (A), CONFUCIUS (B), LAO TSE (C)
(According to Kircher, *China Monumentis Illustrata*)

ledge of it was in a great measure lost, during the many fatal revolutions of the empire.

From the observatory we ascended, by a broad rising passage, to the top of the city-wall; where we saw about fifteen horsemen riding their rounds; which, we were told, they performed day and night, at stated times. The wall is built of brick, and is about twenty-five or thirty feet high; having embrasures, and square towers, at equal distances; and a wide deep ditch, which may be filled with water at pleasure. On the top of the wall there is a pleasant walk, broad enough for fifteen horsemen to ride a-breast. I suppose the whole is, perhaps, not composed of solid bricks, but the middle filled up with earth and rubbish.

The 25th, we went to all the three convents, and took leave of our friends the missionaries.

The 26th, the ambassador went to the tribunal for foreign affairs, and received a letter from the Emperor to his Czarish Majesty. On this occasion the president acquainted his excellency, that he must consider this letter as a singular mark of favour to his master, as their Emperors were not in use to write letters of compliment to any prince; or, indeed, to write letters of any kind, except those which contained their orders to their subjects; and, that the Emperor dispensed with so material a custom, only, to testify his respect for his Czarish Majesty.

The original of this letter was in the Chinese language, and a copy of it in the Mongalian. It was folded up in a long roll, according to the custom in China, and wrapped in a piece of yellow silk, which was tied to a man's arm, and carried, in procession, before the ambassador. All persons on horseback, whom we met, dismounted, and stood till we had passed them. Such veneration do these people pay to every thing belonging to the Emperor.

The same day, the ambassador had a visit from a young gentleman, a descendent of the famous Chinese philosopher Confucius; whose memory and works are greatly respected in China. From what I could learn of this eminent philosopher, he appears to have been a person of extraordinary parts, extensive knowledge, and examplary virtue. On account of such rare qualities, his family is still honoured and esteemed even by the Emperor himself.

30. THE GREAT WALL OF CHINA
   (*Photo*: John Massey Stewart, 1964)

31. THE GREAT WALL OF CHINA
(*Photo*: Fitzroy Maclean, 1964)

CHAPTER XII

Some account of the present Emperor of CHINA, *the* CHINESE *wall, &c.*

Before we leave China, I shall make a few general remarks, on the people and country, drawn from the best information I could procure; and shall begin with the long wall.

The long, or endless wall, as it is commonly called, encompasses all the north and west parts of China. It was built, about six hundred years ago, by one of the Emperors, to prevent the frequent incursions of the Mongalls, and other western Tartars, who made a practice of assembling numerous troops of horse, and invading the country in different places. The Chinese frontiers were too extensive to be guarded against such bold and numerous enemies; who, after plundering and destroying a wealthy country, returned to their own, loaded with spoils.

The Chinese finding all precautions ineffectual to put a stop to the inroads of such barbarians, at last resolved to build this famous wall. It begins in the province of Leotong, at the bottom of the bay of Nankin; and proceeds a-cross rivers, and over the tops of the highest mountains, without interruption, keeping nearly along the circular ridge of barren rocks that surrounded the country to the north and west; and, after running southwards about twelve hundred English miles ends in impassable mountains and sandy deserts.

The foundation consists of large blocks of square stones laid in mortar; but the rest of the wall is built of brick. The whole is so strong, and well built, as to need almost no repair; and, in such a dry climate, may remain in this condition for many ages. Its' height and breadth are not equal in every place; nor, indeed, is it necessary they should. When carried over steep rocks, where no horse can pass, it is about fifteen or twenty feet high, and broad in proportion; but, when running through a valley, or crossing a river, there you see a strong wall, about thirty feet high, with square towers, at the distance of a bow-shot from one another, and embrasures at equal distances. The top of the wall is flat, and paved with broad free-stone; and where it rises over a rock, or any eminence, you ascend by a fine easy stone-stair.

The bridges, over rivers and torrents, are exceedingly neat, being both well contrived and executed. They have two stories of arches, one above another, to afford sufficient passage for the waters on sudden rains and floods.

This wall was begun and completely finished in the space of five years; every sixth man in China being obliged to work himself, or find another in his stead. It is reported, the labourers stood so close, for many miles distance, as to hand the materials from one to another. This I am the more inclined to believe, as the rugged rocks would prevent all use of carriages; nor could clay, for making bricks or cement, of any kind, be found among them.

The building of this wall, however, was not the only burden the Chinese supported, on this occasion. They were also obliged to keep a numerous army in the field, to guard the passes of the mountains, and secure the labourers from being interrupted by their watchful enemies the Tartars, who, all the while, were not idle spectators.

I am of opinion, that no nation in the world was able for such an undertaking, except the Chinese. For, though some other kingdom might have furnished a sufficient number of workmen, for such an enterprise, none but the ingenious, sober, and parsimonious Chinese could have preserved order amidst such multitudes, or patiently submitted to the hardships attending such a labour. This surprising piece of work, if not the greatest, may justly be reckoned among the wonders of the world. And the Emperor, who planned and completed it, deserves fame, as much superior to his who built the famous Egyptian pyramids, as a performance of real use excells a work of vanity.

Besides the main wall, there are several semicircular walls, which have the long wall for their diameter, at the places least fortified by nature, and at the open passes of the mountains. These are strongly built, of the same materials and architecture with the long wall, and are of considerable extent, sometimes on one side of the main wall, and sometimes on the other. In these walls are strong gates, constantly defended by a numerous guard. They are intended to prevent a surprise, and stop sudden irruptions of the enemy. Even these lesser bulwarks seem works of great expence and labour; but nothing in comparison with the long wall.

After the Chinese had finished their wall, they had respite for a considerable time, from the invasions of their enemies, reaping the fruits of their labour in peace and quietness. However, about five hundred years ago, the western Tartars found means to get through the wall, and, with a powerful army of horse, entered the country, carrying terror along with them wherever they went. They, at last, became masters of the greatest part of China, and kept possession of it for many years, till the Chinese, exasperated by their tyranny, took advantage of their negligence, and drove them back, with disgrace, to their ancient habitations in the deserts. The Chinese now began to re-establish their former government, to rectify disorders, and repair desolations made by the Tartars. From this time they enjoyed long peace, till the fatal year one thousand six hundred and forty, when the Mantzur Tartars conquered the whole empire of China; which conquest they retain to this day; and, by their prudent management and mild government, seem in a fair way to keep it.

I shall briefly relate in what manner this strange revolution was brought about, by so small a nation as the Mantzurs; a people whom the Chinese despised, and who bear no greater proportion to the Chinese than the inhabitants of Wales to the rest of Great Britain.

It happened, during a time of profound peace, that a certain prince of Mantzur, going to fetch his bride, from a place bordering on the province of Leotong, was, without provocation, attacked by a party of Chinese, and slain, with most of his attendants; against all laws of justice and good neighbourhood.

The Tartars, though highly exasperated, behaved with uncommon moderation on this occasion. Before proceeding to make reprisals, on taking any step whatever with that view, they sent ambassadors, to the court of Pekin, demanding satisfaction for the outrage committed upon one of their princes. Their complaints were neglected, and the matter, under various pretences, delayed, from time to time, till the Tartars, losing all patience, and positively insisting on an answer to their demands, were affronted, and contemptuously dismissed by the Chinese ministry, to whom the Emperor had referred them. This treatment highly enraged the whole race of the Tartars; who immediately vowed revenge; and, having got an army together, entered the province of Leotong, which lies without the wall, wasting all with fire and sword.

Besides this war with the Tartars, several other circumstances concurred to bring about a revolution in the empire; for, at the same time, there happened a great insurrection in China, which, at last, became general. The rebels were commanded by one named Li; who, after having defeated the imperial army sent to oppose him, invested and took Pekin itself. And the Emperor, rather than fall into the hands of his furious subjects, first hanged his daughter, and then himself, on a tree in his own garden.

The Emperor's general, Usangue, still kept the field with the small remains of his troops; but altogether unable to resist the powerful army of the rebels. He therefore retired northwards; and, all hopes of success being lost, came to a resolution of calling in the Tartars to his assistance. He promised them many rewards, and, particularly, the province of Leotong; if, by their aid, he succeeded in forcing the rebels to obedience. Kum-Ti, the Tartar chief, readily hearkened to the proposal, and the terms were soon settled between the parties.

In consequence of this agreement, the new allies joined armies, which were both commanded by the Tartar, and advanced towards the long wall. But, before they reached the gate, Kum-Ti, the Tartar Prince, died, and left his son Xungsti, a child of seven years of age, for his successor. This accident did not retard the progress of the expedition; for this child was left to the guardianship of his uncle; a man of great abilities and address, and perfectly qualified to conduct the important project then on foot.

Immediately after the death of Kum-Ti, the young Prince was proclaimed King of the Mantzurs, and commander in chief of the combined army of Tartars and Chinese. In order to magnify the number of Tartars in the army, and consequently render themselves more formidable to the rebels, they luckily fell upon a stratagem; which was, to dress all the Chinese soldiers in Tartar habits. And, at entering the wall the real Tartars, in the army, did not exceed eight thousand men; though, indeed, they were followed by strong reinforcements.

When they arrived at the wall, the Chinese, who kept guard, seeing a child at the head of such an army, which they imagined to consist wholly of Tartars, were so surprised, that they immediately opened the gates, without the least resistance, crying out, long live the Emperor. This circumstance, added to the reports of so formidable an army of Tartars, increasing daily by reinforcements, struck such terror into the rebels, that many of them forsook their leader. The Tartars still advanced, and had daily skirmishes and several battles with the rebels, in which the latter were defeated. In the mean time, the guardian took care to leave garrisons in all the towns through which they passed, with strict orders, to use the inhabitants with the greatest humanity. Such mild behaviour gained the affection of the nation in general. And thus he proceeded, from one province to another, till the whole empire submitted to his jurisdiction.

The war, which had lasted some years, being now at an end, and peace re-established, the Chinese thanked the Tartars for their good services, and desired they would return to their own country. But the Tartar chief, on various pretences, delayed his departure, till such time as he found his party sufficiently strong to fix his nephew, Xungsti, on the imperial throne of China.

Xungsti died a young man, and left his second son, Kamhi, to

. THE FORBIDDEN CITY. This shows a ceremonial reception for the Russian Envoy Ides, in 1693. (From Ides, *Three Years' Travels*, 1706)

. THE OBSERVATORY AT PEKIN (see page 172)
   (From Du Halde, *Description de la Chine*, 1735)

34. K'ANG HSI. The Emperor in his Old Age
(A contemporary portrait reproduced from Fu Lo-Shu, *A Documentary Chronicle*)

succeed him. On finding himself at the point of death, he called for his eldest son, and asked him, whether he would take upon him the government? but, being young and modest, he was unwilling to accept, and begged his father would excuse him on that account. Then Kamhi was called, and asked the same question. He was better instructed, and briskly answered, he was ready to obey his father's commands, and would take the weight of the government upon him. This answer so pleased the Emperor, that he named him his successor; and, accordingly, on the death of his father, he was proclaimed Emperor; and his behaviour has shown him altogether worthy of that honour. It is, it seems, agreeable to the laws and customs of China, that the Emperor chuse, for his successor, which of his sons he pleases without regard to primogeniture.*

Although the Emperor's name is Kamhi,† the western Tartars call him Boghdoy-Chan, signifying chief governor; but the Chinese, in talking of him, say Vansuy, which signifies, many times ten thousand years; meaning, let the Emperor live so long. This is a high title in the Oriental phrase. His sons are called Van, signifying ten thousand years; and are distinguished by the names of Van the first, Van the second, &c. according to their age.

Kamhi, the present Emperor, has about twenty sons, and, it is said, he intends the fourteenth for his successor. He is a prince eminent for prudence and valour; and had, at this time, the command of an army against the Kalmucks.

Kamhi hath yet the remains of a graceful person. His countenance is open, his disposition generous, and he gives great application to business; qualities absolutely necessary to manage the great affairs with which he is instructed. His reign has been long and prosperous, though sometimes disturbed by dangerous insurrections, and open rebellions; but his good fortune, and prudent conduct, overcoming all difficulties, restored publick tranquillity, and he has now, for a considerable time enjoyed perfect peace and happiness. Although the government of China is absolute, it requires no small sagacity and skill to rule an empire of such extensive dominions, and containing so numerous subjects.

---

* K'ang Hsi's succession to Shun Chih (Xungsti) was more probably due to the fact that his elder brother was the son of an inferior concubine.

† 'K'ang Hsi' (Kamhi) is of course a reign-name, not a personal name. In the eulogy that follows, Bell hardly overstates the achievements of this great man, the greatest, probably, of all Chinese Emperors. For a full outline of his deeds and character see Hummel, *Eminent Chinese of the Ch'ing Period*, under *Hsüan-yeh*.

After Kamhi had settled his affairs at home, the first step he took was to gain the western or Mongall Tartars to his friendship. The Chinese had no enemies so formidable. The Emperor knew their valour, and had employed many of them in his army, who did him signal service on many occasions. To effect this, he began to form alliances with their princes and chiefs, by inter-marriages between their families and his, where these could take place; others he allured by rich presents; so that they are, at present, little better than his subjects. And, by this masterpiece of politicks, he succeeded more effectually than if he had employed the whole force of China. The friendship of the western Tartars is of great importance to the Emperor; for they not only supply Pekin with provisions, the produce of their flocks; but, upon any emergency, can bring to his assistance fifty thousand horse, on a short warning.

It may easily be imagined, that great armies and strict discipline are necessary to guard so extensive territories, and keep such a numerous people to their duty. The number of soldiers, reported to be in the empire, is prodigious, and almost incredible. I am well informed that the single province and city of Pekin contain no less than one hundred and twenty thousand effective men, all well paid, cloathed, and armed.

Notwithstanding the vast revenues which are necessary for the support of the government, the duties on inland trade must be very easy; for I was told by a merchant, that he could live in the capital, and trade in what branches of business he pleased, for paying only one ounce of silver annually to the Emperor. Such easy taxes show the great oeconomy and moderation of Kamhi whose reign is called the reign of great peace and rest; in Chinese *Tay-ping*.

The Tartars call China Kitay, and the people Kitaytzi; but the Chinese call themselves Chum-Quotigen, that is, the people of the middle region.

The empire of China is, in a manner, separated from all the rest of the world; situated in a fine and healthy climate, surrounded by the ocean to the east and south; by a chain of high rocks and barren mountains on the north and west, along which runs the famous wall as an additional defence. But what, in my opinion, is a greater security to the empire against invaders, than any thing yet mentioned, is the barren desert, stretching for several hundred miles westward, where none but Tartars can subsist, and which scarce any regular army can pass. The seas, to the south and east, are, indeed, open; and China might be attacked on that side; but, I am persuaded, no prince will think it proper to disturb his own repose, and that of such a powerful people

35. A CHINESE HUNTING SCENE
A blue and white plate of the K'ang Hsi era

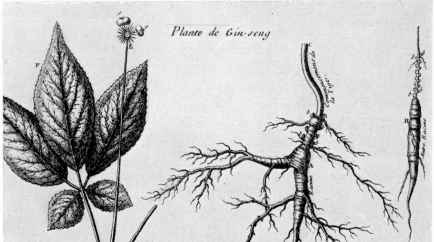

Plante de Gin-seng

36. THE TEA PLANT (see page 181)
   (From Kircher, *China Monumentis Illustrata*, 1667)

37. GINSENG (see page 185)
   (From Du Halde, *Description de la Chine*, 1735)

inclined to peace with all their neighbours; and satisfied, as they seem, with their own dominions.

I know but one nation who could attempt the conquest of China, with any probability of success, and that is Russia; but the territories of that empire are so extensive, in this quarter of the world, as to exceed even the bounds of ambition itself; and the Russians seem to entertain no desire of extending them farther.

What part of China I saw is mostly plain, interspersed with hills and rising grounds. The whole is pleasant and well cultivated, producing wheat and other grain, together with abundance of cattle and poultry.

Besides the necessaries, the Chinese have also many of the super-fluities of life; particularly, fine fruits, of various kinds, too tedious to mention. They have likewise mines of gold, silver, copper, lead, and iron. They set a greater value on silver, in proportion to gold, than the Europeans do; so that gold is exported to good advantage.

In China are many navigable rivers, and canals, cut to great distances, for the convenience of water-carriage. The merchants are immensely rich by their inland and foreign trade, which they carry on, to great extent, with the Russians and Tartars; besides the vast sums of money they receive annually from the Europeans, in exchange for tea, China-ware, and other merchandise. The trade also to Japan, and the neighbouring islands, is very considerable. What is most remark-able in their payments, is, that they receive only dollars, crown and half-crown pieces; undervaluing smaller coins, of equal weight and standard, though they melt all down directly into bars of different sizes.

Tea is universally used, at all time, and by persons of all ranks. Both the green and bohea grow on the same tree, or rather shrub, called by the Chinese tzay. The green tea is called tzin tzay, and the bohea ouy-tzay. When the leaves are gathered, at the proper season, they are put into large kettles, and dried over a gentle fire; which makes them crumple up, and prevents their crumbling to dust; which they would infallibly do, without this precaution.

What is designed for bohea, is mixed, in drying, with the juice of a certain plant, which gives it the colour and flavour, and qualifies that sharpness, which, in constant drinking, is hurtful to some tender con-stitutions. The cultivating, gathering, dressing, and packing of this useful plant, must employ a great number of hands; and particularly, of old and young people, who would be unfit for harder labour.

The high rates, at which tea is sold in Europe, are a little surprising considering the prices in China. For, at Pekin, the price of the best tea, either green or bohea, is half an ounce of silver the Chinese pound;

N

which is equal to what it would be at two shillings a-pound in England. And allowing the freight and duties to be high, yet the profits seem somewhat extravagant. I shall only add, on this subject, that the tea, commonly sold at Pekin, is preferable, in quality, to what is imported to Europe from Canton; and, that the Chinese drink it without sugar, though sugar is a produce of the country, and consequently very cheap.

Several of the Chinese manufactures are brought to great perfection; especially that of weaving silk, damasks, and other stuffs; which are partly worn by the natives, and partly exported. Silks are the common dress, of the better sort of people, of both sexes; and coarse cotton-cloth that of the lower class. They use almost no woolen cloths; because, they say, in their climate they gather too much dust. They have great abundance of raw silk. They make no muslines, nor fine chints; neither are these much used.

The Chinese, it is well known, are excellent performers in several mechanic arts; particularly, as potters, dyers, japanners, joiners, and paper-makers. In the article of paper-making they excel even the Europeans.

Their workmanship in metals is but clumsy; except only founding, at which they are very expert. The arts of statuary, sculpture, and painting, have made but small progress among them. They have excellent water-colours of all sorts, but none in oil. The chief study of their painters seems to be landskip-painting; and I have seen some of their performances, in this way, very natural.

They have many quarries of fine marble, of different colours; but not so much as a single statue is to be seen in the Emperor's garden.

The making of clocks and watches was lately introduced, under the protection of the present Emperor; who, at his leisure hours, amuses himself with whatever is curious either in art or nature.

The Chinese are a civilized and hospitable people; complaisant to strangers, and to one another; very regular in their manners and behaviour, and respectful to their superiors; but, above all, their regard for their parents, and decent treatment of their women of all ranks, ought to be imitated, and deserve great praise. These good qualities are a natural consequence of the sobriety, and uniformity of life, to which they have been long accustomed.

The general regularity, and decency of manners, among the Chinese, is obvious to all who see and observe them with the least attention. And, as they are singular, in many things, beyond most other nations; they are so, likewise, in this point of polity, which I cannot omit taking notice of in my transient remarks.

It may easily be imagined, that, in so populous a city, there must be many idle persons of both sexes; though, I believe, fewer than in most other cities of the world, even in those of much less extent than that of Pekin. In order to prevent all disorderly practices, as much as possible, the government have thought fit to permit, or connive at, certain places, in the suburbs, for the reception and entertainment of prostitutes, who are maintained by the landlords of the houses in which they dwell; but not allowed to straggle abroad. I have been informed, that these ladies of pleasure have all separate apartments; with the price of each lady, describing, at the same time, her beauties and qualities, written, over the door of her apartment, in fair legible characters; which price is paid directly by the gallant; by which means, these affairs are conducted without noise in the houses, or disturbances in the neighbourhood. Noisy brawls are very seldom, hardly ever, known at Pekin ; those who are found offending, in this way, undergo very severe penalties. It is likewise to be observed, that these houses are calculated for the meaner sort of people only; so that any person, who hath the least regard to his credit or reputation, carefully avoids being seen in them.

I must, however, take notice of one shocking and unnatural practice; which appears more extraordinary in a country so well regulated and governed as China. I mean, that of exposing so many new-born infants in the streets. This, indeed, is only done by the poor, who have more wives than they can maintain. To prevent the death of these children, there are publick hospitals appointed for their reception, and people sent out through the streets, every morning, to pick up, and carry thither, such children as they find exposed. The missionaries also send out people to take up such as have been neglected, who are carried to a private hospital, maintained at their charge, and educated in the Christian religion. And of such persons do the greatest part of the Chinese Christians consist.

I shall now make a few remarks upon the ladies, who have many good qualities besides their beauty. They are very cleanly, and modest in their dress. Their eyes are black, and so little, that, when they laugh, you can scarce see them. Their hair is black as jet, and neatly tied up, in a knot, on the crown of the head, adorned with artificial flowers of their own making; which are very becoming. The better sort, who are seldom exposed to the air, have good complexions. Those who are inclined to the olive, take care to add a touch of white and red paint, which they apply very nicely.

The ladies of distinction are seldom permitted to stir abroad, except to visit their nearest relations; and, on these occasions, they are always carried in close chairs, and attended by their servants. The women of all ranks stay pretty much at home. The smallness of their feet, which renders them unable to walk to any considerable distance, makes their confinement less disagreeable. As soon as a girl comes into the world, they bind her tender feet with tight bandages, which are renewed as occasion requires, to prevent their growing. This custom prevails universally, the Tartar ladies, residing in China, only excepted, who appear to have no inclination to conform to this fashion.

This fashion was introduced into China by a great Princess, who lived some ages ago. She was a lady of extraordinary beauty and virtue, and has obtained the reputation of a saint; but, it is reported, her feet resembled those of birds; on which account she kept them always carefully wrapped up, and concealed even from the Emperor her husband. The ladies of the court followed her example; which, of course, soon became general. The Chinese women never pare their nails; but suffer them to grow to the full length. This proves no impediment in embroidery, and other needle-work, in which they are constantly employed. These they finish with extraordinary neatness, as fully appears from some specimens of them brought to Europe.

The Chinese deserve great praise for their patience in finishing, completely, every thing they undertake. And, what is still a greater recommendation, their labours are not the effect of whim or caprice, but calculated to serve some useful purpose. The publick works, about the city of Pekin, are instances of these observations. The streets, in particular, are the finest in the world. They are spacious, neat, and straight. The canals, which supply the city with water, have, at proper distances, commodious stone-bridges over them; and these canals are not only built with free-stone, on the sides, but the bottoms of them paved with broad cut-stones, in the neatest manner imaginable. There are but few springs of soft water in Pekin. And the water, in general, though a little brackish, is by no means unwholesome.

The Chinese are generally of a middle size, and slender make; but very active. They are honest, and observe the strictest honour and justice in their dealings. It must, however, be acknowledged, that not a few of them are much addicted to knavery, and well skilled in the arts of cheating. They have, indeed, found many Europeans as great proficients in that art as themselves. And if you once cheat them, they are sure to retaliate on the first opportunity.

As to the religion of the Chinese, I cannot pretend to give a distinct account of it. According to the best information I could procure, they

DAME TARTARE   FILLE DE MENAGE   BONZESSE   VILLAGEOISE

MANDARINS   DE GUERRE   BONZE   VILLAGEOIS
Chinois.   Tartare.

38. CHINESE AND TARTAR COSTUMES
(From Du Halde, *Description de la Chine*, 1735)

39. CHINESE AND TARTAR COSTUMES
(From Du Halde, *Description de la Chine*, 1735)

are divided into several sects; among which, that of the Theists is the most rational and respectable. They worship one God, whom they call Tien, the Heaven or the highest Lord, and pay no religious homage to the images of their countrymen. This sect has subsisted for many ages longer than Christianity, and is still most in vogue; being embraced by the Emperor himself, and most of the grandees, and men of learning. The common people are generally idolaters. The few Jews and Mahometans, residing here, are supposed to have entered China about six or seven hundred years ago, in company with the western Tartars. There is a very inconsiderable sect, called Cross-worshippers. They worship the holy cross; but have lost all other marks of Christianity; which makes it probable the gospel was preached in this country before the arrival of the missionaries; but by whom is uncertain. The Christians, at present, are computed to amount to one hundred thousand, of both sexes. I have been told, the Chinese have also some Atheists among them.

I had several opportunities of talking with their physicians. They, generally, both prepare and administer their own prescriptions, and are very little acquainted with the medicinal system practised in Europe. As they have but few chymical preparations, their chief study is the virtues of plants, which they apply on all occasions, and often with success. They feel the patient's pulse for four or five minutes, and very seldom let blood, even in high fevers. They compare a fever to a boiling pot, and chuse rather to take the fire from it than diminish the quantity of liquor it contains, which would only make it boil the faster. Bathing and cupping are much practised; and they even apply fire in some cases, particularly for pains in the joints, and gouty disorders. On these occasions they apply a lighted match, composed of the downy substance that grows on mugwort, to the part affected; which, making a scar, either entirely removes or considerably mitigates the pain.*

I cannot but take notice, on this occasion, of a famous plant, called gingsing, which grows in the province of Leotong. The root of this plant is so much esteemed for its physical virtues, that it is gathered by people, appointed by the Emperor, for this purpose only; and is valued at the rate of about twenty five pounds Sterling the pound weight. It is so rare, that the Emperor sent two pounds of it only in a present to his Czarish Majesty. There are two sorts of it; one looks as if candied;

---

* This is a clear reference to the traditional Chinese medical treatment of 'moxibustion', still very much alive in modern China. One can only regret that Bell does not mention the equally venerable and today even better known treatment of acupuncture. See *Chinese Therapeutical Methods of Acupuncture and Moxibustion*, Peking, Guozi Shudian, 1964.

the other like small parsley roots, and has something of the same taste. They slice down or pound it; and, after infusion and slight boiling, give it to the patient. I could never learn from their physicians, what specific qualities this plant possessed, only that it was of universal use. I have heard many stories of strange cures performed by it; that persons, seemingly dead, have, by its means, been restored to health. I believe, indeed, it may be a good restorative plant; but, if it really has any extraordinary virtues, I could never discover them, though I have made many experiments on it, at different times. I should imagine this rare plant might be cultivated, with success, in the country where it grows naturally; and it appears improbable the Chinese would neglect such a sovereign remedy.

The great men in China follow the example of the western Asiatics, in keeping eunuchs to attend them; who are their counsellors, and chief confidants, on all occasions. Their business is to take care of the women; and, being in a manner detached from the world, they are much respected. Castrating is a trade in China; and so skilful and dexterous are the performers that few die under their hands. I knew a man, who, being reduced to low circumstances, sold himself to be made a eunuch, after he was thirty years of age.

The language of the Chinese is composed chiefly of monosyllables, and, seems to me, easily acquired; at least as much of it as is sufficient for conversation. The difficulty of learning their letters, or rather marks for words, cannot be so great as is commonly represented; for you scarce meet a common hawker who cannot read and write what belongs to his calling. It requires, indeed, much labour, and considerable abilities, to acquire the character of a learned man in China.

I have mentioned above a few only of their manufactures. I cannot omit taking notice of their paper, which is made both of silk and cotton, and is remarkably clean and smooth. They had been in possession of this art, for many ages, before they had any intercourse with the Europeans, as appears from their records. Their sheets are made larger than any I ever saw in Europe; and, though they generally write with hair pencils, I have seen Chinese paper that bore our pens and ink very well.

Their ink, called *toush*, is well known to our painters and designers. I was told, the chief ingredient in it, is the burnt bones of animals. They have several sorts of it; but the best is very cheap, and is made up in pastes of various figures, stamped with characters or letters. It is generally put up in little flat boxes, sometimes double the value of the ink they contain.

I shall here insert a specimen of Chinese numbers, and a few capital words, with those of several other Asiatic nations.

CHINESE numbers

1	Iga	16	Shileoga
2	Langa	17	Shiziga
3	Sanga	18	Shispaga
4	Siga	19	Shizuga
5	Uga	20	Shielga
6	Leoga	30	Shinshiga
7	Tziga	40	Tzeziga
8	Paga	50	Ushiga
9	Tziuga	60	Leoshiga
10	Shiga	70	Tzishiga
11	Shiyga	80	Pashiga
12	Shierga	90	Tzioshiga
13	Shisenga	100	Ibay
14	Shisga	1000	Itzen
15	Shiuga	10000	Van

A specimen of ENGLISH and CHINESE words

God	Foy	Wind	Fung
The heavens	Tien	Rain	Eu
The earth	Tiye	Good	Cho
The sun	Shilo	Bad	Pu
The moon	Jualang	A good friend	Cho-pung-yu
The stars	Tzising	Farewell	Mansay-lea
The devil	Kuy	Fire	Choa
Water	Shuy	Bread	Bobon

The MANTZUR's numbers

1	Emu	6	Nynguin
2	Dio	7	Naadan
3	Ilan	8	Iaachun
4	Tuin	9	Une
5	Suindja	10	Ioan, &c.

The MONGALL's numbers, and some of their words

1	Neggea	11	Arba-neggea	30	Gutshy
2	Choir	12	Arba-choir	40	Dutshy
3	Gurba	13	Arba-gurba	50	Taby
4	Dirbu	14	Arba-dirbu	60	Dira
5	Tabu	15	Arba-tabu	70	Dala
6	Zurga	16	Arba-zurga	80	Naya
7	Dolo	17	Arba-dolo	90	Irea
8	Nauma	18	Arba-nauma	100	Dzo
9	Jussu	19	Arba-jussu	1000	Minga
10	Arba	20	Choiry	10000	Tumea

God	Burchan
The heavens	Tengery
The earth	Gadzar
The sun	Narra
The moon	Shara
The stars	Odu
The clouds	Ulea

The TANGUT's numbers

1	Dgi	6	Duk
2	Neé	7	Dunn
3	Sum	8	Dja
4	Che	9	Gu
5	Gno	10	Dju-tamba, &c.

Numbers of INDOSTAN

1	Eck	6	Tzo
2	Duy	7	Tateé
3	Tin	8	Aatsa
4	Tzar	9	Nouy
5	Penge	10	Dass, &c.

The people of Indostan have little or no correspondence with China; being separated from it by impassable mountains and barren deserts. They call China by the name of Kitat; and the Emperor, Amola-Chan.

The Indians call Russia Olt.

The first great Lama, or high Priest, near the borders of India, is called Beyngin-Bogdu; and hath his residence at a place called Digerda.

The second is the Delay-Lama, residing at Lahassar; the Indians call him Tamtzy-Kenna. From Digerda to Lahassar is a month's journey on foot.

The third is the Kutuchtu, called by the Indians Tarranat, who resides at the Urga, not far from Selinginsky.

The present Great Mogul is called Sheyhalim Patisha. The Indian married priests are the Brachmans; their monks are called Atheits, and their military men Resput.

The Indian and Tangut numbers, together with these few notes, I had from the Faquir, at Selinginsky; who told me, that the greatest penance that could be imposed on any of their order, was a pilgrimage to visit these three high priests. Though I have hinted something concerning them, during my stay at Selinginsky, yet, as I shall have no opportunity in future to learn any thing more about those great men, I think it will not be unacceptable that I have inserted the foregoing short notes.

I had, from my early youth, a strong inclination to visit the eastern parts of the world; and providence afforded me an opportunity, far beyond my expectations, of gratifying my curiosity in the most ample manner. For never, perhaps, were those countries in a more flourishing condition than under the famous Emperors, Kamhi and Peter the first; and, perhaps, such another conjuncture of circumstances may not happen for several ages. I have now finished my account of the observations I made during my residence in China; and, had we returned by the same route we went eastward, I should here conclude my journal; but, as our route was different in many places, particularly, in our passage, by water, from Selinginsky to Tobolsky, I shall proceed to make my remarks on such places and things, only, as I have hitherto had no opportunity of mentioning.

CHAPTER XIII

Our departure from PEKIN, *Occurrences, &c. during our journey back towards* MOSCO

March 2nd, we sent off our heavy baggage, early in the morning; and, about noon, left the fine city of Pekin, accompanied by several Chinese gentlemen, who were to return with Mr de Lange, whom his Czarish Majesty had appointed to remain, as his agent, at the court of Pekin. In the evening we reached a large town, called Sangpingju, where we lodged.

The 4th, Mr de Lange and our friends returned to the city, and we continued our journey. I have already mentioned most of the remarkable towns through which we passed; and, as little happened on the road worth notice, I shall only observe, that we were entertained, by the governors, in the same hospitable manner as before.

The 9th, we arrived at Kalgan, the last town of any note, and about three miles distant from the long wall. We staid here two days, in order to provide bread, rice, and other provisions, for our journey over the Hungry Desert.

Next day, the governor waited on the ambassador, and invited him to see some Chinese troops perform their exercise. We accordingly walked into an adjacent field, where we found about four thousand infantry drawn up in six lines. All their guns had match-locks. The field-officers were on horseback, armed with bows and arrows; but the subalterns on foot, having spears, longer or shorter, according to their rank. All the troops kept a profound silence, till the commanding officer ordered the signal to be given for beginning the exercise; which was done by firing a small gun, mounted on the back of a camel. Upon this signal, they advanced, retreated, and performed their evolutions, according to the discipline of the country, in a very regular manner. After finishing this exercise, the whole corps, at last, divided itself into companies of fifty men each; and, kneeling as close to one another as possible, continued in this posture for some minutes; they then rose, and, running to their former stations, quickly formed themselves, without the least confusion. From what I observed of their motions, I am of opinion they might easily be taught any exercise whatever.

The 12th, we arrived at the gates of the main wall, which we found open. Here the commander, and several officers of the guard, met us, and invited the ambassador to walk into the guard-room, and drink a dish of tea. After this repast we proceeded a few miles farther; but, as it was too late to get over the mountains that night, we took up our quarters at a village where we had lodged in going to Pekin.

Next morning early we left the village; and travelled along the banks of a torrent, which runs through a narrow valley, between the mountains. For conveniency of the road we crossed this rivulet several times. The weather was very fine and warm, and the face of the country extremely pleasant. On the sides of the rocks we saw scattered many neat cottages, surrounded with little gardens and crooked trees, which the Chinese have naturally designed on some of their japanned and China-ware. After travelling about a dozen of English miles, we ascended the rocks by a winding path, formed by art; and, as soon as we reached the summit, we entered on the plain; for there is little or no descent into the desert from the opening between the rocks. I observed, that all the rivers spring from the mountains on the north and west of China, run towards the south and south-east; and those that rise westward of the desert, direct their courses, through Siberia, to the north and north-west; which makes it evident, that the rocks and desert are higher than any places either in China or Siberia. We now felt a very sensible change in the air. In the morning, we left a warm climate; but here, we found the desert all covered with snow. We travelled about five miles farther, and then pitched our tents on the banks of a small rivulet.

The ambassador, considering, that to travel along with the heavy baggage would render the journey, at this season, tedious and disagreeable, resolved to leave it under a proper guard, and proceed, by the shortest and speediest way, to Selinginsky. Lomy, our former conductor, being appointed in the same station, was consulted on this occasion; and agreed to make one of our company; while the Chinese guard, commanded by another officer, took care of the baggage. Our party consisted of the ambassador, Mr Krestitz, myself, and four servants. We packed up beds, and a few necessaries, and set out directly.

We rode very hard all the fourteenth; and, in the evening, took up our lodgings in a Mongalian tent, along with the family. The outside of the tent was hung round with several pieces of horse-flesh; on which our landlord and his wife supped, and invited us to share their repast; but, as we had provisions of our own, we desired to be excused. The disagreeable smell of this supper made us resolve to sleep in the fields for the future, till we came to Selinginsky; for although the nights were somewhat cold and frosty, the weather was dry and pleasant.

Next day, having got fresh horses, we proceeded on our journey. Nothing of moment occurred till the third of April, when we arrived, before noon, on the banks of the river Tola. It was now nineteen days since we left our baggage, during which time we rode very hard, changing horses generally three or four times a-day, and this was the first running water we had seen. I cannot help taking notice of the pleasure that appeared in every face at the sight of this stream; and I need not mention how chearfully we regaled ourselves on this occasion. For my own part, I thought the most delicious wines of Ispahan and Thiras, not worthy to be compared to this simple element; so little prized by those who enjoy it in plenty. Our bread was all spent some days before; however, we had still some mutton, with which we had been supplied, from time to time, during our journey. All this time we observed no road; but kept mostly about one, or sometimes two days-journey to the northward of our former route. The greatest danger, attending this way of travelling, arose from the arrows which the Mongalls had set in strong bent bows, covered with sand, for killing antelopes. One of our horses happened to tread on one of these bows; the arrow immediately flew out, and, most fortunately, hit the stirrup iron; otherwise the horse or rider would have been killed upon the spot. We had, indeed, guides to conduct us, from place to place, but they were unacquainted with any snares laid beyond their own bounds.

This day, about noon, some Mongalls unluckily set fire to the long grass before us, which, by means of a strong wind, soon spread to a great distance. We immediately retired to the top of a neighbouring hill; (for now the grounds begin to rise, and the soil is much better near the river;) and, setting fire to the grass around us, travelled near a mile in a dismal cloud of smoke. Some of our people who were behind us, and unprovided with flints, were put to hard shifts, having their hair and cloaths all singed. We forded the Tola in pretty deep water, and continued our journey through pleasant valleys, between gently rising hills, some of whose tops were adorned with woods, which looked as if planted by art.

Nothing worth mentioning occurred, till the morning of the 6th of April, when we reached the river Iro; but found the ford so frozen that we could not ride it. As our provisions were now nearly all spent, and we were quite tired of lying in the open air, we wanted to pass the river at any rate. After long search for a ford, we, at last, found a place clear of ice; but excessively deep. We immediately stripped off our cloaths, mounted our horses, and swam a-cross the river; which was at this place about forty yards broad. After getting all safe to the other side, we lighted a great fire of sticks to dry and warm ourselves; and then set forward to the rivulet Saratzyn, the boundary between the Russian and Chinese territories, which we reached in the evening. From the Tola to this place we had seen no inhabitants; but here we found a few Mongalls, subjects of Russia, who hospitably entertained us with such fare as the place afforded.

The 7th, we set out early, and, at noon, came to a zimovey, (a single house built for the accommodation of travellers,) inhabited by a Russian, who entertained us with good bread, and other homely fare. After a short stay we mounted, and, at night, came to another of these houses, belonging to the commissary, Mr Stepnikoff, of the caravan where we were well provided with necessary accommodations.

Next day, we arrived in good health at the town of Selinginsky; and all of us had good reason to return our most grateful thanks to the almighty Disposer of all events, who conducted us safe through so many dangers, without the least accident befalling any of our company.

The 12th, the ambassador having made the conductor an handsome present, and thanked him for his trouble and obliging behaviour, that gentleman took leave, and returned to China.

Next day, we set out, on horse-back, for Irkutsky. We lodged every night in villages till the 16th, when we arrived at the Possolsky monastery, situated on the south shore of the Baykal sea, as formerly observed. The superior received and entertained us with great hospitality; and furnished us horses and sledges for passing the sea upon the ice, which we found perfectly firm, though the people on the south shore were ploughing and sowing their oats.

April 7th, having taken leave of the monks, we placed ourselves in the sledges, and drove along a pathway upon the ice. We found several large gaps in the ice, which run for many miles a-cross the sea, and are generally from two to five, or six feet, wide. These we passed on long boards, which we were obliged to carry along with us, for that purpose. They are made, I conjecture, by the air; which, being pent up under the ice, bursts out through these apertures. I observed also a number of small round holes, which are made by the seals, who come thither for breath and to bask themselves in the sun. These circumstances render travelling on the ice extremely dangerous, except in day light, and clear weather. Towards evening the ambassador and myself, being provided with light sledges, put on at a great rate, in order to get in with the shore before night. This we happily accomplished, and arrived at a fisherman's house, near the mouth of the Angara; where we found a warm room, and a boar's head, hot from the oven, for supper. But, a

little before sun-set, a thick fog arose to the westward, accompanied
with terrible thick drifts of snow, which soon covered the road upon
the ice, and filled every gap and hole. Our poor people, who had not
yet reached the land, were caught in the storm, forced to stop short,
and ly on the ice all night, with their horses and carriages. We had,
indeed, dispatched the fishermen to conduct them to the shore; but the
snow continuing to fall very thick, they returned without being able to
find them. This disappointment created in us some uneasiness; but
there was no remedy. We were obliged to wait patiently till the morning, when they arrived in a very distressed condition; half dead with
cold and wet. However, by proper accommodation, and some warm
liquor, they soon recovered.

Next day, we sent back the sledges to the monastery; and, after our
people had refreshed themselves with a little sleep, about noon, we
mounted, and proceeded about four miles, to the small chapel of St
Nicolas. We had now passed all the cataracts, and there was no ice
to be seen in the river; we immediately, therefore, got boats and rowed
down the stream. In the evening, we put ashore at a small village, where
we lodged; and were plentifully provided with variety of excellent fresh
fish for supper.

The 19th, in the morning, we went again on board; and, about two
in the afternoon, landed at Irkutsky, and dined with our old friend,
Mr Rakitin, the commandant, who met us on the river, about two
hours before we landed. Some days after our arrival, Mr Ismayloff
was seized with a fever; which went off in a few days, without any bad
consequences. We waited here for our baggage, which did not arrive
till the second of July. During this time, little remarkable happened.
We diverted ourselves with hunting and fishing; and, though we lived
much at our ease, the time grew tedious, and we wanted much to be
gone.

About the 10th of May, the ice began to break up, in the Baykal,
and continued floating down the river, for some days, in great shoals.
The weather was very hot, before the ice came down; but when this
happened, an alteration was sensibly felt; for the air, about the sides
of the river, became extremely chilly. A small part only of the ice,
about the mouth of the Angara, floats down that river, the rest, being
scattered along the shore by the winds, is melted down as the season
advances. This is accounted the most unhealthy season of the year; as
people, notwithstanding all possible precautions, are very apt to catch
cold. I have already made some remarks on Irkutsky, and the country
adjacent; I shall therefore only add, that in summer, which is very hot,

the country is much pestered with swarms of muskitoes and large gnats; which are so troublesome, that those who have occasion to go into the fields are obliged to wear nets of horse-hair, to defend their faces from the attacks of these insects.

July 2nd, the barks arrived safe from Selinginsky, with our people and baggage. They told us many dismal stories of the hardships they had suffered in passing the desert; but, on comparing notes, the difference was not great between their misfortunes and our own.

After our people had rested a few days, and necessaries were procured for the voyage, on the 5th, they shoved off, and rowed down the Angara. The ambassador, myself, and two servants, staid behind, in order to proceed in a small shallop, which had a little cabbin in the stern, and was rowed with ten oars. The commandant caused it to be built for our use; and as it sailed quick, and was rowed by our own men, we could pursue the voyage, at pleasure, without being confined to attend upon the heavy barks.

The 7th, we went on board, accompanied by the commandant and several other gentlemen, and fell down the river to a monastery in the neighbourhood, where we were invited to dine with the superior, who made us a grand entertainment of excellent fish; and furnished us, besides, with store of provisions for our voyage. In the evening we took leave of the abbot, and the rest of our friends; and, being assisted by a rapid current, went down the river at a great rate. At night we put ashore, and took up our quarters in a village.

As little of importance occurred during the progress of our voyage, I need not be particular in describing it. The banks of the river, on both sides, are pleasant and fruitful, and beautifully diversified with tall woods, villages, and corn-fields; and we found every-where great abundance of fish. But what renders this fine country extremely disagreeable, is the swarms of muskitoes, with which every part of it is infested. The gnats, about Ilimsky in particular, are of a much larger size, and are reckoned more venomous than any in Siberia; but have this good quality, that they never enter houses, as the muskitoes do. The Tonguses, when they are angry with any person, wish that an Ilimsky gnat may sting him. This may appear but a slight punishment; but it marks the character of these simple people.

The 9th, we sailed the whole day, with a fair wind and strong current; and, in the evening, overtook our barques. Next day, we came to a great cataract, called Padun from the steepness of the fall. This fall we passed safely, as there was water enough upon the rocks for our vessels. The next cataract we met with, which, from its great length, is called Dolgoy, was reckoned more dangerous; for, besides the length and deepness of the passage, it was extremely crooked, winding from one side to another by turns, among rocks and great stones. In passing these cataracts, the pilot sits upon the bow of the vessel, and makes signs, with his cap, to the people at the helm, which way to steer; for the waters, dashing against the rocks and great stones, make such an hideous noise, that not a single articulate sound can be heard. The oars, besides, must be plied very hard, in order to prevent the vessel from running to either side; for if once she touches the rocks, all the goods must infallibly be lost, and, perhaps, the mens lives; of which disasters there are many examples.

The 11th, we passed another cataract, called Shamansky, which is reckoned the most dangerous of them all, the channel being very narrow and crooked. Some of our company chose to walk along the banks, rather than run the risque of passing by water; but they repented of their resolution; for they were obliged to scramble over rocks and through thickets, where they saw many vipers, and other venomous creatures. We stopped, at the bottom of the fall, to take them on board, and refresh our rowers. As the ambassador staid on board, I remained along with him.

Besides these three great cataracts, there are many lesser ones, called by the country-people Shivers; but, as the passing them is attended with little danger, I make no mention of them.

It is surprising that loaded vessels should pass these falls against the stream. They are commonly warped up by means of strong anchors and cables; and on the goodness of the tackle all depends; for should it chance to give way, all is lost. This is a laborious piece of work, though not very costly in these parts; and the navigation of this river is attended with no other inconvenience, except that of striking against stumps of trees hid under the water.

The 14th, we left the Angara, and entered the Tongusky, a mighty stream, formed by the Angara, and another small river called Elim. The Tongusky points to the northward of the west, and is well stored with excellent fish.

We went ashore, this day, at a little village, called Seeza, situated on a high bank of the Tongusky. Here we were met by our old acquaintance General Kanifer, who came from Elimsky to see Mr Ismayloff. I took notice of having seen this gentleman in our journey eastward. We dispatched our barques, and staid with him two days. After which we proceeded down the river; and he returned to Elimsky by water, attended only by his own servants; for, though he was a prisoner, he

40. THE SCHAMANSKY WATERFALL (see page 196)

41. OSTEAKS (see pages 201-202)
    (Both from Ides, *Three Years' Travels*, 1706)

42. A TONGUSE (see page 197)
   The basket of smoking coals was carried to ward off mosquitoes
   (From Ides, *Three Years' Travels*, 1706)

had liberty to go where he pleased, as an escape was impracticable in such remote parts.

The 17th, we set sail with an easterly wind, and a strong current, which carried us along with great velocity. We passed many villages, and some Tongusian huts, upon the banks, to which we made several visits. We found the men generally employed in fishing in their little canoes, and the women in looking after their children and rain-deer, which, at this season, lie near the huts, because the gnats will not suffer them to stay in the woods. In order to banish these troublesome vermin, they light fires all around the place of their abode; and the insects, unable to endure the smoke, immediately fly off. For the same reason, no person stirs abroad without carrying, in his hand, a small earthen pot filled with smoking coals. The canoes skim upon the water very swiftly, but the least touch of an unskilful hand oversets them. The Tonguse places himself on his knees, in the middle of his boat, keeping it as even balanced as possible; and, with a little paddle only, ventures to cross the greatest rivers. I have seen them haul to the side a sturgeon of great weight. When a Tonguse wants to go from one river to another, across a neck of land, he takes his boat upon his back, and carries it whither he pleases.

The 19th, we were overtaken with such a heavy shower of rain, in the middle of the river, that, before we could reach the bank, our boat was half full, notwithstanding all hands were employed in rowing, or scooping out the water. However, after much labour and difficulty, we at last got to land, wet to the skin; and, what was much worse, all our bedding thoroughly drenched in water. After we had hauled up our boat, and fastened it to a tree, we went into a thick wood, and kindled a great fire to warm and dry ourselves; but, the rain being abated, a violent storm of wind arose from north-west, so that we were forced to remain all night in this dismal place, at a great distance from any village. In this condition we lay, round a great fire, till next morning.

The 20th, early in the morning, we left the woods, went on board our boat, and proceeded down the river. About noon, we reached a village, on the right hand, where we halted some hours to refresh ourselves, and dry our cloaths. In the evening, we pushed off again, and came to another village, where we lodged. On this river are great numbers of water-fowl, of different kinds, which come hither to hatch their young in summer; and fly off, to the south, at the approach of winter. I observed, also, a large fowl, of a grayish colour, about the size of a kite; after it has hovered for sometime upon the wing, if it spies a fish in the water, it stoops suddenly, strikes it's prey, and even

o

dives below water to catch it; after which it flies to the bank, and eats it.

There are also wild goats upon the rocks along the shore. They are very large animals, with long and thick horns. Their shaggy coat is brownish, having a black ridge down the back. They have long beards like common goats, but are twice as large. It is surprising to see them leap from one rock to another. They go in pairs about this season; but, towards winter, retire, in herds, to the south. On the hills, and in the woods, are all sorts of game, and wild beasts, natural to the climate.

The 21st, we overtook our barques, and kept in company with them till night, when we arrived at a village, where we lodged. In this river are many islands, some of which are very large, and others surrounded with high rocky shores. Most of them are covered with tall birch and pine trees, fit for masts to the largest ships; and form a beautiful prospect. We had no need to go ashore in order to seek sport, as we found plenty of wild ducks, and other water-fowl, wherever we came. As to fresh fish, we had more of them, in every village, than we could consume.

The two following days we continued our voyage, without meeting with any thing worth mentioning; and, on the morning of the 24th, arrived at the conflux of the rivers Yenisey and Tongusky, where the latter loses it's name; and, both joined, retain the name of Yenisey. The Yenisey falls into the Tongusky from the south, and its course is then turned northward by the current of the other; which, in my opinion, is the larger of the two. It is observed, that the Yenisey does not afford such plenty of fish, nor so good of their kinds, as the other rivers of this country. These two rivers, joined, form a mighty stream; among the greatest in the world. I think it larger than the Volga at Astrachan. It continues its course to the north-west, daily augmented by other considerable rivers, till it falls into the Icy sea.

In the evening, we arrived at the town of Yeniseysky, where we were met by our friend Mr Becklimishoff, the commandant, who conducted us first to our lodgings, and then to his own house to supper. Our barques also arriving in the evening, the whole company met again at this place; not a little happy at having safely passed the water-falls, and escaped the dangers to which we had already been exposed; though we were still above a thousand leagues from the end of our journey.

As we had no time to lose, our baggage was landed next day, and the barques discharged. The packing the baggage, for land-carriage, took up two days; after which it was transported to a place called Makofsky, on the river Keat, where it was again put on board other barques, which lay ready for that purpose. The road lies to the westward, mostly through thick and dark woods; in dry weather, it is tolerably good; but in heavy autumnal rains scarce passable. We staid at Yeniseysky, through the persuasion of our hospitable landlord, the commandant, till we heard all was ready at Makofsky.

Having formerly mentioned the pleasant situation of Yeniseysky, and the fertility of the soil about it; I shall only add, that the harvest, at this place, was already far advanced; the barley being all reaped, and the people at work in cutting their oats. This seems very early, in a climate so far to the north, and must proceed from the heat of the summer, and the soil being fertilized by the nitrous particles of the snow, which lies so long upon the ground.

August 2nd, we left Yeniseysky on horse-back, accompanied by the commandant, who staid with us all night, at a village about ten miles from town. Next morning, we took leave of our friend, and proceeded to Makofsky; where we arrived in the evening, and found the barques ready waiting for us.

The 4th, early in the morning, we went on board, and, pushing off from the shore, rowed down the river Keat. The water being shallow, we made but little way the first day; but, as we advanced, it increased daily, by rivers and brooks from both sides. Before we left Makofsky, we laid in provisions for three weeks, in which time we computed we would enter the Oby; for, during this long navigation, there is not a single house, nor village, to be seen, except one religious house, possessed by three or four monks resembling more an hermitage than a monastery.

The Keat is really a most dismal river. It is not above the flight of an arrow broad, and so overshadowed with tall trees, that you can scarce see the sun. The banks are a perfect wilderness, and so intangled with bushes, that no creature can pass along them but wild beasts; with which these woods greatly abound. Near the edge of the river, we found great quantities of black currants upon the bushes, the largest and best I ever saw. I was told the bears feed much on this fruit.

The river Keat takes its rise from a lake at a small distance from the Yenisey; and were a canal cut between them, which might easily be done, there would be a passage, by water, from Verchaturia to the borders of China. But his Czarish Majesty was, at this time, employed in works of the same nature, of much greater importance to his country.

The Keat runs in a crooked channel, pointing, in general, to the west. The bottom is ouzy, and sometimes sandy. The barques, at first, run often a-ground on the sand banks, and the people were obliged to get into the water, and heave them off, by main force, with levers and setting poles; besides these little inconveniencies, we were molested with gnats and muskitoes, in this confined place, more than we had formerly been in any part of our journey. They were not, indeed, so numerous as they had been in the heat of summer; for the nights began to be cold, and the wind northerly. However, no wind could reach us in this close place; and I even wished myself in the desert again, where I might breath the fresh air. In short, the appearance of this place put me in mind of the descriptions, given by the poets, of the river Styx.

During our tedious voyage down the dark Keat, our only diversion and exercise was shooting wild-ducks. One day Mr Ismayloff and myself went down the river in a small canoe, rowed by two soldiers, at some distance before the barques. We met with a large flock of ducks, which swam up a narrow creek in order to avoid us. We sailed a little way after them; and, in the mean time, our barques passed us, and continued before us till night, still imagining they had not overtaken us. This day's sport cost us dear; for, our rowers being quite fatigued, we were obliged to relieve them, and row in our turns, till at last we came up with the barques, both hungry and tired. To make some amends, we had a good dish of wild-ducks for supper.

The 20th, we met with two Osteaks in their canoes, who had come from the river Oby, to catch fish and kill ducks; and had their fishing-tackle, and bows and arrows along with them. We were glad to see any human creature. We called them on board, and they willingly staid with us till we entered the Oby, and supplied us with plenty of fish and wild fowl. These were the first of the tribe of the Osteaks I had seen. I shall give some account of them, when I describe our voyage down that river, on the banks of which they have their habitations.

I formerly mentioned the great abundance of black currants growing on the banks of the Keat. We found them an excellent and wholesome fruit; many of our people eat great quantities of them without the least bad effect.

After a tedious voyage, with little variety, we arrived, on the 28th, at a village called Ketskoy, a few miles distant from the Oby. After procuring, at this place, what necessaries we wanted, and refreshing ourselves a few hours, we continued our voyage, making what way we possibly could; for fear of being frozen up, near some desert place on the Oby, before we came to Tobolsky, where we intended to land. We had no rain all the time we were upon the Keat; which was a lucky circumstance, as our oars were upon deck. Had our barques drawn only about eighteen inches water, as was intended, we should not have been above fourteen days on this river, and thereby saved much time and labour; but, coming from China, every person in the retinue had a little, which overloaded the vessels, and retarded their progress. The next day, we entered the famous river Oby, which, from its breadth and deepth of water, appears, at least, equal to the Volga or Yenisey, and could carry ships of considerable burden.

The 30th, we reached the first town upon the Oby, called Narim situated on the north bank, about a gunshot from the river, and a few miles from the mouth of the Keat. It commands a fine prospect, up and down the river, and of the woods to the south. Near the town, are a few corn-fields, and garden grounds, abounding with greens and roots. This place has a small fortress governed by a commandant. The inhabitants are generally dealers in furs, which they buy from the Osteaks; and either carry them themselves to the borders of China, where they are exchanged for the commodities of that nation, or dispose of them to merchants going thither.

The 31st, we dined with the commandant, and spent the rest of the day in laying in a stock of provisions. We found, at this place, plenty of fine fish; particularly sterlet, sturgeon, and mucksoon, and many more too tedious to mention; the last is peculiar to the Oby and Irtish.

Here I met with Mr Borlutt, a native of Flanders, who had been a major in the Swedish service, and sent to this place a prisoner of war. He was a very ingenious gentleman, and had a particular turn for mechanicks. The commandant treated him more like a friend than a prisoner; which, indeed, was the case of most of those unfortunate gentlemen, whom the fate of war had sent to this country. His Czarish Majesty, well considering their circumstances, sent them to a plentiful country, where they could live at their ease till peace was restored.

September 1st, having provided ourselves with necessaries, and got new rowers, our former ones returning to Yeniseysky, from whence they came, in the evening we went again on board; and, putting off in fine calm weather, rowed down the Oby at a great rate; our course being much favoured by the rapidity of the current. We passed several villages, and a little monastery called Troytza. The banks to the north are pretty high, but to the south flat; by which means, on the melting of the snow in the spring, they are overflowed to a great extent. The river runs towards the north-west, with little variation. We continued our voyage night and day, except in great darkness, or a gale of contrary wind, when we were obliged to ly by in some creek.

The Osteaks, I mentioned above, differ from all the other tribes of natives in Siberia, both in complexion and language. Many of them are fair, resembling the people of Finland, and they have many Finnish words in their language. Their manner of life is nearly the same with that of the Tonguse, who border with them to the eastward. In summer, they live in the woods, in huts covered with birchen bark. In winter, they dig pits, across which they lay stakes, above them spread earth, to keep them warm. They have a fire in the middle, and a hole in the roof to let out the smoke. During this season they live chiefly on fish, dried and smoked, wild fowl, or what else they catch in hunting. Many of them are stout fellows, fit for any service. Two of them, with their bows and arrows, a short spear, and a little dog, will attack the greatest bear. They are dexterous archers and fishermen. We had always a number of them, in canoes, round our barques, who supplied us with plenty of fish and wild fowl, of various sorts, at an easy rate. Give them only a little tobacco, and a dram of brandy, and they ask no more, not knowing the use of money.

The Osteaks, though a savage people in their manner of life, are far from being barbarous; for a single Russian will travel about all their abodes, in order to purchase furs, without fear of any violence. They are also remarkable for their honesty; and the small tribute of furs, which they pay annually to his Czarish Majesty, they bring punctually to the place appointed.

In summer, they wear nothing but coats and short drawers, made of fish-skins, dressed after their fashion; but, in winter, are clothed with skins of deer and other wild beasts.

They have no cattle except rain-deer, which supply their children with milk; and are, besides, of great service to them on many accounts.

As to their religion, they are ignorant heathens, like the rest of the natives of Siberia. They have many both male and female shamans, who are in great esteem among them. These shamans have many small images, or rather blocks of wood, rudely cut with a knife or hatchet, representing a human figure, dressed up in rags of various colours, by which they pretend to foretell future events, such as the good or bad luck of those that go a-hunting. But these are no better than others of the same species, already mentioned, who impose on the ignorance or credulity of their neighbours.

From what I have now and formerly said concerning these poor savage tribes, it will appear that they are involved in the most profound ignorance. Their manners are so rude, and minds uncultivated, that many of them seem stupid, and altogether unmindful of any thing beyond their present employment. I have, however, met with men of reflection among them, who agreed with the rest of mankind, in acknowledging one great almighty Creator of this world, and of every thing else.

The archbishop of Tobolsky has, of late, baptised many of the Osteaks, and other natives, in a tour he made through Siberia with that view; and it is to be hoped his successors will follow his laudable example.

CHAPTER XIV

Our arrival at the town of SURGUTE, *our journey thence to* MOSCO,
some account of the creature called mammon, &c.

After a voyage of ten days from the town of Narim, during which
little remarkable happened, we arrived, on the 11th of September, at
another town, called Surgute, situated on the north bank of the Oby,
and defended by a small fort. The inhabitants, like the people of
Narim, are mostly traders in furs. The adjacent country, on both sides
of the river, is overgrown with dark and tall woods, where there is
no cultivated ground, except a few gardens. Bread is got, at a small
charge, by water-carriage, from Tobolsky, and other places on the
river Irtish.

In the banks of the Oby, about this place, are found great quantities
of that kind of ivory called, in this country, mammon's horn. Some of it,
also, is found on the banks of the Volga. Mammon's horn resembles,
in shape and size, the teeth of a large elephant. The vulgar really
imagine mammon to be a creature living in marshes and under ground;
and entertain many strange notions concerning it. The Tartars tell
many fables of its having been seen alive. But to me it appears that this
horn is the tooth of a large elephant. When, indeed, or how, these
teeth came so far to the northward, where no elephants can, at present,
subsist during the winter-season, is what I am unable to determine.
They are commonly found in the banks of rivers which have been
washed by floods. The commandant of this place had his entry ornamented with several very large ones, and made me a present of one of
them.

I have been told by Tartars in the Baraba, that they have seen this
creature, called mammon, at the dawn of day, near lakes and rivers;
but, that on discovering them, the mammon immediately tumbles into
the water, and never appears in the day-time; they say it is about the
size of a large elephant, with a monstrous large head and horns, with
which he makes his way in marshy places, and under ground, where he
conceals himself till night. I only mention these things as the reports
of a superstitious and ignorant people.

I have observed, in most of the towns, we passed, between Tobolsky
and Yenesiesky, many of these mammons horns, so called by the
natives; some of them very entire and fresh, like the best ivory, in every
circumstance, excepting only the colour, which was of a yellowish hue;

others of them mouldered away at the ends, and, when sawn asunder, prettily clouded. The people make snuff-boxes, combs, and diverse sorts of turnery ware, of them.

They are found in the banks of all the great rivers in Siberia, westward of Irkutsky, when the floods have washed down the banks, by the melting of the snow, in the spring. I have seen of them weighing above one hundred pounds English. [I brought a large tooth, or mammon's horn, with me to England, and presented it to my worthy friend Sir Hans Sloane, who gave it a place in his celebrated Museum; and was of opinion, also, that it was the tooth of an elephant. This tooth was found in the river Oby, at a place called Surgute.]*

The 12th, after we had been supplied with a fresh stock of provisions and fresh rowers, we proceeded towards the next stage, called Samarofsky-Yamm, near the conflux of the Oby and Irtish. The wind being contrary, we made but slow progress. The near approach of winter, which usually begins about the first of October, made us hasten forward as fast as possible.

Next day, the wind being easterly, we hoisted our sails, and run along at a great rate; and, the 14th, arrived at a small village on the north shore. The south bank still continued low and flat. At this village we saw great quantities of wild geese, picked, and smoked, and hung in shades, for winter-provisions. We had some of them dressed; but I cannot much praise them for agreeable food. The people of this place catch vast numbers of them in day-nets, more on account of the down and feathers, than of their flesh, which is but of small value. We let our barques proceed; and detained a boat to follow them, as soon as we had seen the method of catching the wild geese. The sportsman conducted us into a spacious open plain, encompassed with woods and water. Here he had his large nets, with wide meshes, spread; and a small hut, made of green branches, to conceal himself. Upon the grass were scattered about a score of geese-skins stuffed, some of them standing, others sitting, in natural postures. As soon as he sees a flock flying over his head, he calls, with a bit of birchen bark in his mouth, exactly like

* Bell's mammoth's tusk was to figure prominently in eighteenth-century learned discussions on the mammoth question. Thus William Hunter, MD, FRS, in a paper read to the Royal Society in 1768 said: 'The supposed elephant's tusk which was brought from Siberia by Mr Bell, and presented to Sir Hans Sloane, and of which we have a description and figure in the Memoirs of the Academy of Sciences at Paris (An. 1727, p. 309) is evidently twisted like the tusk of the *incognitum*, and not at all like any elephant's tusk which I have ever seen. This proof will have considerable weight with those who will take the trouble to examine that tusk in the British Museum' (*Annual Register*, 1769, p. 76). I am sorry to say I have had no success in trying to track down Bell's tusk in South Kensington today.

the wild geese. On hearing the call, they take a turn round, and then alight among the stuffed skins; which being perceived by the sportsman, he immediately draws a string, and claps the nets over the whole flock, or as many of them as are within their reach. The geese always alight and rise with their heads to windward; to prevent, therefore, such as escape the day-net from flying off, he has a deep long net placed, on tall slender poles, to windward, which intangles great numbers in their rising. I am persuaded this method might easily be practised, in other parts of the world, to greater advantage; though, I believe, there are no where such quantities of water-fowl, especially geese of different kinds, as in these northern climates; where, free from annoyance, they bring forth their young among woods and lakes, and, at the approach of winter, fly off to the Caspian sea, and other southern regions.

There is here one species of geese, called kazarky, of a size less than the common wild goose, having beautiful scarlet spots about the head, and some feathers of the same colour in its wings. Of this sort I saw great flocks about the Caspian sea in winter. Besides these, there are numbers of swans, and all sorts of water-fowl natural to the climate.

The woods are stored with game, and various sorts of wild fowl; particularly, the coc-limoge, the heath-cock, and several others too tedious to mention. The manner in which the coc-limoge is caught, by the Osteaks, is somewhat curious.

They make a paling, about four or five feet high, running from any wood, along a sandy bank, to the edge of the river, having the stakes set so close that the fowls cannot pass between them. In this paling they leave openings, at certain distances, large enough to afford a passage for these birds; and, rather than take the wing, the cock will seek a passage from one end of the hedge to the other. In these openings are set springs, on bent branches, which, as soon as touched, fly up, and catch the fowl, either by the neck, or feet. The Osteaks brought us these, and other wild fowl, in great plenty.

The 15th, in fine weather, we continued our voyages; using our sails or oars, by turns, as circumstances obliged us. Little material happened till the 19th in the evening, when we left the Oby, and entered the Irtish; and, night coming on, we put ashore, where we staid till next morning. On entering the Irtish, we had a strong current against our course, which had been down the stream, in all the different rivers, from Selinginsky to this place.

Before I proceed farther, I shall take a view of the famous Oby. It is one of the largest rivers in the world; and runs as long a course as any in Siberia, or perhaps in any other quarter of the globe. It rises in the desert, several hundred miles southward of the Baraba; and is daily augmented, by many streams of different names, till it reaches a place called Belogarsky, where it takes the name of Oby, at the conflux of two large rivers, the Alley and the Tzaritt. These rivers joined form the Oby. The Oby signifies *both* in the Russian language. But I am of opinion, this river had that name long before Siberia was known to the Russians; as the natives still give it that name.

In going eastward, we passed the Oby upon the ice, at a place called Tzausky Ostrogue; where it made no great appearance, in comparison of what it does after receiving the rivers Tom, Tzulim, Keat, Irtish, and many others; when, indeed, it may be reckoned in the number of the largest rivers in the world. It points generally to the north, with various windings, till it meets the Keat, when it turns to the north-west; and runs in that direction many miles, till, meeting with the Irtish it turns short, in a rapid current, towards the pole, swallowing up many rivers and brooks in its course; and, at last, it discharges itself into the Northern ocean, at a great bay called Obskaya-Guba, or the Lips of the Oby.

Few rivers in the world contain greater plenty and variety of fish than the Oby. The banks to the south produce woods in abundance, interspersed with cornfields, and good pasturage. I have been informed that in these parts are rich mines of copper and iron, and even silver.

At the conflux of the Oby and Irtish are several large islands; and farther north, several villages; but only one town of any note, called Bercosa, situated on the left hand.

I may here observe, that geographers generally agree, that a line drawn from the place where the river Tanais, now called Don, discharges itself into the sea of Azof, or the Black sea, to the mouth of the Oby, is the proper boundary betwixt Europe and Asia.

The 20th, early in the morning, we shoved off from the shore, and made the best of our way up the Irtish. In the evening, we reached Samariofsky-Yamm, where we lodged this night.

Next day, having taken on board fresh labourers, and the wind being northerly, and very cold, we put off in haste, hoisted sail, and went along at a great rate. The wind continuing from this point, was a certain sign that winter was at no great distance; and, that we might soon expect to be met by shoals of floating ice.

The 22nd, the north wind still continued very strong, to our great joy. For, although there are many villages on the Irtish, we dreaded the being frozen up near some desert place.

Next day, there fell a little snow, which softened the coldness of the air; but, at the same time, the wind unfortunately chopped about to the westward, and retarded our progress.

The 24th, we continued our voyage; and, next day, the wind again becoming northerly, we used our sails all that day and night. We proceeded, without any thing material happening, till the 29th, when we reached Demiansky, a town standing on the eastern bank.

Next day, we set out immediately, after taking in fresh rowers. The fields were now covered with snow, and the frost so strong, that the ice began to float in the river; and we expected every day to be frozen up.

These signs, of approaching winter, influenced Mr Ismaylof to leave the barques, to follow as should be possible for them, while himself made the best of his way to Tobolsky, in a small boat. Accordingly, carrying me along with him, we immediately set out towards that place.

October the first, we continued rowing along, near the banks, and took in fresh rowers as occasion offered. The river was full of great shoals of ice, the frost strong, and much snow. In the evening, we arrived, cold and wet, at a small village, where we lodged in a warm room, about fifty verst from Tobolsky.

Next day, the river was so covered with ice that we could proceed no farther in our boats; but luckily, in the night, there fell snow enough for sledges. We soon got horses, and such open sledges as the place afforded, and, in the evening, arrived safe at the city of Tobolsky. We went immediately to the palace of Prince Alexie Michaylovitz Cherkasky, the governor, who was an intimate friend of the ambassador. This Prince was much esteemed for his capacity, as well as his great probity and honour. We supped with him, and then retired to our lodgings; but could not avoid commiserating the fate of our fellow travellers, labouring with the ice, and afraid of being frozen up every minute.

The 3rd, we sent some soldiers to meet the barques, and assist them in coming up the river. And on the 5th, they arrived safe at Tobolsky; where they were, next day, discharged.

We were obliged to stay for the falling of the snow, in order to proceed on sledges, the common method of travelling in winter. At this place, we thought ourselves at home, having good lodgings, good company, and plenty of provisions; so that we waited patiently for the setting in of winter; besides, we had now a frequented road, lying through a well inhabited country, all the way to Mosco.

During our stay at Tobolsky, I was informed, that a large troop of gipsies had been lately at that place, to the number of sixty and upwards, consisting of men, women, and children. The Russians call these vagabonds tziggany. Their sorry baggage was carried on horses and asses. The arrival of so many strangers being reported to Mr Petroff Solovoy, the vice governor; he sent for some of the chief of the gang, and demanded whither they were going? they answered him, to China; upon which he told them, he could not permit them to proceed any farther eastward, as they had no passport; and ordered them to return to the place whence they came. It seems these people had roamed, in small parties, during the summer season, cross the vast countries between Poland and this place; subsisting themselves on what they could find, and on selling trinkets, and telling fortunes to the country people. But Tobolsky, being the place of rendezvous, was the end of their long journey eastwards; and they, with no small regret, were obliged to turn their faces to the west again.

Before I leave this new world, as it may be called, of Siberia, I think it well deserves a few general remarks; besides the particulars mentioned in my journal.

This vast extent of eastern continent is bounded by Russia to the west; by Great Tartary to the south; on the east and north by the respective oceans; its circumference is not easy to ascertain. Foreigners commonly are terrified at the very name of Siberia, or Sibir as it is sometimes called; but, from what I have said concerning it, I presume it will be granted, that it is by no means so bad as is generally imagined. On the contrary, the country is really excellent, and abounds with all things necessary for the use of man and beast. There is no want of any thing, but people to cultivate a fruitful soil, well watered by many of the noblest rivers in the world; and these stored with variety of such fine fish, as are seldom found in other countries. As to fine woods, furnished with all sorts of game and wild fowl, no country can exceed it.

Siberia is generally plain, sometimes varied with rising grounds; but contains no high mountains, and few hills, except towards the borders of China, where you find many pleasant hills and fruitful valleys.

Considering the extent of this country, and the many advantages it possesses, I cannot help being of opinion, that it is sufficient to contain all the nations in Europe; where they might enjoy a more comfortable life than many of them do at present. For my part, I think, that, had a person his liberty and a few friends, there are few places where he could spend life more agreeably than in some parts of Siberia.

Towards the north, indeed, the winter is long, and extremely cold.

There are also many dreary wastes, and deep woods, terminated only by great rivers, or the ocean; but these I would leave to the present inhabitants, the honest Osteaks, and Tonguses, and others like them; where, free from ambition and avarice, they spend their lives in peace and tranquillity. I am even persuaded, that these poor people would not change their situation, and manner of life, for the finest climate, and all the riches of the east; for I have often heard them say, that God, who had placed them in this country, knew what was best for them, and they were satisfied with their lot.

During our stay at Tobolsky, a messenger arrived from court, with the glad tidings of peace being concluded between his Czarish Majesty and the crown of Sweden, after a destructive war, which had raged above twenty years. This was very agreeable news to every body, particularly to the officers who had remained so long in captivity. The peace was proclaimed with firing of guns, and other rejoicings usual on such occasions.

November 18th, all the roads being now firm, and fit for sledges, we left Tobolsky in a strong frost. As we returned by the same road we went to the eastward, which I have already described, I shall not repeat the particulars, but only name the towns through which we passed, viz. Tumeen, Epantshin, Verchaturia, and Solikamsky. The weather being excessively cold, we remained two days at this place. From thence we came to Kay-Gorod, then to Klinoff; from which, instead of going towards Cazan, we proceeded straight through the woods towards the town of Nishna-Novogorod, situated at the conflux of the Volga and Ocka. This road is nearest, but very rough and narrow in many places, the country being overgrown with large tall woods, of different kinds, according to the nature of the soil. The principal inhabitants are the Tzeremish, who afford but indifferent accommodation for travellers; however, the people are very courteous and hospitable. Among them are scattered a few Russ villages, and a very few Russ towns of small note; for which reason, I shall only mention the names of such as lay in our road from Klinoff to Kusma-Damiansko, (which last place is situated on the east bank of the river Volga) viz. Bistritsky, a large village; Orloff, a small town; Yuriefsky, a village; Kotelnitzy, a small town; a village called Tzorno-Retzky; a large village called Voskresensky; Yaransky, a small town; Tzarevo-Sanchursky, another small town; Shumetrey, a village. Besides these, and some others, we passed through many villages, inhabited by Tzeremishian and Tzoowashian Tartars, to mention which would be too tedious. These people, having destroyed the woods about their villages, live much at their ease, have plenty of corn and cattle, and great numbers of bee-hives, whereby they furnish the markets with great quantities of honey and bees-wax. They also furnished us with changes of horses, whenever we had occasion for them; but their tackling of harness, &c. is so bad, that much time was lost in accommodating them to our heavy carriages; so that we thought ourselves happy when we met with Russian villages, which are far better provided in that respect, and more accustomed to travelling, than those poor people, who never go far from their own home.

After a tedious journey, we came out of the woods, to the Volga, and travelled along upon the ice; which, in some places, was not very firm. In the evening we reached Nishna-Novogorod; where we staid some days to refresh ourselves, and kept our Christmas with the commandant.

We proceeded again on the 28th, and, little material happening, arrived safe at the capital city of Mosco, on the 5th day of January, 1722; where we found his Czarish Majesty, and all the court, who had lately arrived from St Petersburg; and preparations were making for grand fire-works, triumphal arches, and other marks of joy, on account of the peace. With which I shall conclude my journal.

I think it will not be unacceptable to the reader, if I subjoin a list of the places and distances between St Petersburg and Pekin. They are as follows.

It is to be noted, that the distances between St Petersburg and Tobolsky in Siberia, are all measured in versts; each verst being 500 Russ fathoms, each fathom consisting of 7 feet English measure; so that a Russian verst measures exactly 1166⅔ yards.

	Versts		Versts
From St Petersburg		to Yazhetbeetsach	39
to Yeshore	35	Zemnigorskom	23
Tossinsky-Yam	23	Edrovo	22
Lubany	26	Kotelofsky	35
Chudova	32	Vishny-Volotshoke	36
Spaskoy Poliste	25	Vidropusko	33
Podberezwa	23	Torshoke	36
Novogorod	22	Medna	33
Bronitza	35	Tweer	28
Zaitsoff	30		
Kristitskom	31	To be carried over	567

	Versts		Versts
Brought over	567	Slobodsky	28
Gorodna	31	Selo-Prokofiefsky	30
Zavidova	27	Selo-Solovetzkoy	33
Klinn	27	Troitska-monastery	22
Peshka	30	Kruto-Gorsky	25
Tshorny Graz	24	Katharinsky-	
City of Mosco	28	monastery	25
Novo-Derevenoy	27	Tikofsky	35
Bunkovo	26	Leonsky	25
Kyrzatsky	29	Kay-Gorod	35
Lipnach	28	Reka Volva	34
Undola	17	Korish Retska	
Volodimer	22	Beresofsky	25
Selo-Sudogda	34	Selo Ysinofsky	30
Moshkach	30	Zezefsky	15
Selo-Dratshevo	26	Selo-Kossinsky	36
Murom	30	Logginoff	32
Selo-Monachovo	25	Selo-Syrinsky	28
Selo-Pagosty	29	Nikonoff	25
Selo-Bogoroditzky	39	Town of Sollikamsky	30
Nishna Novogorod	28	Martinskoy	25
Zyminka	25	Yanvey	35
Selo-Tatintza	31	Moltzanoff	35
Belozerika	35	From Moltzanoff to Verka-	
Fokina	29	turia are five stages,	
Selo-Sumkach	34	making	181
Kosma-Damiansko	20	thence to Saldinskaya	
Bolshoy Rutky	10	Pogostia	27
Kumea	50	Maggnevoy	46
Shumetrey	30	Fominoy	28
Zarevo-Santzursky	30	Babichinoy	53
Potavinoy-Vrague	47	Turinsky	53
Yaranskey	29	Slattkoy	50
Selo-Voskresensky	34	Selo-Roshdesvinsky	50
Tshorna-Retzka	47	Tumeen	51
Kotelnizy	46	Sossnovoy	46
Yuriofsky	20	Pokrofska-Slaboda	31
Orloff	26	Iskinskoy	35
Selo-Bistritz	21		
Klinoff	30	To be carried over	2977

	Versts		Versts
Brought over	2977	Dechterevo	39
Backsarino	34	City of Tobolsky	43
Shestakovo	26		
			3119

From St Petersburg	to Mosco	734
From Mosco	to Kusma-Damiansko	564
From Kusma-Damiansko	to Zarevo-Santzursky	120
From Zarevo-Santzursky	to Sollikamsky	813
From Sollikamsky	to Tobolsky	888
		3119

It will be observed, that, in our journey outwards to China, we went by Cazan; which must make the distance, we travelled, between St Petersburg and Tobolsky, more than the above (which is the shortest road) by, at least, 200 versts.

The route continued from Tobolsky, eastward, down the river Irtish, and up the rivers Oby and Keat, by water.

From Tobolsky	Versts
to Samariofsky-Yamm	570
the town of Surgute	262
the town of Narim	590
the town of Makofsky, up the river Keat	1480
by land, to Yeniseysky	92
to Elimsky, along the river Tongusky	627
to Irkutsky	450
cross the Baykall lake, to Selinginsky	394
to Saratzine, the boundary between Russia and China,	104
to the river Tola	467
to the wall of China, cross the Hungry Stepp, or Desert,	1212
to the city of Pekin	200

From Tobolsky to Pekin	6448
From St Petersburg to Tobolsky	3119
	9567

N.B. The versts between Tobolsky and Pekin are computed, which generally exceed the measured verst.

It will be noted, that the route above-recited is that by which we returned from China.

P

IZMAILOV'S EMBASSY – A JESUIT ACCOUNT

[Chapters XIX and XX from *Memoirs of Father Ripa during thirteen years residence at the Court of Peking in the Service of the Emperor of China*, London 1844. Selected and translated from the Italian by Fortunato Prandi.]

O N the 29th of November of the same year, 1720, Count Ismailof, who was sent on an embassy to his Celestial Majesty by the Czar, Peter the Great, made his public entry into Peking with a retinue of ninety persons, and the sound of trumpets, drums, and other military instruments. He was on horseback, and had a man of gigantic height on one side of him, and a dwarf on the other, both on foot. His retinue partly preceded and partly followed him; some on horseback, and others on foot; all with drawn swords, and in splendid array. Count Ismailof had a fine person and a noble expression of countenance: he spoke German, French, and Italian, and had some slight knowledge of Latin.

To conduct the negotiations with this ambassador the Emperor appointed a commission, consisting of a mandarin and two courtiers, all personages of great authority; and deputed five Europeans and a Chinese to serve as interpreters. Being one of the number, I had the honour of waiting on Count Ismailof together with the others. After an exchange of compliments, the ambassador said he had a letter from the Czar, which he was instructed to deliver into his Celestial Majesty's own hands; and on being questioned as to its contents, he produced a copy, and gave it to the commissioners. Louis Fan, the Chinese interpreter, was desired to read it; but the letter was written in Latin, and the poor man knew so little of this language, that he had been obliged to petition the Pope for a dispensation from reading mass every day. He muttered and mumbled till he wore out the patience of the bystanders; and when at length he was pressed to tell the meaning, he was obliged to confess that he could not make it out. The letter was then handed to us, and we immediately read the contents. It imported that the Czar, being desirous to strengthen the good understanding in which he had hitherto lived with the Emperor, had sent Count Ismailof as his ambassador, requesting his Majesty to listen to all the details that he would have to submit to him, and not to send him back to Moscow before the business on which he had been dispatched was completely arranged.

The commissioners were incessant in their inquiries respecting the business alluded to in the letter; but the wary Ismailof constantly replied that he was forbidden to speak upon the subject until the letter had been received by the Emperor, and his diplomatic capacity acknowledged. As however the commissioners insisted upon having the first information, the ambassador, being at length overcome by their troublesome importunity, stated that the whole business consisted in the establishment of a treaty between the Russians and the Chinese, in order to avert any future misunderstanding. Whilst we were engaged in conversation with the ambassador, the dinner sent him by his Majesty arrived; and when he was requested to return thanks, by making the accustomed prostrations, he refused, alleging that he represented his sovereign, who was on equal terms with the Emperor; but that he would make an obeisance according to the custom of his country. The commissioners could not obtain any further concessions, and were obliged to be satisfied.

The Emperor having been immediately informed of this, was as much satisfied with the contents of the letter, and the business on which the ambassador had been sent, as he was displeased to hear of the reluctance which he had shown to perform the indispensable prostrations. But he dissembled; and in order to obtain his object without coming to a rupture, he resorted to the stratagem of inviting Count Ismailof to a private audience, saying that he would receive the Czar's letter upon a subsequent occasion. The ambassador immediately perceived the snare, and returned thanks to his Majesty for the honour he was willing to grant him as a private individual; but added that, as he was in the service of his sovereign, he must first beg to present his letter.

The Emperor then ordered us to inform the ambassador that, as he declined being presented to him before delivering the Czar's letter, his Majesty would neither receive the letter nor the gifts sent him by the Czar; and that he might therefore return to Russia. To this Ismailof replied that, before executing the commission he had received from his sovereign, he could not receive any personal distinction; and when he was asked whether, in presenting the letter he would perform the prostrations, he answered that he would not; but that he would make the obeisance which European ambassadors made before the princes to whom they were sent.

Upon this the Emperor commanded one of his principal eunuchs, a page, the master of the ceremonies, and the five European interpreters to inform the ambassador that, out of regard to the Czar, he had been induced to do him the honour which he had refused; that, according to the immutable ceremonial of China, it was incumbent upon ambassadors to make the prostrations, and to place the letter upon a table, whence it was taken by a great officer of state, and presented to his Majesty; that although such was the custom, he would waive it on that particular occasion, and receive him in the great hall: that, besides this manner of presenting anything written to his Majesty, there was also the official channel of his government; and that he could choose which of the two ways suited him best. To the suggestion of the official channel, the ambassador replied with a smile; and with respect to the other, he answered that he was commanded by his master to deliver the letter into his Majesty's own hands, and that he could not take upon himself to depart from his instructions. The eunuch then told him that, if neither of these ways satisfied him, he might endeavour to meet the Emperor, as he was coming to Peking, and kneeling down before his Majesty, present him the letter on the public road. Count Ismailof also rejected this advice as indecorous towards his own sovereign, and persisted in saying that he would deliver the letter into the Emperor's own hands, in the place where he was accustomed to receive the ambassadors of other powers. At this presumption, highly offensive to Chinese pride, the eunuch smiled, and the page said the ambassador must be mad; whereupon, without saying one word more, we all rose and broke up the conference.

The interpreters were again summoned to the palace, and a decree, written by the Emperor himself, was given to them for translation, with the injunction that they should represent it as the work of his Majesty's ministers, and should request the ambassador to reply, categorically, to every particular. The translation was executed by one of us who was not in sufficient possession of the Tartar language to render several parts of the manifesto very clearly.

The subject of this imperial edict, which was supposed to be addressed by the Foreign Office to the ambassador, was as follows:— 'The Emperor had hitherto received, and treated with great honour, all envoys of foreign powers; and as during many years he had been on a good understanding with the Czar, as soon as he was informed of the approach of his ambassador to Peking, he had sent some mandarins to meet him, furnishing him with horses, and whatever else was necessary in the journey. On the ambassador's arrival in Peking, one of his Majesty's eunuchs was sent to him with dishes from the imperial table, and a message that after a few days he would be received at court. His Majesty thought that all these favours might have induced him to give up his unreasonable pretensions of delivering the letter with his own hands, as he was no more than a representative of his master. This circumstance had awakened much suspicion upon his conduct. If he expected to receive the same honours as those that would be paid to the Czar if personally present in Peking, the marks of respect hitherto shown him were certainly insufficient, and other forms and ceremonies must be put in practice. He however was not the Czar, but merely his envoy, and even for that his Majesty did not consider the credentials as entirely satisfactory. Although he had boasted of being not only an ambassador, but also a prime minister, he might be a merchant, who, the better to succeed in his traffic, had disguised himself as an ambassador. But granting that he had really been dispatched by the Czar, and that he was in fact his ambassador, yet he ought not on this account to be so presumptuous, nor insist upon presenting his letter with his own hands, as one familiar friend would to another, without observing any of those ceremonies which in China are indispensable, as must have been known not only to him, but to the Czar also. In this manner it was impossible that he should ever attain the object of his embassy.'

Such was the purport of this imperial manifesto, which concluded by directing that, as the conduct of the ambassador was so suspicious, the Foreign Office should make strict inquiries into the matter, and exact from him detailed explanations on every point.

When the translation was completed, the eunuch asked us whether the ambassador and the gentlemen of his suite understood the Latin language, and as we replied that they did but very little, he then desired me to make it in Italian. Fearing the Count Ismailof might suspect that I had some share in the invectives contained in the decree, and excite the Czar's hatred against the Propaganda, in whose service I was, I replied that the ambassador was better acquainted with the French than with Italian. Upon this the eunuch immediately ordered that the translation should be executed in the French language, and the task was accordingly confided to Father Parrenin. It was fortunate for me that he relieved me from this duty, as Count Ismailof actually conceived suspicions of the other interpreters, but never of myself. Had this been otherwise, it would have grieved me much, for afterwards he was recommended to me by the Bishop of Peking in the name of the Propaganda.

The French translation of the imperial decree, together with the original copy in Tartar characters, was conveyed by the mandarins to the ambassador without the aid of the interpreter. I was however informed that he did not appear in the least surprised at the blame thus bestowed upon him, and that he again expressed his determination not to make the required prostrations, and to present the letter with his own hands.

The mandarins returned to the ambassador with an answer also written by the Emperor himself, but with more condescension, and in the name of the government. Count Ismailof again declared in the same manner, that he would not make the prostrations, and demanded permission to place the Czar's letter himself in the hands of the Emperor.

His Majesty perceiving that the ambassador firmly persisted in this resolution, no longer corresponded with him in the name of the government, but sent several mandarins, accompanied by interpreters, of whom I was one, immediately from himself. We stated that the Emperor considered the family of the Czar as his own, and that the Czar's honour was equally dear to his Majesty, with many other similar expressions which were made to bear upon the pending question. We added, that whenever he should send an ambassador to the Czar, he promised that his representative should stand uncovered before him, although in China none but condemned criminals exposed their heads bare, and should perform all the other ceremonies customary at Moscow. No sooner had we arrived at these words, than the chief mandarin instantly took off his cap before the ambassador; and the latter being thus satisfied, promised to perform the prostrations according to Chinese custom, and also to place the letter upon the table in sight of the Emperor sitting on his throne, so that one of the courtiers might afterwards convey it to his Majesty. The mandarin farther stated, that the ambassador had the imperial permission to repair to the gate of the palace in the same state as he had entered Peking, namely with drawn swords, music, and other distinctions. After this Count Ismailof endeavoured to justify his conduct, and produced the original instructions confided to him by the Czar, in which, among other things, he was commanded not to perform the prostrations, and to insist on delivering the letter himself into the hands of the Emperor. It was finally arranged that the ceremony should take place on the 9th of the same month.

On the appointed day Count Ismailof went to the palace to present the letter to the Emperor, with the usual ceremonies and prostrations, as had been agreed; and the presentation took place in the manner which I am about to describe.

After the ambassador and the ninety men of his suite had been kept waiting a good while in the open vestibule of the Great Audience Hall, the Emperor entered it, followed by the principal officers of state, and mounted his magnificent throne by some steps on the left, whilst every one else ascended on the right. His Majesty took his place in a chair gorgeously decorated, having on his right three of his sons seated upon cushions, and a little farther off, the halberdiers, pages, eunuchs, chief courtiers, and ourselves, all standing; we interpreters wearing the dress and insignia of great mandarins. At the foot of the throne, on the floor of the Great Hall, sat upon cushions, in distinct rows, the first mandarins of the empire, the Koong-yeh, or lords of the imperial family, and many other mandarins of inferior rank. Before the throne, near the entrance of the Great Hall, stood a table prepared with sweetmeats for his Majesty. In the open vestibule, which was a few steps lower than the Great Hall, there was another table beyond which Count Ismailof was standing. According to Chinese etiquette, the ambassador should have placed the letter upon this table, kneeling down in the vestibule; but the Emperor ordered that the table should be brought into the Audience Hall, and that the ambassador should also advance, which was a mark of great honour.

Count Ismailof then entered, and immediately prostrated himself before the table, holding up the Czar's letter with both hands. The Emperor, who had at first behaved graciously to Ismailof, now thought proper to mortify him, by making him remain some time in this particular posture. The proud Russian was indignant at this treatment, and gave unequivocal signs of resentment by certain motions of his mouth, and by turning his head aside, which under such circumstances was very unseemly. Hereupon his Majesty prudently requested that the ambassador himself should take up the letter to him, and when Count Ismailof did so, kneeling down at his feet, he received it with his own hands, thus giving him another mark of regard, and granting what he had previously refused.

After the presentation of the letter, the ambassador, attended by the master of the ceremonies, returned to his former place in the open vestibule. Shortly after, he moved to the centre opposite the chair in which the Emperor was sitting; behind him stood his principal attendants, and further back a number of soldiers and servants.

When all present were thus marshalled in due order, at particular signals given by the master in chief of the ceremonies, they all went down upon their knees, and after the lapse of a few minutes, beat their heads thrice to the ground. After this all arose upon their feet, then again kneeled down and prostrated themselves three times. In this manner they kneeled thrice, and performed nine prostrations.

The ambassador was then conducted again to the Emperor's feet, and was asked by his Majesty, through us interpreters, who were standing, what request he had to make. Count Ismailof answered in the French language, that the Czar had sent him to inquire after the health of his Majesty, and to confirm the friendly relations that existed between them ; and that he himself also took the liberty of inquiring after the state of his Majesty's health.

To these inquiries the Emperor replied in a very courteous manner; and then added, that it being a feast day, it would not be proper to discuss business, for which an audience would be granted at another opportunity. He then commanded Count Ismailof and his attendants to be seated. The ambassador was then permitted to sit down upon a low cushion at the end of the row in which were the Koong-yeh, as mentioned above, and four of his principal attendants were placed behind him at the extremity of the next row. All his other followers were directed to remain in the vestibule. When they were all seated, his Majesty began to speak, addressing his discourse to the ambassador, and said that he was not to be surprised at seeing the European missionaries of our party habited in the dress and decorations of great mandarins: that we were not mandarins, but only apparelled as such by his command, so that we might take part in the ceremony, to which none but persons in that costume could be admitted; but that although we were not mandarins, it was not to be inferred that we were unworthy of such distinction, but merely unwilling to be elevated to this dignity, as well as other honours, which he would otherwise gladly have bestowed. He also wished the ambassador not to feel surprised at our being placed nearer to the throne than himself, or the great mandarins and lords, as ours was an exceptional place, granted only for that particular occasion, while that occupied by Ismailof was in the rank of his own grandees. He moreover desired him to understand that we Europeans were not residing at Peking by force or constraint, like prisoners of war, and so brought to the capital, but that we had come from distant countries of our own free-will to offer him our services; and that even on that day we had assisted him as interpreters not by command, but merely by invitation. He lastly declared, that during the whole of his reign we had committed no fault deserving even a reprimand; and that he gave us such marks of his affection because he wished to gain ours. His Majesty was pleased on that day to say from his throne these and many other things in praise of the Europeans, not only for the information of the ambassador, but also to justify himself before his courtiers, who were astonished to see us so highly honoured.

When the Emperor had finished his eulogy of the Europeans, he put many questions to the ambassador upon various subjects. After these he called him to the throne, and with his own hands gave him some wine in a gold cup, an act of condescension which he also bestowed on his four principal attendants above-mentioned. He then commanded his great officers of state to summon the remaining persons composing the ambassador's suite to the door of the Great Hall, in parties of five, and to serve them with drink. In the meantime a table of sweetmeats was conveyed to the ambassador, and then another upon which were dishes from the Emperor's own table. As all the company were seated in the Tartar fashion, that is, with the legs crossed, and upon very low cushions, the tables were scarcely a foot high. All those who were seated on the floor of the great Hall, as well as ourselves, were each furnished with a little table, and thus we all ate and drank, his Majesty continuing on the throne.

During the repast, the Emperor ordered his musicians to play and sing in the Chinese fashion; and after this two youths were introduced, who danced with so much elegance, that we Europeans were much astonished at the performance. In the vestibule, where the ambassador's suite was entertained, the same kind of amusements were provided; and after two hours had been thus passed, the Emperor retired, and we proceeded to another part of the palace to join the other Europeans. Here we all prostrated ourselves before the mandarins, and returned thanks to his Majesty for the honour he had done us by the great eulogy above-mentioned. His Majesty sent a message to us by the eunuch Ching-foo, importing that he had thus spoken in our favour, in order, by making our good qualities generally known, to palliate anything of a contrary nature; and that although he had punished Pedrini, that fact must be considered as a family transaction, for he had behaved towards him as a father to his son, without any publicity.

On the following morning the Emperor sent a dinner to the ambassador and the whole of his suite; and as his Majesty was at Chanchoon-yuen, and the ambassador at Peking, we were obliged to perform a journey of three hours on horseback. The eunuch put so many questions to the ambassador, partly by command and partly to satisfy his own curiosity, that we were detained till three o'clock in the afternoon. We then returned to the palace at a gallop; and as I had not yet broken my fast, I found myself so weak, that it was with great difficulty I could keep my seat upon the horse. This kind of hardship I experienced very often, but I only mention it to show the kind of honourable galley-slaves we were at the imperial court.

Upon a certain day appointed for the purpose, the ambassador presented the gifts sent by his sovereign, consisting of two watches studded with diamonds, a clock in a case of crystal, containing a portrait of the Czar, which was not at all relished by the Chinese, who did not like to see the portrait of the Czar thus publicly exhibited; a beautiful casket likewise adorned with crystal; eight large mirrors, some cases of mathematical instruments, a large hemisphere, a level, a microscope, some telescopes, a hundred sable skins, the same number of ermine and of fox; and some articles turned by the Czar himself. His Majesty accepted all these presents, which, as I said elsewhere, was a mark of especial honour; and gave the ambassador, and each of his four principal attendants, an enamelled snuff-box, made in his imperial manufactory.

When the Emperor had accepted these presents, the ambassador and two gentlemen of his suite were again received by his Majesty in his private apartments, where, after performing the usual prostrations, they were again invited to a repast, of which we interpreters were also allowed to partake. Upon this the conversation turned exclusively on the peace which it was expedient to preserve between the two monarchies, during which the Emperor repeatedly commanded the Russians to listen in silence, and to write in their language what he was going to say, so that they might report it to their master. He likewise ordered the Tartars to record it in their language, and us Europeans in ours, and to furnish the ambassador with an accurate translation, that he might carry to his sovereign the important piece of advice he wished to send him. His Majesty then began to speak, and after a bombastic preamble, said that the peace and welfare of the two nations depended on the Czar's health; and that, having heard how he delighted in marine excursions, he was desirous to warn him against the inconstancy of the sea, lest he should thus expose himself to destruction. At the conclusion of this solemn illustration of the old saying, 'Parturiunt montes, nascetur ridiculus mus,' Count Ismailof had great difficulty in refraining from laughter, as he himself afterwards told me.

As the Emperor's elephants are kept near the house of the Portuguese Jesuits, his Majesty ordered that upon a certain day the ambassador and the four principal officers of his suite should be entertained by these missionaries, and then escorted to see the imperial stables. There were thirty-three elephants instructed to perform various feats and tricks, which they executed in the presence of the ambassador, blowing trumpets with their trunks, and kneeling or dancing at the command of their keepers.

The day after we returned to the palace with Count Ismailof and his secretary, when his Majesty gave each of them a superb dress of sables, a vase of fine metal, and two glasses of wine.

The ambassador was also invited to dine at the residence of the French Jesuits, who gave him a sumptuous entertainment, enlivened by the best music to be found in those parts, which is not at all disagreeable to the ear; this was followed by dances, and tricks of legerdemain, which excited the admiration of all the company.

On the 13th of March, 1721, Count Ismailof departed with his train from Peking on his way back to Moscow, taking with him many valuable presents sent by the Emperor to the Czar. As my attention was then engrossed by other matters, I will not attempt to describe these presents, or any other transaction of the embassy, lest I should commit any error. I will only add one incident, which may perhaps give an idea of the immense wealth of the Chinese monarch. One day I was commanded to show to the ambassador and some of his attendants his Majesty's collection of clocks and watches. On entering the room, Count Ismailof was so astonished at the number and variety of these articles displayed before him, that he suspected they were counterfeit. I then requested him to take some of them in his hand, and having done so, he was surprised to find them all perfect. But his astonishment increased still more when I told him that all the clocks and watches he now saw were intended for presents, and that his Majesty possessed a still greater number, placed in various parts of his palaces for his own use.

THE SUBSCRIBERS *to the* 1763 *Edition*

A

The right hon. Earl of Aylesford
George Abercromby of Tillibody, Esq.
Isaac Akerman, Esq., Fenchurch-street
Ralph Allen, Esq., Prior-park; 2 sets
Sir John Anstruther of Anstruther, Bart.;
  2 sets
John Anderson, Esq., London
Sir Charles Asgill, Bart.; 2 sets
Mr Hugh Atkins, merchant, London; 4
  sets

B

The right hon. Lord Belhaven
The right hon. Lord Bruce
The hon. George Brown of Coalston,
  senator of the College of Justice
The rev. Thomas Bagshaw, D D
The hon. George Baillie of Jerviswood,
  Esq.
William Baird of New-Baith, Esq.
Henry Baker, Esq., F R S
James Barclay, Esq.
John Barclay, Esq.
David Barclay, junr., Esq.
The rev. Dr Barclay, Fellow of Merton-
  coll. Oxon.
James Robinson Barclay of Kevle, Esq.
Richard Becher, Esq.
Thomas Becket, bookseller, London
Peter Bell, senr., Esq., Glasgow
Peter Bell, junr.
William Bell, merchant at Leith; 3 sets
The rev. Mr William Bell, minister at
  Campsey
Mr William Bell of Guernsey
Archibald Bell at Manchester
Capt. Thomas Bennet, London
James Benson, Esq., London
Thomas Best, Esq.
Capt. Leonard Bazer, London
Dr Birch, secretary to the Royal Society
Dr Blair
          Blount, apothecary to the Devon-
  hospital, Exon.
Charles Bouchier, Esq., Edmonton
The rev. Mr Bouchery, Swaffham

John Bond of Grange, Esq.
The hon. Alex. Boswell of Auchinleck,
  senator of the College of Justice
          Boyd of Trochrig, Esq.
Sir Brook Bridges, Bart.
Isaac Hawkins Brown, Esq.
The rev. Mr John Bradfute
Thomas Berney Bramston of Skreens, Esq.
Alexander Brown of Ardrie
Jacob Bryant, Esq.
James Buchanan of Drumpellier, Esq.
Arch. Buchanan of Drummikil, Esq.
The rev. Dr Buckler, Fellow of All-Souls,
  Oxon.
Mrs Buchanan of Auchinreoch
Merrick Burrell, Esq.
James Burnet of Mountbodo, Esq.
The rev. Mr Bush of London
John Byrom, M D, Manchester
Edward Byrom of Manchester
Mr   Bruch
James Bell of Kirkton, Esq.
Matthew Bell, Esq., of Newcastle
Andrew Burnet, merchant of St Petersburg

C

The right hon. Earl of Cardigan
The right hon. Earl of Chesterfield
The right hon. Earl Cowper
The right hon. Countess-dowager of
  Carlisle
The right rev. Bp. of Carlisle, F R S
David Cadder of Inchbruch
William Caddle, junr., of Carron
John Cameron of Carntyn
Mrs Mary Campbell of Balquhane
The hon. John Campbell, junr., of Stone-
  field, senator of the College of Justice
Dr John Campbell
Alex. Campbell, surgeon at Pool
Daniel Campbell, Esq.
John Campbell, Esq.
Daniel Campbell of Shawfield, Esq.
Pryce Campbell, Esq.
Lieut.-Col. Robert Campbell
John Callendar of Craigforth, Esq.

John Carmichael of Castlecraig, Esq.
James Carmichael of Hales, Esq.
John Cathcart, Esq.
James Caulet, Esq.
John Cayley, merchant, St Petersburg
James Cheap of Sawchy, Esq.
The rev. Dr Samuel Chandler
Alex. Chancelour of Shielhill, Esq.
Joseph Chippendall of Manchester
      Cholwell, Esq., of the Temple
Richard Champion, Esq., of Bristol
William Champion, Esq., of Bristol
Sir James Clark of Pennycook, Bart.
Dr Matthew Clarke
The rev. Mr John Clayton of Manchester
Benjamin Coole of St Petersburg, merchant
Dr John Cook of Hamilton
Peter Collinson, FRS
William Colquhoun of Gar scadden, Esq.
Andrew Cochrane, Esq., late provost of
    Glasgow
Peter Colvil, junr., of Ochiltrie, Esq.
John Cornwall, Esq., of London
James Corbett of Tolcross, Esq.
James Corbett, merchant in Glasgow
Josiah Cotton, Esq., Old Jewry
Hosea Coates, Esq., of Dublin
Oliver Coult, Esq.
Nicholas Crisp, Esq.
Crayle Crayle, Esq.
John Cruikshank, merchant of London;
    6 sets
William Cumming, MD, of Dorchester
Alex. Cunningham, Esq., of Edinburgh
Mr   Currie
John Campbell of Clathick, Esq.
John Campbell, Esq.
James Campbell of Ardkinlas, Esq.
Mrs Campbell of Menzie
Alan Cuthbertson, merchant in Glasgow

D

Her Grace the Dutchess of Douglas; 6 sets
The right hon. the Earl of Dunmore
Baron De Witz, minister from Mecklenburg
The right hon. Robert Dundas of Arniston,
   Lord President of the Court of Session
Sir David Dalrymple, Bart.
Theophilus Daubuz, Esq.
Robert Davenport, merchant in London
John Davie, merchant in Edinburgh
Andrew Devisme, Esq., London
John Deponthieu merchant, London

John H. Demorin, merchant, St Petersburg
Simon Desnizkoi, from the university of
   Mosco, at present student at the Univer-
   sity of Glasgow
Robert Dingley, Esq., London
Henry Digge, Esq.
John Dickson of Kilbucko, Esq.
The rev. John Dickenson, AM, Wisbich
      Dickenson, Esq., Lincoln's Inn
Sir Alex. Dick of Prestonfield, Bart.
Alex. Donaldson, bookseller, Edinburgh
Mrs Duncan at Edinburgh
The rev. Christopher Duffield of Feather-
   stone
George Drummond of Blairdrummond,
   Esq.
Alex. Duff of Hatton, Esq.
Thomas Dundas of Quarrell, Esq.
Henry Dundas, Esq., advocate; 2 sets
The rev. Dr Dumaresque
Governor Dinwiddie
John Drummond of Logie-Almond, Esq.

E

The right hon. Earl of Elgin
The right hon. Earl of Errol
The hon. Charles Elphinstone of Cumber-
   nauld, Esq.
The hon. James Erskine of Barjarg, senator
   of the College of Justice
John Erskine of Carnock, Esq.
Mr David Erskine, writer in Edinburgh
Peter Eaton, Esq.
Godolphin Edwards, Esq.
George Edwards, Esq.
John Erskine of Cardross, Esq.
James Erskine, Esq., advocate
Thomas Eyre, Esq.
Miss Nelly Edmonston, of Newton

F

The hon. Edward Finch, Esq.
The hon. Mrs Finch
      Fall, Esq., provost of Dunbar
Peter Fearon of London
William Fergus of Kirkintilloch
Sir Adam Ferguson of Kilkerran, Bart
Robert Ferguson, Esq., Austin-friars
Thomas Forester of Denovan
John Fordyce, Esq., merchant in Edinburgh
The rev. Mr Forester, rector of Passenham,
   Northamptonshire
Robert Fordyce, merchant in Aberdeen

Dr William Freer, Edinburgh
Miss Freame
Robert Freeland of Kirkintilloch
Joseph Freame, Esq., of London
Moses Franco, Esq.
James Frampton of Mozeton, Esq.
George Fraser of Edinburgh
George Fullerton, Esq., at Leith
William Frederick, bookseller, Bath

G

The right hon. John Earl of Granville,
 Knight of the Garter, President of the
 Privy Council, &c.; 50 sets
The right hon. Earl of Granard
The right hon. Earl of Glencairn
The right rev. Bishop of Glocester
The hon. William Grant of Preston-
 Grange, senator of the College of Justice
Francis Garden, Esq., one of his Majesty's
 sollicitors
Dr Gardiner of Great Massingham, Nor-
 folk
Robert Gardiner of Edinburgh
Alexander Garden of Troup, Esq.
John Gibson, broker in London
Osgood Gee, Esq.
Phil. Gell, Esq., of Hopeton, Derbyshire
John Garshore of Garshore, Esq.
Alex. Gibson, junr., of Durye, Esq.
Mr John Glassford, merchant in Glasgow
James Glen, Esq., late governor of S.
 Carolina
Thomas Goldney, Esq., of Clifton
Mrs Ann Goldney of Clifton
Mrs Gordon at Glasgow
Chamberlain Godfrey, Esq.
Joseph Godfrey, Esq.
Peter Godfrey, Esq.
Edmund Godfrey, Esq.
Thomas Godfrey, Esq.
Richard Gough, Esq.
William Gomm, junr., merchant, St
 Petersburg
John Gordon, Esq.
Charles Gough, Esq., London
James Grieve, MD, St Petersburg
Silvanus Grove, Esq.
James Groset of Breadisholm, Esq.
David Graham of Micklewood, Esq.
Sir Archibald Grant, Bart.
The rev. Mr Andrew Gray, minister of
 New Kilpatrick

The rev. Dr Green, rector of Bell-
 Broughton, Worcestershire
William Graham of Airth, Esq.; 2 sets
David Graeme of Orchill, Esq.
Henry Graeme, Esq.; 2 sets
John Galbreath of Balgare, Esq.
Library of the University of Glasgow

H

The right hon. Earl of Hyndford
The right hon. Countess of Hyndford
The right hon. Earl of Haddington
The right hon. Earl of Holdernesse
The right hon. Earl of Home
The hon. James Hamilton, Esq.
Charles Hamilton of Wishaw, Esq.
Lady Hamilton of Rosehall
Henry Hamilton, Esq., Londonderry
Robert Haldane of Glenegy, Esq.
Patrick Haldane, Esq.
Capel Hanbury, Esq.
Jonas Hanway, Esq.
Alex. Hay of Drummellier, Esq.
Will. Hay, junr., of Drummellier, Esq.
Rev. Mr Harden
John Hardman of Manchester
George Hay of St Petersburg
George Gottfried Harenfeller of St Peters-
 burg
Rev. Dr Harrison of C.C.C. Oxford
William Havard of London
The hon. Dr Hay
John Hay of Belton, Esq.
William Heron, Esq.
James Henckell, Esq., London
Rev. Mr Humphrey Henchman
Sir Robert Henderson of Fordell, Bart.
Thomas Hepburn, merchant in Edinburgh
Patrick Heron of Heron, Esq.
Richard Hoare of Boreham, Esq.
William Hog and son, of Edinburgh
William Hope Wier, Esq.
Edmund Holme of Manchester
Charles Grave Hudson, FRS
William Hudson, FRS
 Haldane, junr., of Lanerk, Esq.
Robert Hudson, Esq.

I

Archibald Ingram, Esq., present Lord
 Provost of Glasgow
James Jackson, merchant of St Petersburgh
William Johnston of London

K

Robert Kennedy of Aughtefardel, Esq.
James Kennedy of Kayly, Esq.
Thomas Kennedy, junr., of Denure, Esq.
Kincaid and Bell, booksellers in Edinburgh;
  6 sets
E. King, Esq., of Lincoln's Inn
Marsden Kenyon of Manchester
John Kincaid of Kincaid, Esq.
Mr George Kippen, merchant in Glasgow
Henry Klaufing of St Petersburg, merchant
Sir Wyndham Knatchbull, Bart.
Thomas Knight, Esq.

L

The right hon. Earl of Leven
William Lenox of Woodhead, Esq.
T. Llewellin, LLD
W. J. Liebman, London
Sir David Lindsay, Bart.
William Loch, writer, of Edinburgh
Library of Liverpool
John Lockhart of Lee, Esq.
James Livingston, writer at Falkirk
Thomas Lockhart, Esq.
Theodore Luders, Esq., counsellor of the
  embassy from the court of Russia
Rev. Mr Jonathan Lypeatt, of Boringer,
  Essex
John Lenox, Esq.
Gilbert Laing, merchant in St Petersburg

M

His serene highness Prince Charles of
  Mecklenburgh-Strelitz
His serene highness Prince Ernest of
  Mecklenburgh-Strelitz
His grace the Duke of Montrose; 6 sets
The right hon. Earl of Marchmont
The right hon. Earl of Macclesfield, PRS
The right hon. Earl Mareschal
The right hon. Lady Mansfield
Right hon. and rev. Bishop of Meath
The Laird of McFarlane
Dr McFarlane, of Edinburgh
Dr McFarlane, junr., of Edinburgh
William McFarlane, Esq., of Aymouth
Robert Mackye, Esq., of London; 4 sets
Ebenezer McCulloch of Edinburgh
Norman McLeod of McLeod, Esq.
Library of Manchester
Robert McNair of Falkirk
Robert McQueen, Esq., advocate

Arthur Maister, merchant of St Petersburg
George McDougal of Makerston, Esq.
Sir William Maxwell of Springkell, Bart.
Sir James McDonald, Bart.
John Major, Esq., of London
          Marks, Esq., of London
Lascells Metcalf, Esq., of London
Robert Menzies of Coulterhall, Esq.
Michael Miller, Esq., of Bristol
John Misenor, Esq., of London
Richard Milles, Esq.
John Mills of London
George Middleton of Seaton, Esq.
John Moor of Falkirk
Dr Mounsey, late director general of med-
  icine in Russia
Sir Roger Mostyn, Bart.
John Moor, Esq., rear-admiral
Henry Moor, Esq., of Jamaica
David Moncrief, Esq., deputy remem-
  brancer of the exchequer, Scotland
James Montgomery, Esq., one of his
  Majesty's sollicitors general
James Moor, LLD, professor of Greek in the
  University of Glasgow
William Murray of Touchadam, Esq.
Ja. Murray, Esq.
John Muirhead, Esq., of Gorbals
The reverend Dr Musgrave, provost of
  Christ's College, Oxford
Henry Muilman, Esq., of London
          Monro of Auchinbowie, Esq.
Mr George Muirhead, professor of Hum-
  anity in the University of Glasgow
James Mathias, Esq., of London
James Murray of Abercairn, Esq.
Anthony Murray of Dollerie, Esq.
Alexander Munro, merchant in Glasgow
          More of Leckie, Esq.

N

The right hon. Lord Napier
The rev. Mr William Nairn, MA, of Poole
John Napier of Bolikinrene, Esq.
Lt.-Colonel William Napier; 2 sets
Miss Jenny Napier
Doctor Napier of London
Sir James Naismith of Posso, Bart.
Robert Nettleton, Esq., governor of the
  Russia Company
Nathaniel Newberry, merchant of London;
  2 sets
John Nourse, King's bookseller, London

James Norman, Esq., London
Henry Norris, Esq., London
Wm. Northey, Esq., Grosvenor-square
Lt. John Napier of Craiganet
Houston Stewart Nicolson of Carnock, Esq.

O

The right hon. Earl of Orford
Archibald Ogilvie of Rothemay, Esq.
Charles O'Hara, Esq., of Dublin
Leak Okeover of Okeover, Esq., Stafford-
shire
George Ouchterlony, Esq., of London
Library of C.C.C. Oxford

P

The right hon. Lord Chief Justice Sir
Charles Pratt
David Paterson of Bannockburn, Esq.
Robert Patrick, Esq., of Dublin
Doctor Park of Kilmarnock
Thomas Penn, Esq., of London; 6 sets
The right hon. Lady Juliana Penn
Miss Penn
Richard Penn, Esq.
Rev. Roger Pettyward, DD
Richard Pennant, Esq.
George Peters, Esq., of London
Mrs Pickard of Edmonton
William Pickance of Liverpool
Thomas Phipps, Esq.
Charles Pinfold, Esq.
M. de Plescheoff, counsellor to the court of
Russia
Thomas Plummer, Esq.
Honourable Isabella Powlett
David Powell, junr., Esq.
William Palmer of London

R

The most noble Marquis of Rockingham
The right rev. Zachary, Bishop of Rochester
David Rae, advocate
Robert Ramsay, MD, Edinburgh
John Ramsay of Ouchtertyre, Esq.
James Robertson, Esq.
Charles Rogers, Esq., FRS
William Roberton, merchant of Glasgow
Robert Rollo, sheriff-clerk of Clackmannan
Lt.-Colonel William Roy
The rev. Mr James Roy

Q

John Lockhart Ross of Balnagown, Esq.; 3
sets
Andrew Reed, Esq., of London
John Renton of Blackader, Esq.
James Reed of Bristol
Jeremiah Redwood, Esq.
Sir Thomas Reeve, Knt.
John Van Rixtel, Esq., of London
David Ross, advocate
Archibald Ross, merchant, St Petersburg
Dr William Robertson, Edinburgh
Rush, Esq.
Alexander Russel of Stirling
Archibald Roberton, junr., of Bedlay, Esq.
Lorentz Bastian Ritter, merchant, St
Petersburg
Jacob Rigail, merchant, St Petersburg
Mr James Rannie, merchant in Leith

S

Her grace the Dutchess dowager of Somer-
set
The right hon. the Earl of Suffolk
The right hon. Earl of Sutherland
The right hon. Lord Viscount Spencer
The right hon. Lady Viscountess Spencer
Honourable George Sinclair of Woodhall,
senator of the College of Justice
Honourable Mrs Southwell
Sir William Saint Quintin, Bart.
Andrew Saint Clare of Hermiston, Esq.
Robert Salisbury, Esq., of London
Henry Saxby, Esq., of London
Sir John Sebright, Bart.
Hugh Seton of Touch, Esq.
Roger Sedgewick, MD, of Manchester
Doctor Schomberg
George L. Scott, Esq., commissioner of
excise
Henry Shiffner of Pontrylas, Esq.
Mrs Shiffner of Pontrylas
Walter Sharp, Esq., of London; 3 sets
Mrs Shaw of Chishunt
Henry Sharp of Bermondsey, Esq.
William Sloane, Esq., of London
Morgan Smith, Esq., of Bristol
Charles Smith, Esq., of Bulogn
John Smith of Buchanan
John Smith, fellow commoner of Magdalen
College, Oxford
William Somervil, writer in Glasgow
Joseph South, Esq.
Edward Southwell, Esq.

James Sperling, Esq., of London
Charles Spence, Esq., London
Harry Spencer, Esq.
John Russel Spence, Esq.
John Spencer, Esq.
Archibald Stirling of Keir, Esq.
Sir James Stirling of Glorat, Bart.
Lady Stirling of Glorat; 2 sets
Sir William Stirling of Ardoch, Bart.
James Stirling of Calder, Esq.
Alexander Stirling, Esq., of St Albans
William Stirling, Esq.
Tho. Stephens, merchant in St Petersburg
Andrew Stalker, bookseller, Glasgow
William Stewart, writer in Edinburgh
Sir Archibald Stuart of Castlemilk
John Struther, brewer in Glasgow
George Stonehouse, Esq., of Standon, Wilts.
Dr Charles Stuart of London; 3 sets
Alexander Sutherland of Woodend, Esq.
Daniel Swaine of Laverington, Esq.,
   Cambridgeshire
The rev. Mr James Stodart, minister of
   Kirkintilloch
Swaffham Book-club
Dr Matthew Stuart, Prof.M., Edinburgh
Samuel Swallow, Esq., consul general in
   Russia
John Syme, writer to the Signet
Walter Syme, merchant at Carronshore
Walter Sim, merchant in Bothkennar
William Steel, merchant in Glasgow
Dr Walter Stirling of Stirling
Captain Thomas Stirling
William Stirling of Northside, Esq.
James Saffre, merchant in St Petersburg
Mr James Simson, merchant in Glasgow
Adam Smith, LLD, professor of Moral
   Philosophy in the University of Glasgow
James Stirling, Esq., agent for the Scots-
   mining Company at Leadhills
Alexander Stevenson, Esq., clerk to the
   commissariot, Glasgow

T
The right hon. Lord Torphichen
John Thornton, Esq., of London; 2 sets
Sir Peter Thompson of Poole, Knt.
Andrew Thomson, Esq., of London
John Thomson, Esq., of Edinburgh
Alexander Thomson of Edinburgh
Peter Thompson of Bermondsey, Esq.
Capt. William Thornton

Sir Clement Trafford of Dunton-hall
Lady Trafford of Dunton-hall
Robert Tracy, Esq.
The rev. Dr Tracy, fellow of All-souls,
   Oxford
Henry Tuckfield
Godfrey Thornton, merchant, St Peters-
   burg

U
Robert Urie, printer at Glasgow

V
Mrs Vandewall of Greenwich
Honourable James Veitch of Elliock,
   senator of the College of Justice
James Vere, senr.
John Vere of Stonebyres, Esq.
Miss Vere of Stonebyres
William Vigor of Taplow, Esq.
Mrs Vigor of Taplow
Benjamin Vigor, Esq.
Allen Vigor, of Manchester
North Vigor, MD

W
The right hon. Earl of Winchelsea
The right hon. Lord Willoughby of Par-
   ham, FRS
The right hon. Lady Charlotte Wentworth
His excellency Count de Woronsoff; 3 sets
William Wallace of Cairnhill, Esq.
John Watcot, Esq.
Dr William Watson, FRS
John Watson, merchant in St Petersburg
Joel Watson, Esq.
Capt. George Wauchope
Rev. John Warden of Edinburgh
John Weyland, Esq., of London
              Wensbry of Wisbitch
Taylor White, Esq., of London
George Whateby, Esq., of London
Charles White, surgeon of Manchester,
   FRS
Robert Whyt, surgeon at Falkirk
Robert Willock, bookseller, London; 6 sets
Sir Rowland Winn of Nostel, Bart.
Thomas Winn, Esq., of Acton
John Wilkinson, Esq.
John Wills, Esq., of London
Ralph Willet, Esq., of Marly
Thomas Withington of Manchester

John Wilson, writer at Glasgow
Baron Wolff
John Wright
Major White

Y

The right hon. Sir Wm. York, Bart.
William Young, Esq., of Standlinch, Wilts.
Robert Young, merchant at Edinburgh

Q*

INDEX

Figures in italic indicate illustrations

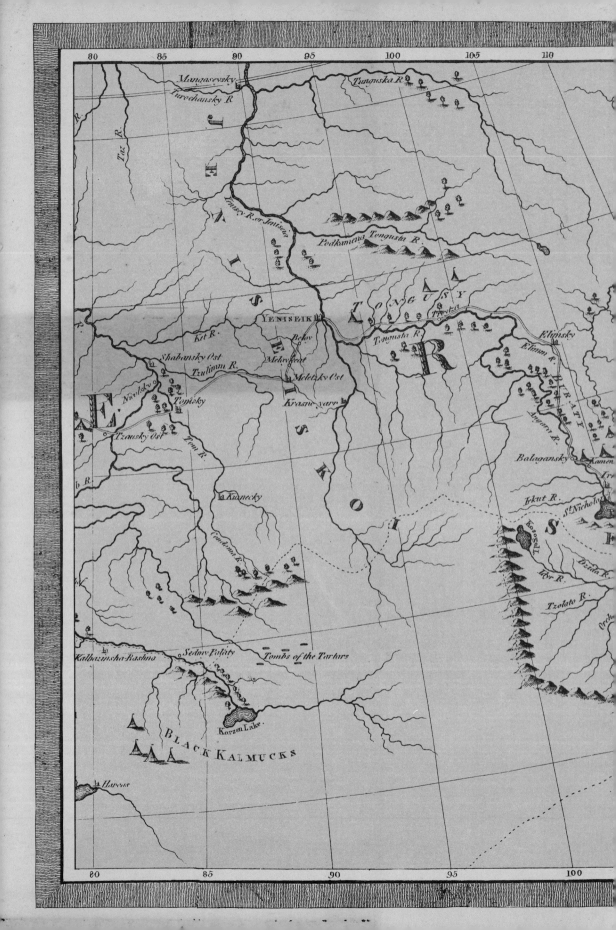

Map labels (reading across the map):

80 85 90 95 100 105 110

Mangasevsky
Turochansky R.
Tunguska R.

Taz R.

Tansey R. or Jenisea

Podkamena Tongusta R.

TONGUSY

YENISEIK

Kit R.
Belov
Tunska
Shabansky Ost
Meloukeat
Tongusta R.
Elimsky
Tzulinm R.
Meletzky Ost
Etimm R.
Nivolsky
Krasne yare
TIRATY
Tomsky
Angam R.
Tzausky Ost
Tron R.
Balagansky
Kamen

Irkut R.
Kuznecky
St. Nicholas

Kosogol L.

Condoma R.
Idyr R.
Dzida R.

Tzolato R.

Kalbazinsha-Rashna
Sednv Palaty
Tombs of the Tartars

Orcha

Korzen Lake
BLACK KALMUCKS

Harcas

80 85 90 95 100